SATIRE
AND THE
HEBREW PROPHETS

LITERARY
CURRENTS
IN
BIBLICAL
INTERPRETATION

EDITORS

Danna Nolan Fewell
Perkins School of Theology,
Southern Methodist University, Dallas TX
David M. Gunn
Columbia Theological Seminary, Decatur GA

EDITORIAL ADVISORY BOARD

Jack Dean Kingsbury
Union Theological Seminary in Virginia, Richmond VA
Peter D. Miscall
St Thomas Seminary, Denver CO
Gary A. Phillips
College of the Holy Cross, Worcester MA
Regina M. Schwartz
Department of English, Duke University, Durham NC
Mary Ann Tolbert
The Divinity School, Vanderbilt University, Nashville TN

SATIRE
AND
THE
HEBREW
PROPHETS

THOMAS JEMIELITY

WESTMINSTER/JOHN KNOX PRESS
Louisville, Kentucky

SATIRE AND THE HEBREW PROPHETS

© 1992 Thomas Jemielity

First edition

Published by Westminster/John Knox Press,
Louisville, Kentucky

This book is printed on acid-free paper that meets the American National Standards Institute Z39.48 standard. ∞

PRINTED IN THE UNITED STATES OF AMERICA
2 4 6 8 9 7 5 3 1

Library of Congress Cataloging-in-Publication Data

Jemielity, Thomas, 1933–
   Satire and the Hebrew prophets / Thomas Jemielity. — 1st ed.
      p.   cm. — (Literary currents in biblical interpretation)
   Includes bibliographical references and indexes.
   ISBN 0-664-25229-X

   1. Bible.   O.T.   Prophets—Language, style.   2. Satire in the Bible.   I. Title.   II. Series.
BS1505.2.J46   1992
224'.066—dc20   92-242

For Barbara

So Jacob worked seven years for
Rachel, and they seemed like a
few days because he loved her.

Gen 29:20 (NEB)

CONTENTS

SERIES PREFACE

New currents in biblical interpretation are emerging. Questions about origins—authors, intentions, settings—and stages of composition are giving way to questions about the literary qualities of the Bible, the play of its language, the coherence of its final form, and the relations between text and readers.

Such literary criticism is rapidly acquiring sophistication as it learns from major developments in secular critical theory, especially in understanding the instability of language and the key role of readers in the production of meaning. Biblical critics are being called to recognize that a plurality of readings is an inevitable and legitimate consequence of the interpretive process. By the same token, interpreters are being challenged to take responsibility for the theological, social, and ethical implications of their readings.

Biblical interpretation is changing on the practical as well as the theoretical level. More readers, both inside and outside the academic guild, are discovering that the Bible in literary perspective can powerfully engage people's lives. Communities of faith where the Bible is foundational may find that literary criticism can make the Scripture accessible in a way that historical criticism seems unable to do.

Within these changes lie exciting opportunities for all who seek contemporary meaning in the ancient texts. The goal of the series is to encourage such change and such search, to breach the confines of traditional biblical criticism, and to open channels for new currents of interpretation.

—THE EDITORS

ACKNOWLEDGMENTS

Unlike Samuel Johnson in his famous letter to the Earl of Chesterfield, I cannot claim seven years' neglect in this undertaking. If I do drown, it is not for lack of help to bring me safe to shore. Thanks are due to the University of Notre Dame for a leave in the Fall 1986, to its Institute for Scholarship in the Liberal Arts, especially to Robert Burke of the Institute, for thrice supporting this research, and to the Indiana Committee for the Humanities for its Summer Research Fellowship in 1988.

Debts to specific persons are many. I apologize for overlooking anyone. Among my colleagues I must thank Joseph Blenkinsopp, Gerald Bruns, Joseph Buttigieg (*Illustre Capo*), and Christopher Fox. Farther away, O. M. Brack, Jr., and John Mulryan helped launch this project. Howard Weinbrot responded often with characteristic generosity along the way. A very special debt is due to Michael Patrick O'Connor, who listened to these ideas and read these pages from *tohu wabohu* onwards. His uncovering my innumerable howlers made me most uneasily aware of the dark side of prophetic laughter. I assume full responsibility for the howlers that remain. A literary scholar's book on the Bible should thank two most exemplary and influential teachers: Monsignor Thomas Kelly of the Diocese of Cleveland, who taught me to know and love Scripture, and M. H. Abrams, who showed this graduate student at Cornell how literary premises could fruitfully approach the biblical text. His is an astonishing erudition. Even more impressive for me was the light and easy way in which he carried it. Cheryl Reed of the Faculty Steno Pool ought surely to list this book as an sin crying to heaven for vengeance. Her sufferings with it have been many. Special thanks at Westminster/John Knox Press are due to Danielle Alexander. David Gunn, my editor, proved a most welcome and appreciated guide through the final stages of this book.

Closer to home are three children, David, Samuel, and Sarah. They encouraged and inspired and, by growing older and commendably self-reliant, left me with time such as I never thought possible for parents. Finally, the deepest gratitude to my wife, Barbara. Even if her repeated questions about the progress of this book were, according to Proverbs, like "a constant dripping" of water, she prompted, spurred, cajoled, suggested, read, threatened, and, along the way, pursued her own career (when I wasn't pestering her about mine). To her this book is genuinely and sincerely dedicated: "song made in lieu of many ornaments."

—THOMAS JEMIELITY
University of Notre Dame
20 August 1991
Feast of Samuel the Prophet

PERMISSIONS

Permission to use copyrighted material has been granted as follows:

From the American Society for Eighteenth-Century Studies to reprint from "Prophets or Projectors? Challenges to Credibility in Hebrew Prophecy," in *Studies in Eighteenth-Century Culture*, 18 (1988), 445-78.

From St. Bonaventure University to reprint from "Divine Derision and Scorn: the Hebrew Prophets as Satirists," *Cithara: Essays in the Judaeo-Christian Tradition*, 25, no. 1 (Nov. 1985), 47-68; and "Prophetic Voices and Satiric Echoes," *Cithara*, 29, no. 1 (Nov. 1989), 30-47.

From Aubrey Williams, ed. POETRY AND PROSE OF ALEXANDER POPE. Riverside Edn. Copyright © 1969 by Houghton Mifflin Company.

From *Satire: That Blasted Art*, eds. John R. Clark and Anna Motto (New York: Putnam's [Capricorn Books], 1973). Copyright © 1973.

From *The New English Bible*. Copyright © The Delegates of the Oxford University Press and The Syndics of the Cambridge University Press 1961, 1970.

From EZEKIEL (ANCHOR BIBLE) A NEW TRANSLATION by Moshe Greenberg. Copyright © 1983 by Doubleday. From HOSEA (ANCHOR BIBLE) A NEW TRANSLATION by Francis I. Andersen and David Noel Freedman. Copyright © 1980 by Doubleday. From JEREMIAH (ANCHOR BIBLE) A NEW TRANSLATION by John Bright. Copyright © 1965 by Doubleday. Used by permission of Doubleday, a division of Bantam Doubleday Dell Publishing Group, Inc.

PREFACE

This study of satire and the Hebrew prophets was prompted by Northrop Frye's describing William Blake's *The Marriage of Heaven and Hell* (1793) as "the epilogue to the golden age of English satire, . . . a vigorous Beethovenish coda . . . big with portents of the movements to follow."[1] Those movements took the form of the prophecies Blake wrote after earlier, satiric ventures like the *Marriage* and the *Songs of Innocence and of Experience* (1794). As a longtime teacher of the classical and eighteenth-century satirists, and even a teacher of courses in the Bible, crosslisted in Notre Dame's departments of English and of Theology, I was most intrigued by this implied connection between prophecy and satire. My teaching of the Hebrew prophets, indeed, reinforced those connections with each return to the material. Frye's analysis of *The Marriage of Heaven and Hell* implies many links between prophecy and satire,[2] yet the connection remains unpursued in his two later books on the Bible, both of which stimulatingly apply literary paradigms to biblical material. The brief analysis of biblical prophecy in *The Great Code* does not mention satire at all, nor does *satire* make it into the index of the second book.[3]

This present book examines systematically the connection between prophecy and satire in a way that neither biblical nor literary scholarship has yet pursued it. If, as prophet and satirist, Blake is inspired with a vision of a more desirable future as well as a searing insight into a stifling, myopic present—a vision, in other words, of the stark contrast between the ideal and the real, the possible and the actual—then Blake certainly embodies the insight and the motivation that impels prophecy and satire. For the insight that judges and thereby proclaims a more desirable alternative is precisely the core, the subject matter of both proclamations. That very criticism is the common denominator that explains in the Hebrew prophets the rhetorical strategies, themes, techniques, and the like familiar in satire. In this basically comparative study of the satirists and the prophets, I propose to pursue those many likenesses in some detail.

Although aware of satire in the prophets, biblical scholarship likewise seems not to have pursued the connection thoroughly. Again, and intriguingly, Robert Alter's few comments about and illustrations of satire in *The Art of Biblical Poetry* appear in his analysis of biblical prophecy, but the connection goes undeveloped.[4] The earlier 1984 number of *Semeia* shows more flirtation, but again no consummation. The entire number takes up tragedy and comedy in various biblical texts. Contributors and respondents alike admit the awkwardness of applying a dramatic paradigm to material that is not drama. In an essay on tragedy and comedy in the Latter Prophets, for instance, Norman Gottwald briefly mentions features of prophecy common to satire—sarcasm, invective, parody, irony, and direct condemnation—without at all considering that the oratorical, rhetorical, and generically indefinite character of satire might be a critically more fruitful paradigm for considering the prophets than the tragic and comic forms he and others in the issue employ yet admit to feeling uncomfortable with.[5]

The collection of essays *On Humour and the Comic in the Hebrew Bible* appeared too recently for me to take advantage of in this study.[6] Although the contributors discuss humor in the Hebrew Bible as a whole, generally and in particular texts, their comments—with one exception—reinforce positions in this book. For example, the editors' introductory essay asserts that "the chief motive for biblical instances of humour appears to be aggression," a claim developed extensively in Chapter One of this book. The laughter of satire is an aggressive laughter. They cite with approval John Miles' insistence that "ancient humour was typically a laughing at rather than a laughing with."[7] That distinction strikes me as very useful in separating the forms and laughter of satire from those of comedy. In a separate contribution, Athalya Brenner's mentioning of numerous humorous passages in the Hebrew Bible observes "that most of them veer towards the 'scorn, ridicule' pole, that is, tendentious and even

cruel and bitter rather than the merry facet of humour"[8]—
again, a major claim in this study. Neither of these two essays,
however, is concerned with satire paradigmatically, nor do they
indicate the extent of satire in the prophets.

The essay in this collection that leaves me very uneasy,
however, is R. P. Carroll's "Is Humour Among the Prophets?"—the collection's one discussion of humor in the whole
range of prophetic texts. At first glance, Carroll supports many
claims made here: "the wide range of satire, irony, bawdy and
ribaldry, taunt and mockery, burlesque and lampoon, parody
and denigration" in the biblical books; the "savage irony" and
"mocking parody" of Elijah's comments to the prophets of Baal
(1 Kgs 18:26-29); "caustic wit and sardonic expression . . .
throughout the prophetic collections"; "a considerable amount
of ironic and satiric material" in Jeremiah; "black and gallows
humour, satire and parody, raging anger and kaleidoscopic
irony [thrice compared to that of Jonathan Swift], harangue and
taunt, invective and cursing, and the whole panoply of deroga-
tory attitudes displayed in the prophetic books"; even an
analysis of the "gallows humour," a favorite phrase of Carroll's,
in Isaiah's "satire on the king of Babylon" (14:4-21).[9] Given
Carroll's extent of reference and the occasional analysis of satire
in the prophets, my uneasiness with this essay might seem at
first inexplicable. Let me explain.

First of all, although Carroll admits that certain passages in
the prophets might strike us as funny, the humor is in the
reader, not in the prophet (or in the prophetic text): "A less
humorous collection of people it would be impossible to find
outside a list of mediaeval bishops,"[10] many of whom I had
always thought led jolly enjoyable lives (Isn't that part of what
the Protestant Reformation was about?). Now Carroll admits that
definition is a key issue here and that "if . . . we confine
humour to some genuine sense of wit and funniness the
prophets must be adjudged to be humourless."[11] What Carroll
calls "humour" I call comedy in the pages that follow. I would
agree with Carroll that the prophetic books have little if anything
in them of the tolerant, genial, expansive, belly-laugh quality of
comedy. But is it safe to assume a genial, harmless, and

13

delightful quality for wit in all its guises? Martin Grotjahn argues that the wit, considered as a person,

> is closely related to the sadist. Under the disguise of brilliance, charm, and entertainment the wit . . . is a sadist at heart. He is sharp, quick, alert, cold, aggressive, and hostile. He is inclined to murder his victims in thought; if he inhibits himself and if he does not succeed in transforming his brain child into a joke, he may develop a migraine attack instead.[12]

The problems with Carroll's essay, moreover, are several. It fails to recognize that not all laughter is genial, and however disturbing the laughter of superiority, of satisfaction at another's misfortunes, of grim, macabre "gallows humour," that laughter is laughter, and the prophetic texts, indeed a good deal of the Hebrew Bible, exhibit the laughter of attack, the laughing at that characterizes satire. I disagree with Carroll's claim that "irony is certainly not humour."[13] The achievements of the Yahwist are peripheral to my concern, but I claim later that his (hers? *pace* Harold Bloom) is a genuine comic irony. The irony of the prophets is grim, macabre, black—Hosea perhaps the most compelling example, as I claim in Chapter Three. One of the advantages of Northrop Frye's paradigm of satire and irony, on which I rely in this study, is its laying the basis for recognizing the many qualities of laughter. If Abraham Heschel is right in his claim, cited later in this book, that many biblical scholars are unwilling to confront the message of the wrath of God in the prophets and prefer to emphasize their message of consolation,[14] perhaps Carroll exemplifies a reluctance to confront the sometimes savage, frequently unsettling laughter that God and his prophets enjoy at the expense of those they deride and scorn. Lastly, Carroll patronizes and condescends to satiric laughter. Surely, in the late twentieth century, biblical and literary scholarship can do more than pass on with approval Joseph Chotzner's description of Ezekiel's humor as "like Swift's, rather coarse, and not altogether palatable." Chotzner sends "the curious" to Ezekiel 16 or 23 with a tone that registers the advisability of tweezers or rubber gloves for any who do read either passage. These comments were made in 1905![15] A study of satire in the Hebrew prophets cannot patronize or wish away the laughter of satire, imply its inferiority by describing the laughter it occasions as "negative,"[16] and, most important, I believe, must come to grips with the ambiguity and dark side of laughter. Satire is great art and needs no apology.

A major premise of this study argues that prophecy and satire are near of kin because both are preponderantly criticism or judgment. The heavily censorious content of the canonical Hebrew prophets is clear, even if, like many of their satiric counterparts, they delineate sometimes explicitly their vision of an ideal order. Prophecy and satire, thus, are both forms or expressions of critical discourse. The classic definition of satire's rhetorical objective—to praise and to blame—applies with equal cogency to prophecy.

Of the five chapters of this study, the first three are concerned with The Message. Chapter One discusses how prophecy, like satire, functions in a society where ridicule looms large as a humiliation to be avoided or as an especially satisfying form of punishment for one's enemies. Originally delivered orally in public forums, prophecy, secondly, shares with satire a very rhetorical character. Like satire, prophecy is generically indefinite, a generic parasite, in fact: it employs and even parodies a wide variety of forms. These concerns I pursue in Chapter Two. Chapter Three takes up the variety of satire and irony in the Hebrew prophets. In Part Two of this book, The Messenger, I turn my attention to the prophet himself as he emerges in the text of Hebrew prophecy. Chapter Four discusses why the prophets, to present themselves favorably, need a rhetoric of credibility. Their self-presentation in the biblical text reflects a strategy designed to counter charges often levelled at them: that they are mad, malignly motivated, or subversive of the public order. These accusations, as I point out, are staples in the attack against satirists. Chapter Five discusses how the Hebrew prophets speak of themselves and their mission in roles very similar to those assumed by satirists. This positive self-presentation is designed, of course, to counter charges levelled against their credibility.

I do not offer any analysis in this book of the satire in

Jonah. Many such discussions are readily available. But, and more to my purpose, with the exception of the Book of Jonah, Hebrew prophecy is mostly in the first person. The prophet speaks in his own voice, or God in his, or the prophet in God's. Narrative satire, like that in Jonah, is rare. No other prophetic text offers narrative satire from beginning to end. Consequently, if prophecy bears strong affinity to satire, the strongest affinity is to first-person satire of the sort that appears in Horace, Juvenal, or the later Alexander Pope (roughly 1728 through 1744). Besides including objects of attack, such satire considerably develops the satirist-speaker's own character in ways I find comparable to what appears in Jeremiah and Amos, to mention but two. Although I draw on narrative satire from the likes of Jonathan Swift or Evelyn Waugh and comment on narrative satire in the prophets—Ezekiel 16, for instance—I am much more concerned with the prophecy and satire that speaks in the critic's own voice.

Because my focus is on the themes, strategies, and techniques that prophecy and satire share, the satire I refer to in this book, admittedly selective, represents a "mainstream" of enormous impact on the tradition: in particular, Horace and Juvenal, Pope and Swift. While other satire certainly exemplifies many of these paradigms, I see no pressing need to multiply examples. Biblical scholars, as a result, will find many of these references already familiar or at least not posing too extensive a challenge. Literary scholars have the reasonably circumscribed provenance of fifteen prophetic texts.[17]

As these remarks imply, *Satire and the Hebrew Prophets* has a twofold audience in mind. I write for biblical scholars who are interested in applying literary criteria and paradigms to the biblical text. Although I work with English versions of the prophetic texts, I have found considerable usefulness in commentaries on the Hebrew original.[18] Biblical scholars much better versed in Hebrew than I may thus pursue closer rhetorical analyses of these texts within the paradigms I use and build on, correct, and move beyond what I here propose. But I write as well for literary scholars of satire. Although some eighteenth-century scholars have analyzed the adaptation, assimilation, and parodying of biblical forms in the English satirists, none has yet considered the extent to which Hebrew prophecy can be interpreted in terms of satiric patterns. Scholars of satire will find in this book as well an indication of extensive resources in the prophets for expanding an awareness of the origin and evolution of satire. The general reader, however, who simply enjoys the Hebrew Scriptures and new ways of looking at them, is also welcome here.

A NOTE ON BIBLICAL CITATIONS

Abbreviations within the text identify the version from which the biblical citation comes: JPS, for *Tanakh: A New Translation of the Holy Scriptures According to the Traditional Hebrew Text* (Philadelphia: The Jewish Publication Society, 1985); KJV, for the Authorized or King James Version; Knox, for *The Old Testament*, tr. Ronald Knox, 2 vols. (New York: Sheed and Ward, 1950); NEB for *The New English Bible* (specifically, *The New English Bible with the Apocrypha: Oxford Study Edition*, gen. ed. Samuel Sandmel [New York: Oxford, 1976]); AB, for the relevant volumes of the Anchor Bible, gen. eds. William Foxwell Albright and David Noel Freedman (Garden City: Doubleday). The individual volumes in this series cited in the text and in the documentation are the following:

Genesis. E. A. Speiser. 2nd ed. 1964.
Judges. Rob`rt G. Boling. 1975.
I Samuel. P. Kyle McCarter, Jr. 1980.
II Samuel. P. Kyle McCarter, Jr. 1984.
Second Isaiah. John L. McKenzie. 1968.
Jeremiah. John Bright. 1965.
Ezekiel. 1-20. Moshe Greenberg. 1983.
Hosea. Francis I. Andersen & David Noel Freedman. 1980.
Amos. Francis I. Andersen & David Noel Freedman. 1989.
Jonah. Jack M. Sasson. New York: Doubleday, 1990.
Haggai, Zechariah 1-8. Carol L. Meyers & Eric M. Meyers. 1987.
Psalms I: 1-50. Mitchell Dahood, S.J. 1965, 1966.

Psalms II: 51-100. Mitchell Dahood, S.J. 1968.
Psalms III: 101-150. Mitchell Dahood, S.J. 1970.
Job. Marvin H. Pope. 2nd ed. 1965.
Proverbs, Ecclesiastes. R. B. Y. Scott. 2nd ed. 1965.
Lamentations. Delbert R. Hillers. 1972.
Esther. Carey A. Moore. 1971.
The Wisdom of Ben Sira. Tr. Patrick W. Skehan. Intro. and
    commentary Alexander A. Di Lella, O. F. M. 1987.
The Wisdom of Solomon. David Winston. 1979.

The fifteen texts which bear a prophet's name are not the written product of the prophet to whom the text has been attributed. Bruce Vawter succinctly observes: "No single prophetic book is the work, or derives from the work, of any one prophetic genius: all of them are works of redaction and supplementation from many hands, prophetic and otherwise." See his *Amos, Hosea, Micah, with an Introduction to Classical Prophecy* (Wilmington: Michael Glazier, 1981), pp. 9-10. The canonical prophets are Isaiah, Jeremiah, and Ezekiel, and the so-called Twelve Minor Prophets (i.e., Hosea, Joel, Amos, Obadiah, Jonah, Micah, Nahum, Habakkuk, Zephaniah, Haggai, Zechariah, and Malachi). Daniel is not numbered among the prophetic texts in the Hebrew Bible, but is found in the Writings.

Although I draw occasionally on prophetic material outside these canonical texts, my study is almost exclusively concerned with them. For convenience, therefore, I accept the traditional view that the persons to whom these texts are attributed are male. That prophecy included women, however, is beyond dispute. The prophetess Huldah, for instance, not only figures prominently in the Deuteronomic Reform under Josiah, but delivers a message essentially critical to the delegation sent to seek her counsel about "the book of the law" (2 Kgs 22:8, NEB) discovered in the Temple (22:3-20). She is, thus, a contemporary of Jeremiah.

PART I

THE
MESSAGE

1

PROPHECY AND SATIRE: SIBLINGS OF SHAME AND POWER

Juvenal's *Satire XV* relates, he claims, "a story . . . hard to believe," a grisly, detailed account of cannibalism among the Egyptians. The comments addressed to Volusius at the very beginning of the satire, however, strongly imply that this "barbarous innovation" in human behavior is a built-in consequence of Egypt's weird, irrational religious practices:

> Volusius, who does not know what monsters lunatic Egypt
> Chooses to cherish? One part goes in for crocodile worship;
> One bows down to the ibis that feeds upon serpents; elsewhere
> A golden effigy shines, of a long-tailed holy monkey!
> Where the magic chords resound from Memnon, half-broken,
> Where with her hundred gates old Thebes lies buried in ruins,
> Whole towns revere a dog, or cats, or a fish from the river.
> No one worships Diana. But they have a taboo about biting
> Into a leek or an onion; this, they think, is unseemly.
> Oh, what holy folk, whose gardens give birth to such gods!
> Lamb and the flesh of kid are forbidden to every man's table;
> Feeding on human meat, however, is perfectly proper.[1]

Although no Hebrew prophet, admittedly, would lament the neglect of the worship of Diana, the battery of complaints, innuendoes, and charges which informs Juvenal's ridicule could easily find a place in any prophetic text. Does Juvenal speak contemptuously of the demeaning, less-than-human forms in which the Egyptians discover and adore divinity—crocodile, ibis, or monkey; cat, dog, or fish? Hosea makes fun of the carved wooden phallic symbols worshiped by a high priest of the Northern Kingdom:

> He makes inquiry of his Wood,
> And his Staff reports to him. [Hos 4:12, AB]

Jeremiah compares these humanly crafted divinities to "scarecrows . . . in a cucumber patch—can't talk! / Have to be carried—can't walk! [Jer 10:5, AB]," while Habakkuk wonders why people expect dumb wooden or stone idols to respond to human entreaty (Hab 2:18-19). This ridiculing of false gods is as much a tradition of prophecy as it is of satire, be it Elijah, urging on the perhaps bathroom-occupied Baal (1 Kgs 18:27), Horace's farting Priapus (*Satires*, I, 8), the worshiped male images of Ezekiel's whore-creation Jerusalem (Ezek 16:17), or Robert Burns' Holy Willie, whose God

> Sends ane to heaven and ten to hell,
> A' for thy glory,
> And no for ony guid or ill
> They've done afore thee!

Does Juvenal sarcastically reduce the trivially and obtusely focused sense of ritual impurity that keeps the Egyptians from eating some forms of animal meat but ignores the barbarity of eating human flesh? Amos echoes this contempt in dismissing the ritually and externally focused propriety of the Israelites: their sacrifices and tithes and thank-offerings. "For you love to do what is proper, you men of Israel!" (Amos 4:4-5, NEB) sneers the prophet, who then excoriates their prostitution of religious and political institutions, their oppression of the poor and the defenseless. Is Juvenal outraged at a religious practice that not only raises no scruple about sacrificing human beings but, in fact, incorporates such barbarity as a welcome feature of its religious worship? In his quasi-allegorical account of Judah's worldwide career of infidelity, Ezekiel speaks Yahweh's blood-curdling accusation: "You took your sons and daughters that you bore me and sacrificed them to [your male images] for food, . . . slaughtered my sons as an offering and delivered them over to them!'' (Ezek 16:20-21, AB). Michael Patrick O'Connor points out that Ezekiel 16 is so gross and shocking, in a detail and vividness I find Juvenalian, that Jewish public worship traditionally avoids the passage. What prompts this outburst in Ezekiel, he further notes, is not the prophet's contempt for sexual misbehavior, but moreso, again like Juvenal, a premeditated taking of human life that subverts elementary human decency and the laws of nations.[2] Echoes of at least six Hebrew prophets sound through these twelve lines of Juvenalian satire, which here, as elsewhere in the Roman satirist, convey the prophet-like suspicion that bizarre forms of cult prompt bizarre and reprehensible forms of conduct.

The Juvenal of the *Satires* would easily find himself at home with the targets and themes of prophetic ridicule: the external, mindless, and quasi-erotic quality of religious practice; unspeakable immorality; the oppression of the poor; the subverting of the nation's institutions by the powerful for their own advantage; the absence of any sense of an earlier, wholesome belief and decent ethical practice; the absence of any expectation that such moral dereliction must produce disastrous consequences. Hebrew prophecy displays a full range of satiric technique, theme, and victim. Hebrew prophecy, however unwittingly and unconsciously, provides abundant evidence of the satiric, or at least the proto-satiric, long before the usually cited and familiar appearance of this evidence among the classical Greeks and Romans. What John McKenzie said, a generation ago, of the incredibly sophisticated and subtle ironist who crafted the tale of the man, the woman, and the serpent is also true, I affirm, for the prophetic message and those who fashioned and preserved it: "Let us not think that wit and irony, profundity and wisdom were beyond the reach of the ancient Hebrew story-tellers; there was genius before Homer."[3] In this chapter, I propose to demonstrate the following: first, that the sense of shame pervasive in the Hebrew Scriptures provides fertile ground for the equivalent of what is later recognized as satire; second, that this shame is often interpreted as a punishment, exploited and presented as such in prophecy and satire; and, finally, that the prophet's and satirist's assuming of a judicial authority appears in the quasi-legal nature of both, one of the most significant common denominators between them.

i.

" . . . *satura . . . tota nostra est.*"
Quintilian, *Institutio oratoria*

To look for the genius of satire in the text of Hebrew prophecy, however, flies in the face of the scholarly consensus that the Romans invented satire in the first century BC (and that the Greeks probably invented irony about three centuries earlier).[4] How then can Hebrew prophecy be satiric when its near-finished textual form antedates the Greeks and the Romans, for the most part, by some centuries?[5] James Ackerman, for example, who studies "elements in the story [of Jonah] that bring it close to classical satire," finds, nevertheless, "no evidence of cultural contact between the writer and the classical satire that was probably *evolving* [my emphasis] in other parts of the Mediterranean world at that time," i.e., in the sixth and fifth centuries BC, when Ackerman assumes Jonah was written. For a variety of characteristics, however, he insists that *satire* gives "the modern reader the most useful handle on the story."[6] *A fortiori*, no evidence of such contact appears in the canonical prophets, the text of virtually all of whom antedates Jonah (with the possible exception of Malachi, Haggai, and Zechariah). Like Ackerman, though, I find *satire* a most useful handle on the techniques of ridiculing criticism that pervade Hebrew prophecy.

I do not claim that satire and prophecy are always interchangeable or formally equivalent terms. However, I do claim that Hebrew prophecy often displays the nature, qualities, techniques, themes, and patterns of satire, but, more to the immediate point, I do not argue that the satire of Hebrew prophecy is a conscious literary device. In the present state of biblical knowledge, no one can assert that those responsible for preserving, amplifying, and passing down the prophetic text deliberately wrote satire. Nor is such an affirmation essential to my argument. If, as I believe, literary qualities and patterns can appear unconsciously, then the critical impulse and prompting as central to prophecy as to satire can, not surprisingly, antici-

24

pate the deliberate artistic fashioning of ridiculing judgment called satire.[7]

A cautionary guess, however. The Hebrew Scriptures are replete with stories of reversal, the stuff of irony: Yahweh achieves his ends, despite human proposing, interposing, and disposing. The so-called Yahwist, one of the first known Hebrew writers, crafting his tales in the shadow of the Davidic monarchy in the tenth or ninth century BC, masters ironic narrative and subtle humor. His contribution to the Jacob-Esau story (Genesis 27), after all, provides one of the earliest instances of a classic eiron-alazon encounter where dissembling and shrewdness overcome physical superiority.[8] Several centuries later the writer of Esther fashions a hilarious, near low-burlesque tale in which every anti-Jewish trick of Haman backfires upon him until he, finally, hangs from the very gibbet he had prepared for Mordecai. The author of this story, so Carey Moore claims, was "primarily concerned with telling an interesting and *lively* [my emphasis] story . . . ."[9] The entertainment value of the Hebrew Scriptures for its audience should not be dismissed: they may please as well as teach, and in delighting, show a concern, however unconscious, with the pedagogical insinuation achieved by the craft which is art. My first insistence, then, is that however usefully and defensibly *satire* describes much Hebrew prophecy, that satire is most likely an unconscious literary product in texts that display the patterns in which satire emerges. In later deliberate craft, these patterns produce the *satura* of artists like Horace and Juvenal. Is Juvenal, then, among the prophets? Several centuries earlier, he might have been.

ii.

"I have become a laughingstock to my friend . . . ."
Job 12:4 (JPS)

In *The Power of Satire*, Robert Elliott traces the evolution of satire from the curse, from the fearful belief that words can effect harm and even death. To approach "the question of the malign efficacy of satire" from a direction other than his analysis of early Greek, Arab, and Irish cultures, Elliott also analyzes the role of ridicule in what he calls shame-oriented cultures: those that "rely on external sanctions to govern behavior: what other people will think or say, whether they will praise or blame—these are the over-riding considerations." In a guilt-oriented culture, on the other hand, admission of wrongdoing, with the appropriate punishment, restores the culprit to society. In a shame culture, wrongdoing leads to criticism, humiliation, and rejection. In such a culture "one of the most powerful of all forms of public disapproval is ridicule."[10]

The Hebrew Scriptures—a source of evidence Elliott considers only in passing—afford abundant witness to the power of ridicule: to the humiliation felt at misfortune, almost invariably interpreted as a sign of divine disfavor at wrongdoing, and to keenly anticipated, even vindictive satisfaction at the discomfiture of others, assumed in their bad fortune to be suffering the consequences of reprehensible behavior. Much in the Hebrew Scriptures confirms Elliott's assertion that "few horrors are more to be dreaded by members of a shame culture than to be publicly laughed at."[11] To adopt for a moment the phraseology of the Bible itself, being a laughingstock and a byword can even be fatal.

The consciousness in the Hebrew Scriptures of the power and attraction of ridicule spans nearly the full chronological extent of its composition, from the last centuries of the second millennium BC to the Maccabean period about a millennium later. The pervasiveness of this sense of shame explains, I believe, the frequency of satire and irony in the Hebrew Scriptures and in the prophetic texts that are my particular concern. The emotions registered by victim or by perpetrator are vindictive, intense, and violent. Perpetrator sees the misfortune of the victim as effected curse; victim, especially if convinced of innocence, utters hair-raising curses on the perpetrator in the expectation that his own misfortune, a momentary aberration in the scheme of justice, will be lifted and he will be vindicated. My particular concern is with the derision, scorn, contempt, and the like that often form an integral part of the hatred and sense of injury the Scriptures consider, for these emotions and attitudes are especially associated with satire and the belittling, unsympathetic, and judgmental laughter it seeks to evoke. To laugh at, to be laughed at—the Hebrew Scriptures speak often, feelingly, and perhaps disturbingly of such experiences. Elliott's tracing of satire from the curse would find much evidence of such a connection and evolution in the Hebrew Scriptures.

a.

> You made us the taunt of our neighbors,
>> the derision and scorn of those about us.
> You made us a byword among the nations,
>> a laughingstock among the peoples.
>> Ps 44:14-15 (AB)

Because the Book of Psalms is itself, as the NEB points out, "a collection . . . of poems from all periods of Israel's history" and a liturgical resource for the latter part of that history,[12] it affords a chronological panorama of the ubiquity of the power of ridicule in the Scriptures of Israel. Particularly apt is the "sixth-century lament" which, according to Mitchell Dahood, "*prays* [my emphasis] for vengeance on Israel's enemies—the Babylonians and the Edomites—who destroyed Jerusalem in 587/6 BC"[13] Psalm 137, in other words, is subsequent to and set in the aftermath of the great catastrophe warned about in the prophets and especially in Jeremiah. It laments the disaster that vindicated the pre-exilic prophets.

> Beside the rivers in Babylon,
>> there we sat;
>> loudly we wept,
> When we remembered you, O Zion!
> Beside the poplars in her midst
>> we hung up our lyres.
> For there our captors demanded of us
>> words of song,
>> and our mockers songs of gladness:
> "Sing for us a song of Zion!"
> O how could we sing Yahweh's song
>> upon alien soil?
> Should I forget you,
>> O Jerusalem,
> Let my right hand wither!

> Let my tongue stick to my palate,
> > should I remember you not!
> If I do not raise you,
> > O Jerusalem,
> Upon my head in celebration!
> Remember Yahweh, O sons of Edom,
> > the day of Jerusalem!
> You who said, "Strip her, strip her,
> > to her foundation!"
> O Daughter Babylon, you devastator,
> > blest he who repays you
> > the evil you have done us!
> Blest he who seizes and dashes
> > your infants against the rock. [Ps 137, AB]

Set in the past, the poem engages memory: the experience of the Exile itself, within which the psalmist recalls the taunting of the Babylonian captors; the Edomites urging on of the Babylonians at the Fall of Jerusalem; and, lastly, most powerfully and ominously, the memory petitioned for, Yahweh's remembering it all. When God remembers, things happen. As Exodus recounts, God "heard their groaning and remembered his covenant with Abraham, Isaac, and Jacob; he saw the plight of Israel, and he took heed of it" (Exod 2:24-25, NEB). Divine memory initiates divine deliverance. Psalm 137 implores Yahweh to remember so that he may deliver.

The psalm also abounds in contrasts, moving climactically to the prayer-curse of its last two verses: two cities, Jerusalem and Babylon; two times, the painful past, the painful present; two mockers, the Babylonians taunting the Israelites in their present distress, the Edomites, urging on the destruction of Jerusalem; two desires, the Babylonians for song, the Israelites for revenge; two songs, the taunts of the captors, the songs the Israelites cannot bring themselves to sing;[14] two curses, what the Israelites condemn themselves to should they sing, what the Israelites pray Yahweh to effect on the Babylonians; and two memories, Israel's helpless consciousness of its catastrophe, Yahweh's efficacious remembrance.

Central to what precedes and what follows, to the memories and the contrasts, to the curse which concludes the poem:

"When we remembered you, O Zion!" The remembrance of things past, however, gradually shifts from the pain and poignancy of the present and the taunting devastation of the past to a deeply desired, yet ominous future, at least for the Babylonians. For with no infants, Babylon will have no future. The river along which the Israelites sit and weep figures the continuity and causal connection of past, present, and future. The cursed byword Israel was once, and is now, embodies the cursed byword Babylon will become. But "blest," not cursed, is "he who seizes and dashes / your infants against the rock."

Emotionally central to this lament is the satisfaction the psalmist anticipates for the agent of Babylon's doom and, by implication, for the Israelites themselves.[15] A prayer-curse like Psalm 137 assumes, furthermore, moral justification for the hatred and satisfying vindictiveness directed at the enemy, an assumption inescapable in the laughter satire seeks to direct at others. Even satire's supposed founder, Archilochus, delighting in the exquisite sight of the curse fulfilled upon his enemy, quickly adds moral justification:

> for he abused me and trampled underfoot our bond—
> he, who formerly was my friend.[16]

As a prayer-curse, Psalm 137 certainly holds its own against anything Archilochus can utter, even in his most vitriolic moments. Somewhat uncomfortably, I sense, Mitchell Dahood urges that "the shocking form in which [the psalmist] expresses his desire for the extermination of his country's destroyer must be judged in light of customs prevailing in his age."[17] True, but Psalm 137 does not uniquely instance such curses in the Hebrew Scriptures and the satisfaction taken in them.

Psalm 109, for instance, is prompted by the psalmist's awareness of how "the mouth of the wicked / and the mouth of the deceitful" (Ps 109:2, AB) are turned against him. He urges Yahweh to cut short the days of his enemy, to widow his wife and orphan and beggar his children, to despoil his property, to deny him kindness and his children pity, to remember the wrongdoing of his father and mother, and to blot out his name from memory on the earth.

So let them curse [he can confidently conclude],
    as long as you bless;
Let them rise up, only to be humiliated,
    while your servant rejoices.
May my slanderers wear their disgrace,
      may they put on humiliation as a garment. [28-29, AB]

The curse which forms the concluding verses of Psalm 83 the NEB calls "a characteristic curse."[18] The lamenting psalmist in Psalm 73, conscious of sneer and calumny, observes with Dickensian grotesqueness that "their eyes gleam through folds of fat" (Ps 73:7, NEB). Psalm 35 can move quickly from its piercing sense of being ridiculed—

When I stumbled they gathered with glee,
    smiters gathered about me,
And they whom I did not know
    tore me to pieces,
And did not desist from slandering me.
My encircling mockers gnashed their teeth at me.
         [Ps 35:15-16, AB]

—to its plea that Yahweh reverse fortunes—

Let all be put to shame and confusion,
    who rejoice at my misfortune;
Let them be clothed with shame and infamy,
    who calumniate me. [Ps 35:26, AB]

With much intensity, more than two dozen psalms repeatedly and urgently beg Yahweh for the satisfaction of seeing misfortune fall on enemies, particularly to repay them in kind for their self-assured mocking and gloating over the discomfiture of the just.[19] Mark Van Doren and Maurice Samuel point out how a major theme in the Book of Psalms is the harm done by the tongue, how frequently the word *adversary* appears there, and how a pervasive attitude of deep moral indignation, most apparent in the curses of the just upon the evil, highlights what they call "the dark side" of the psalms.[20] The Cankered Muse of Satire often sings the songs of Israel's liturgy, where, in their confusion and shame, the just seek the satisfaction of revenge, the discomfiture of the foe by a vindicating triumph. Even the

supposedly idyllic Psalm 23—"The LORD is my shepherd"—
thanks and confides in Yahweh because, among other things,

> You prepare my table before me,
>   in front of my adversaries, [Ps 23:5, AB]

who, I assume, are not at all pleased by the scene.[21] To look,
then, in the Hebrew Scriptures for the ridicule that feeds on a
sense of shame and enjoys the power of humiliation—for what
literary criticism later calls satire—is no anachronism. A thorn by
any other name would pierce as sharply.

b.

> . . . when she saw that she was pregnant, she
> looked upon her mistress with contempt.
>
> Gen 16:4 (AB)

The power and attraction of shame and ridicule do not confine
themselves to Israel's liturgical poetry. They figure as well in
biblical narrative and in wisdom literature, as even the briefest
résumé reveals. The conflict between Sarah and Hagar, in Genesis 16, provides only the earliest instance—the Yahwist again
—of what Robert Alter calls but "a special variation of the re-
current story of bitter rivalry between a barren favored wife and
a fertile co-wife or concubine."[22] The "bitter rivalry," however, has touches of a situation comedy. The suggested cohabita-
tion with her "Egyptian maidservant" comes from Sarai (later
Sarah) to begin with. She tells her husband: "Look, Yahweh
has restrained me from bearing. Cohabit then with my maid.
Maybe I shall reproduce through her." But when Hagar "saw
that she was pregnant, she treated her mistress with contempt."
Sarai blames Abram (his name then) for this turn of events!
"This outrage[23] against me is your fault! I myself put my maid
in your lap. But from the moment she found that she had con-
ceived, she has been looking at me with contempt." Is it a
frustrated Abram who tells his wife: "Your maid is in your
hands. Do to her as you like"? The result? "Sarai then abused
[Hagar] so much that she ran away from her" (Gen 16:1-6, AB).
    In the fortunes of politics and warfare, however, the fear of
ridicule operates with a more obviously violent potentiality that

does not exclude suicide, whose motive, in a shame-oriented society, for this "*honored* [my emphasis] custom," is, according to Elliott, "the avoidance of public humiliation and shame."[24] As first king of Israel, Saul is the most striking example. Defeated in battle by the Philistines, he commands his sword-bearer: "Draw your sword and run me through with it, lest the uncircumcised [i.e., the Philistines] come and have their way with me." In the face of his sword-bearer's unwillingness, "Saul took the sword himself and fell upon it" (1 Sam 31:1-4, AB). What the Philistines were capable of doing for amusement at the expense of their prisoners appears earlier in Judges. They call the captive Samson to make sport for them—just before he brings the roof down on their heads: "When they were good and jolly, they said, 'Summon Samson! Let him entertain us!'" (Judg 16:25-30, AB). This is the same mood of triumphant vindictiveness that dominates, in Psalm 137, the Babylonian desire for songs from the captive Israelites as well as their own desire for revenge. Despite the fact, furthermore, that Saul and Samson, in a way, are suicides, the Hebrew Scriptures clearly regard them as heroes of Israel.[25]

Suicide prompted by what the Hebrew Scriptures unequivocally present as disgrace is the final act of Ahitophel, one-time advisor to David, who joins Abishalom in the rebellion against his father. Ahitophel's counsel, 2 Samuel notes, is respected "as if the word of God had been consulted." But working finally to frustrate the uprising against David, Yahweh sees to it that a specific recommendation of Ahitophel's is rejected in favor of a plan of the Hushai secretly in league with David: "Ahitophel, when he saw that his counsel was not acted upon, harnessed his ass and went up to his home in his own city. Having given instructions concerning his estate, he hanged himself and died" (2 Sam 16:23–17:23, AB).[26]

Not at all devoid of an awareness of the power of disgrace in scenes domestic and political, the wisdom writings of the Hebrew Bible, in which, says R. B. Y. Scott, "'the wise man's counsel' is most prominent,"[27] also command particular attention for feelingly emphasizing a theme prominent in the satires of Juvenal: the indignity one suffers merely for being poor.

Peter Green speaks, for example, of "the nightmare obsession," in the early Juvenal, "with poverty and degradation" and claims that "one of Juvenal's most valid points against excessive money-grubbing is the way it corrupts personal relationships."[28] The extra-canonical Wisdom of Ben Sira (i.e., Ecclesiasticus) develops this very point in an extended section (13:1-14:2, AB) that warns against relationships with the rich man, here called a "scoundrel." Such associations are like the blackened hands that come from touching pitch. Throughout this admonition Ben Sira assumes a necessary inequality in such connections that finally humiliates, manipulates, and even destroys the poor: wronged only to be forced to ask pardon; exhausted in human and material resource; tricked, intimidated, and gloatingly impoverished:

> [The rich man] will gloat over you,
>   pretend to be angry with you,
>   shake his head at your downfall
>   and finally laugh you to scorn. [13:7, AB]

No trust or intimacy is possible in such a finally devouring relationship, which Ben Sira compares to alliance between a lamb and a wolf, "peace between the hyena and the dog." This satire on the insolence, contempt, and self-assurance of the wealthy points out, on the other hand, the impunity with which the rich can shame and ruin the less fortunate. The degradation of the poor, of course, is a frequent theme in the laments of the Psalter, itself one of the Hebrew wisdom writings. The Ben Sira who earlier warns not to "mock the poor person's life" (4:1) enforces this caution by recalling the humiliating reversals often effected by the LORD:

> The oppressed often rise to a throne,
>   and some that none would consider wear a crown.
> The exalted often fall into utter disgrace;
>   the honored are given into enemy hands. [11:5-6, AB][29]

So convinced is Ben Sira of the efficacy of shame as a spur to righteous behavior that he also dwells on the difference between true and false shame (41:14-42:14, AB), that is, about specific forms of moral wrong like deceit, crime, disloyalty, and theft about which any individual ought properly to be embarrassed.[30] The public advantage of such a true sense of shame is clear:

> Thus you will be truly refined[,]
>> and recognized by all as discreet. [42:8, AB]

Even the fearful consequence of female immorality is the damage to the father's reputation:

> My son, keep a close watch on your daughter,
>> lest she make you the sport of your enemies,
> A byword in the city and the assembly of the people,
>> an object of derision in public gatherings. [42:11, AB][31]

When Ben Sira concludes this writing so aware of a good and a bad name, he thanks God who has delivered him from evils like "the slanderous tongue," "the lips of lying miscreants," "Malicious lips, slimy deceivers, / [and] arrows sped by treacherous tongues" (51:2, 5-6, AB).

Among the canonical wisdom writings, however, the Book of Proverbs is very conscious of the effects upon reputation of the use of one's own tongue and offers an enhanced name as an inducement to good conduct: "Wise men will inherit honor," it insists, in one of its characteristic contrasts, but "fools will but heighten their shame" (Prov 3:35, AB). Throughout the canonical and extra-canonical wisdom writings, in fact, the fool's public recognition as an ass repeatedly underscores the urging of wise behavior. Wisdom serves as shield, for

> When a fool talks they take a stick to his back,
> Whereas the words of wise men are their protection. [14:3, AB]

The metonomy of the tongue throughout Proverbs, as the instrument affecting one's good name, almost reifies it as the agent of reputation. Proverbs repeatedly makes counsel about how to speak. Even the much more circumspect, hesitant, and questioning wisdom of Qoheleth in Ecclesiastes does not overlook the effect upon reputation of immoral or imprudent behavior. Indeed, one of the specific thrusts Qoheleth directs at more self-assured wisdom like that of Proverbs notes the failure of vicious action to damage the reputation of the wicked: ". . . I saw wicked men borne to their tombs, and as men returned from the sacred place, they were praised in the very city where they had acted so" (Eccl 8:10, AB). None of this résumé, of course, is meant to suggest that vindictiveness, revenge, and a concern with reputation and social proprieties are the center of the ethics of Israel. It points out only that in the midst of sometimes comparatively sophisticated ethical promptings and concerns the ethics of Israel does not overlook the power of shame.[32]

The wisdom writing that speaks most vividly and harshly of the power of shame is, of course, Job. Although its dialogs are a lengthy, non-narrative center in what is, finally, a very brief story, Job is the longest single biblical tale dealing with a response to the continuing humiliation associated with and integral to dreadful misfortune. Believing himself, as his friends also assume, cursed by God, Job responds as we might expect the victim of the curse of Archilochus to respond.

The dialogs that form the book's core (3-31) are framed with self-imprecation. In his very first remarks, Job curses the day of his birth in terms that reverse God's creative act:

> Why not pardon my fault,
> Forgive my iniquity,
> That I might now lie in the dust,
> And you seek me but I would not be? [Job 7:21, AB]

The annihilation sought here reduces Job to a void like that which precedes God's creation in Genesis. The concluding self-imprecation (31) calls curses down upon himself if he can be successfully convicted, as he never is, of specific forms of wrongdoing. The bitterness of his initial self-imprecation continues in his parody of Psalm 8. There, given the overpowering magnitude of the macrocosm fashioned by God, the psalmist cannot contain his awe at Yahweh's special loving concern for the human microcosm. Job, however, wonders why God pays "any mind" to him, why he, like the Satan who prompted this misfortune, inspects Job "every morning" and tests him "every moment." This God, Job charges, is the "man watcher," targeting the human being for every possible misdeed (7:17-18, 20, AB).[33] This bleakly ironic view of a malignly suspicious God grimly contrasts with the divinity celebrated in Psalm 8.[34]

In the framework of these self-imprecations, parodies, and final oath, Job repeatedly expresses his sense of the shameful thing he has become:

> A derision to his neighbor I am become,
> One whom God answered when he called,
> The just and perfect a derision. [12:4, AB]

> They gape at me with their mouth,
> They slap my face in scorn,
> Together they mass against me. [16:10, AB]

> He has made me a popular byword,
> One in whose face they spit. [17:6, AB]

Perhaps sensing the mood of his friends, Job can insist:

> Only mockers are with me,
> My eye dwells on their hostility. [17:2, AB]

For Eliphaz, Bildad, and Zophar—like Job, at least until now—have always assumed that only the wicked suffer. If Job's claim of innocence is true, however, the friends' assurance must disintegrate. What has happened to Job can happen to them. Job knows how that assurance responds to the threatening:

> The comfortable hold calamity in contempt,
> Fitting for those whose feet slip. [12:5, AB]

Hence, the intensifying sarcasm and exchange of insults that quickly replace Eliphaz' opening deference. Indeed, within moments, Eliphaz can speak in terms that come tastelessly close to Job's misfortune:

> At a breath of God they [who plow evil] perish,
> A blast of His anger, and they vanish.
> The lion may roar, the old lion growl,
> But the young lion's teeth are broken.
> The lion perishes, robbed of prey,
> The lioness' whelps are scattered. [4:9-11, AB]

Bildad is more direct:

> Your children sinned against him,
> And he paid them for their sin. [8:4, AB]

Allegations of the sinfulness of his lost children are followed by direct accusations of his own sinfulness. Eliphaz, in fact, has very specific charges to level against Job (22:6-9), a number of which Job denies in his final oath. Sarcastic, dismissive use of wind imagery is traded back and forth among Job and his three friend-accusers (e.g., 15:2; 16:3) as well as equally contemptuous charges that each side is appropriating wisdom to itself (e.g., 12:2). The increasingly hostile situation climaxes in Job's oath of self-imprecation, which demands, dramatically, that God appear and respond. Moshe Greenberg sensitively phrases it: "there is tension in the air: will the Litigant respond?"[35] Job's lengthy prelude to this oath contrasts the recollection of his days of honor and respect among all levels of society (29) with the derision he experiences in his present anguish (30):

> But now they deride me,
> Men younger than I,
> Whose fathers I had disdained
> To put with the dogs of my flock . . . .
> And now I am become their jest,
> I have become to them a gibe.
> They detest me and stand aloof;
> From my face they spare no spit.
> [30:1, 9-10, AB]

The restoration of Job's fortune restores him as well to the shared life of the community: "All his brothers and sisters and former acquaintances called on him and had a meal with him in his house . . .."[36] No longer a pariah, Job finds his later life blessed "more than his earlier life." The number of his sons and daughters is doubled, he sees "his sons and grandsons to four generations," and dies "old and satisfied with life" (42:12-13, 16-17, AB), no longer a laughing-stock and a byword. If the lexicon of the Hebrew Scriptures does not include *satire* and *irony*, it certainly includes innumerable instances of many words associated with both: *byword, contempt, hate, humiliate, laughingstock, reproach, scoff, shame, taunt*, and related terms like *honor, regard*, and *repute*.[37]

iii.

". . . they have doomed Mistress Prynne to stand only a space
of three hours on the platform of the pillory, and then and
thereafter, for the remainder of her natural life, to wear a
mark of shame upon her bosom."

Nathaniel Hawthorne, *The Scarlet Letter*

The shame and humiliation complained of in the Hebrew
Scriptures regularly assume that suffering punishes wickedness
or is interpreted as doing so. Yet the distress at issue has nothing to do with sentences imposed by human judicial authority.
No incarceration, decree of banishment, fine, or doom of
execution underlies the complaint. Victim and bystander refer
rather to the misfortunes of life: death, especially if sudden and
violent, sickness, the loss of children, the inability to bear
children, the loss of property, and, in the prophets with particular emphasis, exile and captivity. These humiliating mischances
apparently reflect a punishment for wrongdoing effected by
divine judicial authority.[38] Shame is thus integral and related
to an assumed system of divine justice. In some instances, as in
the case of Job, a causal relationship between suffering and
punishment is revealed as groundless. In other cases, however,
the Scriptures affirm the connection. The prophet Nathan, for
example, explains that the death of David's first child by Bathsheba and the rebellion against him within his own household
are punishments for David's treacherously murderous adultery
(2 Sam 11:27-12:13). Then too the Hebrew Scriptures question,
as in Ecclesiastes, whether God's justice operates within any
humanly discernible framework. Suffering, shame, punishment,
and justice—however differently viewed, the relationship among
them is explored throughout the Hebrew Bible.

Like that created by satirists, the shame threatened by the
prophets operates almost necessarily within a quasi-legal framework. Suffering is exemplary: a warning to others of what
evildoing brings on. As Jonathan Lamb observes, Job is being
mocked because his comforters assign his pain "exemplary
status."[39] In the prophets the ultimate exemplary punishment
for the Northern Kingdom (Israel) is its conquest and devastation at the hands of the Assyrians in the late eighth century BC.

As Hosea succinctly puts it:

> Samaria [i.e., the Northern Kingdom] has become guilty,
>   for she has rebelled against her God.
> They will fall by the sword.
> Their infants will be smashed.
>   Her pregnant women will be torn open. [Hos 14:1, AB]

A century and a quarter later, Judah, the Southern Kingdom, suffers the exemplary shame of destruction, captivity, and exile at the hands of the Babylonians. Through Jeremiah, Yahweh warns in graphic contrast:

> For the people of Judah have done what is highly displeasing to me—Yahweh's word. They have placed their detestable cult objects in the house that bears my name, in order to defile it. They have built the high place of Tophet in the valley of Ben-hinnom in order to burn their sons and daughters in the fire—a thing that I never commanded, nor did it even enter my mind.
>
> Therefore, believe me, days are coming—Yahweh's word—when they will no longer speak of Tophet, or of the valley of Ben-hinnom, but of the valley of Slaughter; for they will bury in Tophet till there is no room left. Then the corpses of this people will be left to feed the carrion birds and the wild beasts, for there will be no one to frighten them away. And I will banish from the cities of Judah and from Jerusalem's streets sounds of mirth and gladness, the voice of the bridegroom and bride; for the land will be a desolate waste.
>
> [Jer 7:30-34, AB]

Like other of the prophets, Hosea and Jeremiah announce God's sentence for wrongdoing. Both catastrophes are punishments for sinfulness.

The legal terminology in this analysis and in the biblical texts on which it draws—*wrongdoing, sentence, punishment, guilty,* and the like—is not at all accidental to or loosely figurative in such discourse, because the language of the law underscores the quasi-legal nature of prophecy and satire, one of their most significant common denominators. Both explain, justify, and even fashion shame as a judgment upon wrongdoing. Both prosecute, judge, and deliberate, the prophet explicitly speaking for God, the satirist claiming moral justification, yet both directing violent verbal abuse at wrongdoers, both announcing sometimes violent and debasing sentencing. Prophecy and satire deliberately equate suffering and its attendant disgrace with punishment. They announce, then, a form of justice, even as revenge. For revenge, popularly yet very precisely viewed as getting even, seeks in its own way to restore the equality at the heart of justice, to bring even the fearful emotional energy of justified retaliation to rest.[40] Yahweh himself looks forward to the catharsis of his effected vengeance on Judah: "I will spend my fury against you and my rage at you shall subside; I will grow calm and not be vexed any more" (Ezek 16:42, AB). Although neither prophet nor satirist acts with judicial warrant to sentence, each exposes wrongdoing and publicizes and creates a shame associated with it. Like a prophet, then, Pope can boast, in *Epilogue to the Satires, Dialogue II*:

> Yes, I am proud; I must be proud to see
> Men not afraid of God, afraid of me:
> Safe from the Bar, the Pulpit, and the Throne,
> Yet touch'd and sham'd by *Ridicule* alone.
> [P. 293, 11.209-212]

Behind the boast, the feared efficacy of the word and the humiliation it can effect. Prophecy and satire create exemplary laughingstocks and bywords of wrongdoing. Even if disaster or its threat has passed, later generations can still read the warning. The exemplary fate of Jerusalem does not cease in 586 BC nor that of civilization in *The Dunciad* in 1743.

a.

> A Lash like mine no honest man shall dread,
> But all such babling blockheads in his stead.
> Alexander Pope, *An Epistle to Dr. Arbuthnot*

The argument advanced here—about the exemplary punitive function often associated in the Hebrew Scriptures with wrongdoing—is applying particularly to Hebrew prophecy the stimulating and provocative analysis by David B. Morris which claims that hatred, anger, and the desire to inflict pain are inescapable components of satire.[41] His analysis is prompted by Alexander

Pope's sketch of Sporus in the *Epistle to Dr. Arbuthnot* (pp. 207-208, ll. 305-333). Pope's contemporaries surely had no difficulty in recognizing John, Lord Hervey, an enemy of the poet's, as a basis for the sketch. Like other critics, Morris admits the "withering contempt" of the portrait, but, he adds, "rarely has finesse been wedded to such destructive force."[42] In this limning of a suspiciously attractive, predatory, bisexual cultivator and patron of the arts, images of the insect and the reptile predominate—the Serpent in the Garden of the Arts.[43]

An undesirable consequence, Morris believes, of the earlier focussing on rhetorical strategies in the portrayal—he refers explicitly to Maynard Mack's "The Muse of Satire"—is a very diminished awareness of the violence, the hatred that courses through the lines. Satire, Morris warns, is "an art which relies on its power to offend." Morris asks then if instruction, amendment, and reformation are "the *only* [his emphasis] purposes which animate the muse of satire." As Morris observes, the presence in satire of the violently offensive language society customarily banishes from discourse obviously reflects the satirist's desire to offend.[44] The question Morris directs at the muse of satire can, it seems to me, be directed with equal justice at the muse of prophecy. For the prophecy which seeks to instruct, amend, and reform also seeks to offend.[45]

Morris then connects satire's desire to punish with the treatment of criminals in the eighteenth century when "punishment . . . usually implied the infliction of pain, and satire was widely regarded as an art of punishment." Deterrence, not rehabilitation, was the goal of eighteenth-century justice. The malefactor's suffering was a warning to all. Pope's satires, consequently, have a "legal or judicial basis," something Pope himself announces in claiming as his subject "Crimes that scape, or triumph o'er the Law" (*Epilogue to the Satires, Dialogue I*, p. 286, l. 168). That announcement endorses "the relation between satire and jurisprudence." Then, in comments particularly applicable to Hebrew prophecy, Morris continues:

> The satirical victim has quasi-legal status as a malefactor; his arraignment is a form of poetic justice; and the satirist, after serving first as judge and jury, steps forward to carry out the

necessary punishment, all for the public good. The reader, like the crowd at eighteenth-century executions, holds the uneasy and sometimes alarming role of witness, for whom the spectacle of someone else's punishment cannot be entirely undisturbing.

Indeed, the "mutilation, exposure, and lingering decay" sometimes inflicted on the cadaver of the wrongdoer "extended legal punishment beyond death."[46] This very point, in effect, concludes the mock-lament Isaiah sings as the regal specter, once King of Babylon, enters the land of the forgotten dead (Isa 14:3-21).[47]

As a weapon, Morris insists, "satire . . . constitutes a form of literary discourse uniquely concerned with power" and with directing that power against the "foolish, corrupt, greedy, stupid, and dangerous," the recurring targets of prophetic power. But most striking for me in this conclusion are two serendipities that provide internal warrant for relating the power of Pope's satire to comparable power in the prophets. First, Pope, it seems, linked the whole question of satire's inflicting pain with a biblical question he "had pondered directly." The poet raises this question in a note to Book XIII, line 779, of his translation of *The Iliad*: "*Wherefore doth the way of the wicked prosper?*" The answer Pope finally satisfied himself with, says Morris, is this: "the pain of satire . . . deprives wickedness of its self-insulating complacency. It forces the villainous to experience both the reality of their unhappy state and the unhappiness they cause others." What Morris does not make explicit here, however, and this is the second find, is that Pope's biblical phrasing of the question appears in Jeremiah (12:1). In defending Menelaus' complaint against Jupiter's apparent protection of a wicked people, Pope not only defends Menelaus' remarks as "no more than what a pious suffering Mind, griev'd at the flourishing Condition of prosperous Wickedness, might naturally fall into," but compares this complaint to Jeremiah's:

Not unlike this is the Complaint of the Prophet *Jeremiah*, Ch. 12, V. 1. *Righteous art thou, O Lord, when I plead with thee: yet let me talk with thee of thy Judgments. Wherefore doth the way of the wicked prosper? Wherefore are all they happy that deal very treacherously?*[48]

42

b.

"I hate the man, because he prophesies no good for
me; never anything but evil. His name is Micaiah son
of Imlah."   1 Kgs 22:8 (NEB)

The complaint of Jeremiah with which Alexander Pope bolsters
his defense of Menelaus' frustration at apparent divine injustice
implies that the prophet seeks appropriate divine sentencing for
evil. If not a prosecutor against those "that deal very treacherously," Jeremiah is at least a concerned witness for the prosecu-
tion, even if he has already determined the defendants' guilt.

The legal language and context which appear so clearly in
prophecy are not peripheral to the biblical texts discussed
earlier as instances of the powerful sense of shame operating in
the Hebrew Scriptures. Job and the Psalms are two cases in
point. In drawing attention to the pervasive legal situations
implied in the laments of the Psalter, Lawrence Toombs connects the legal formulas of the laments with the bringing to the
temple "for *adjudication* [my emphasis] by God himself" of
cases "too difficult" for "the elders of the village courts or the
judges of the royal courts in the principal cities." The laments in
the psalter, he argues, even allow a reconstruction of the
otherwise unavailable "ritual for the presentation of a legal case
in the temple." Hence, the "conventional language" of deep
distress, figuratively expressed, the declaration of innocence,
and the invitation of "the searching scrutiny of God to determine guilt or innocence." The quasi-legal context implied in the
laments, consequently, also conveys the sense of shame a
defendant might experience at having to appear in court at all
to petition an acquittal or a righting of wrongs.[49] Like the
satirist then, to recall David Morris' argument, the psalmist goes
to court before a moral authority to seek a vindication which
formal human judiciary does not provide. The pervasive metaphor in the Book of Job is that of a trial: apparent punishment,
repeated accusation, repeated protestation of innocence, cross-
examination, demands for evidence, a formal oath, God's own
testimony. Of all the forms of rhetoric, discourse, or art most
appropriate to apply to Job, the most fitting, it seems to me, is

that of the trial. Job and God have gone to court.[50]

Nor is there need to elaborate biblical scholarship's insistence on the recurring, ubiquitous terms and forms of the law in the Hebrew prophets. True, Gene M. Tucker notes, "the list of genres, genre elements and formulas used by the prophets to express themselves is almost endless," but, he adds, "especially important is the use of the technical, legal language of the court process." So, Tucker notes, as in Micah 6:1-2, Yahweh appears "as the plaintiff arguing a case against his people" with the language of "the official summons to appear in court" and the immediately subsequent "speech of the accuser":

> Hear what the LORD says:
> Arise, plead your case before the mountains,
>   and let the hills hear your voice.
> Hear, you mountains, the controversy [lawsuit] of the LORD,
>   and you enduring foundations of the earth;
> for the LORD has a controversy [lawsuit] with his people,
>   and he will contend with Israel.

Concerned as they are with the laws of Israel and "the crimes of their people," the prophets display a "completely understandable" use of legal language.[51] The Book of Jeremiah almost at once announces Yahweh's *rib*, that is, his case, against his people (Jer 2:9, AB).[52] The prophet comes to accuse, to present evidence, and to sentence. "Come now, let us argue it out," says Isaiah's God (1:18, NEB). Israel, the prophet charges, has done shameful deeds:

> Shame on you! you who make unjust laws
> and publish burdensome decrees,
> depriving the poor of justice,
> robbing the weakest of my people of their rights,
> despoiling the widow and plundering the orphan.
>
> [Isa 10:1-2, NEB]

Amos' opening parallels sentences upon Israel, Judah, and several of their neighbors in the manner of a legal refrain: "For crime after crime . . . / I will grant them no reprieve" (1:3, 6, 9, 11, 13; 2:1, 4, 7, NEB). The doom the prophets come to announce is both content and form, not only, as Johnson's *Dictionary* defines, "determination declared" or "the state to which one is destined," but "judicial sentence," "judgment," and "condemnation" as well. The language and forms of the law in prophecy and in satire arise organically, inevitably, and integrally out of their common content.

This language and these formulas also reflect an origin and evolution common to both. Satire evolves from the curse—the thesis of Robert Elliott's *The Power of Satire*. But Hebrew prophecy also evolves from the belief that words can effect the good or evil they utter. Such is the inescapable conviction that underlies the story of Balaam, who blesses the Israel he was summoned to curse (Numbers 22-24). Balak, the king of Moab, states explicitly in his summons to the seer: "I know that those whom you bless are blessed, and those whom you curse are cursed" (Num 22:6, NEB). Such is the lurking fear of Ahab, who expresses more than mere irritation when he remarks that the prophet Micaiah "prophesies no good for me; never anything but evil" (1 Kgs 22:8, NEB). If the curse evolves into law, then the quasi-legal nature of prophecy and satire is a relationship internally demanded and internally rooted in the common, original belief that words effect the weal or woe they speak of.[53] That, finally, is why the language and the forms of the law are neither accidental to nor loosely figurative in either. The judgment both share as a common content is, thus, not merely a criticism heavily and primarily censorious, the expression of an unfavorable opinion. Judgment is also a legal act and a descendant of the curse.

c.

The LORD is a jealous god, a god of vengeance;
    The LORD takes vengeance and is quick to anger.
                                        Nah 1:2 (NEB)

To align prophecy with effected curse or blessing, to insist on its naturally and spontaneously legal and adversarial quality, to recognize how it often connects humiliation and punishment, to see it as a kind of sentencing, violent and demeaning in the doom it imposes, sometimes on the people as a whole—to affirm all this underscores the applicability to Hebrew prophecy of David Morris' description of satire as "form of literary dis-

45

course uniquely concerned with power."[54] Unique, of course, I contend, not at all. Power is the stuff of prophecy as well. Not surprising then is a parallel reluctance of biblical critics to confront this disturbing power. Not surprising then are comparable strategies in the biblical texts dealing with this power. The distinguished scholar of the prophets Abraham Heschel, for example, introduces his analysis of "The Meaning and Mystery of Wrath" in the prophets by pointing specifically to emphases elsewhere on the more attractive prophetic utterances dealing with justice and divine love. These he sees as opposed to the "usually disregarded" staple of "harsh words, . . . grave threats, . . . relentless demands, . . . [and] shrieks of doom," prophetic characteristics which have caused recoil or repulsion and, by some, allegorical reading. Like Morris, Heschel charges that critics and scholars confronted with disturbing threats of power in effect wish away the text before them. "It is, indeed, impossible," Heschel nonetheless counters, "to close one's eyes to the words of the wrath of God in Scripture."[55]

At times, surely, the prophetic texts seem almost to luxuriate in the violent prospect of an effected doom. Nahum is a particularly striking instance of divine gloating that characterizes the text. At one point Yahweh speaks as a satirist might describing techniques of the most offensive denigration which here, however, is physically threatened:

> I am against you, says the LORD of Hosts,
> I will uncover your breasts to your disgrace
> and expose your naked body to every nation,
>   to every kingdom your shame.
> I will cast loathsome filth over you,
> I will count you obscene
>   and treat you like excrement. [Nah 3:5, NEB]

When Yahweh commands Ezekiel to "clap your hand and stamp your foot and say 'Ah!' over all the evil abominations of the house of Israel [Ezek 6:11, AB]," Moshe Greenberg explains that "the gestures and a similar exclamation recur as expressions of *malicious glee* [my emphasis] . . . . The prophet is to represent God's satisfaction at venting his rage upon Israel." Greenberg notes the text in Deuteronomy: "And as YHWH once

46

delighted in making you prosperous and numerous, so YHWH will now delight in making you perish and destroying you."[56] Mention has already been made of the satisfying violent destruction of Babylon anticipated at the end of Jeremiah.[57] And Obadiah gleefully looks forward to the day when the tables will be turned on the Edom that assisted in the sacking of Jerusalem. It is precisely the Edomites' gloating that Obadiah warns against:

> Do not gloat over your brother on the day of his misfortune,
> nor rejoice over Judah on his day of ruin;
> do not boast on the day of distress,
> nor enter my people's gates on the day of his downfall.
> Do not gloat over his fall on the day of his downfall
> nor seize his treasure
>   on the day of his downfall. [Obad 12-13, NEB]

The very Yahweh sensitive to the ridiculing contempt his people suffer—

> all round you men gloated over you . . . ; your name was bandied about in the common talk of men . . . . Edom . . . seized on my land to hold it up to public contempt . . . . you have had to endure the taunts of all the nations.
>
>   [Ezek 36:3, 5-6, NEB]

—is equally and frighteningly capable of enjoying the very situation he has created.

Small wonder that contemporary critics can mention how readers "depreciate a prophet" like Nahum, "who seems," to them, so Herbert Marks notes, "content to glorify vengeance." Although Marks notes that such a view overlooks the fact that

> in the edited collection [of Nahum], the reader comes to Nahum's vision of martial triumph by way of an independent hymnic composition, celebrating God's supernatural power and presenting his ultimate control of historical ends as an aspect of his primary authority over all creation

—despite this, Marks still asks where "this ecstatic fury of the negative comes from" and insists, in answer, that "the aggression at the root of all poetic enthusiasm . . . burns hottest in the prophets, who themselves afflicted, inflict their word on every-

47

thing about them." Geoffrey Hartman stresses "the ambivalent sympathy shown by the prophet for the powerful and terrible thing he envisions."[58]

In the disturbing force of such prophetic utterance, Heschel, like Morris on the violence of satire, points to what is at least a common strategy of assurance: God's anger is not "unpredictable, irrational, . . . a spontaneous outburst." God's anger—like the satirist's—is "a reaction occasioned by the conduct of man." The anger of prophecy is morally impelled. Indeed, "the call of anger" in the prophets "is a call to cancel anger, . . . a free and deliberate reaction of God's justice to what is wrong and evil." And, more importantly, in the prophets "anger is always described as a moment, something that happens rather than something that abides."[59] So David Morris, speaking of Pope's Sporus portrait, observes, "Pope must also demonstrate that indignation is not his permanent state of mind or an uncontrollable passion . . . ."[60] In these siblings of judgment then, a disciplined moral fury lashes out at moral disaster. Be it Jonathan Swift's searing outrage in the penultimate paragraph of *A Modest Proposal*, as it breaks through the ironic facade of the lunatic humanitarian-and-mass-murderer, or the fury of Jeremiah at the morally criminal behavior of smugly, self-satisfied Judahites who worship regularly in the Temple (Jer 7:1-8:3), the power in such passages draws from the connection with moral purpose. In their most disquietingly severe moments, prophecy and satire convince because their anger appears neither arbitrary nor self-indulgent. Michael Patrick O'Connor provides a caution for those squeamish about the searing, violent quality in texts that judge. The scorching "salvation-history" of Ezekiel 16, he notes—Ezekiel's fantasy of Judah's worldwide career of infidelity—explicitly charges "premeditated murder, of children, in the cult." O'Connor continues:

> It is understandable that many commentators slide by or seek to minimize Israelite child sacrifice. It is more interesting and demanding to realize that the prophets could not overlook it. Gratuitous murder is not easy to talk about. The real danger in Ezek. 16 is its demand that we recognize our history.[61]

In the face of wholesale, colossal victimizing—of children in the worship of Israel and Judah, of the poor in Ireland, of the genocides of our time—isn't it much more disturbing to expect polite civility of satire and prophecy? Some crimes do cry to heaven for vengeance. Shakespeare, after all, insists that "something is rotten" not in the state of Hamlet, but "in the state of Denmark." Search for the perfect accuser, and no criminal will be whipped.

2

OF
JACOB'S
POTTAGE
AND
HORACE'S
FARE

Reason, says William Blake in *The Marriage of Heaven and Hell*, "is the bound or outward circumference of Energy." Power, energy, impulse demand shape. However volatile, intense, and ambiguous the power that drives prophecy and satire, that power finds final expression in the ritual-like form of the text. The impression of explosive spontaneity, of barely controlled power—Jeremiah and Juvenal come easily to mind— is precisely that: an impression belied by the text. Spontaneous anger seldom expresses itself in dactylic hexameter. The text is the "bound or outward circumference" of prophetic and satiric energy. The metamorphosis of volatility into text presents, first of all, the apparent contradiction of formed explosiveness. The text often captures the disparate, contradictory, and hostile impulses that underlie the order of words. A second unique feature of this change denies prophecy and satire, kin in their descent from the curse, any possibility in the concrete for distinguishing between intention and action, plan and execution, desire and deed. Like blessing, curse is efficacious utterance-act. No word, no curse. No curse, no power. To utter is to shape; to shape is to effect. The very appearance of prophetic or satiric word inspires the fear that harm has already been done. So all of the terrifying, aggressive, fear- and shame-manipulating energies common to both necessarily inhere and find their only expression in strategies of rhetoric.

The effects of this metamorphosis on the form and subject matter of prophecy and satire provide thus another significant likeness between them. Curse or blessing, blame or praise—these, generally speaking, are the subject and the aim of prophecy and satire. In asserting their judgment or announcing their ideal, however, prophet and satirist serve up a melange, a potpourri, a stew of matter and form, itself a metaphor for the volatile energy underlying utterance. Words undermine words; form and content are jumbled; prose and poetry interchange. In this chapter, I examine some issues of content and form in prophecy and satire, the open-ended, unresolved nature of both, their shared view of a morally conditioned future, and their similarly prompted address to more than those they hope to reform. A guiding keynote is provided by Bronislaw Malinowski, whose *Argonauts of the Western Pacific* Robert Elliott cites in *The Power of Satire*. The context—familiar from any analysis of the vagaries of structure in prophecy and satire—is the not always logical quality of either. Elliott's reminder of a remote origin in magic includes a helpful warning from Malinowski, who points out that magic

> does not serve to communicate ideas from one person to another; it does not purport to contain a consecutive consistent meaning. It is an instrument serving special purposes, intended for the exercise of man's specific power over things, and *its meaning* [Elliott's emphasis], giving this word a wider sense, can be understood only in correlation to this aim. It will not therefore be a meaning of logically or topically concatenated ideas, but of expressions fitting into one another and into the whole, according to what could be called a magical order of thinking, or perhaps more correctly, a magical order of expressing, of *launching* [my emphasis] words towards their aim.[1]

What, then, does the volatile energy of prophecy and satire do to the form and content of both?

51

i.

"I saw the earth—lo, chaos primeval!"
Jer 4:23 (AB)

Notice, for example, the implications for form of what Walter Brueggemann claims about the power of Jeremiah's word, the Jeremiah in the text whom he regards as "an imaginative literary construction governed by a powerful person of memory." Like a proto-satirist I would add, this Jeremiah "is summoned to *shatter* and form worlds by his *speech* [my emphasis]." His entire life, in fact, "consists in coming to terms" with the "persistent, inescapable, and overriding word" delivered to him. The poetic mode of his prophetic speech is not accidental or incidental to his prophetic office, "not just a skillful or an occasional cloak for an eternal world," but rather "part of the *strategy* [my emphasis] for letting the word make a difference in historical reality." Brueggemann then continues:

> The shattering and forming of worlds is not done as a potter molds clay or as a factory makes products. It is done as a poet "*redescribes* [my emphasis]" the world, *reconfigures* [my emphasis] public perception, and causes people to reexperience their experience. To do that requires that speech must not be conventional, reasonable, predictable: it must shock sensitivity, call attention to what is not noticed, break the routine, cause people to redescribe things that have long since seem settled, bear surpluses of power before routine assessments . . . . Such *speech* [my emphasis] functions to discredit and illegitimate the old, conventional modes of perception. When things are seen in new ways, we become aware that the old conventional slogans (e.g., Jer 7:4) are in fact ideological coverups that no longer claim allegiance. Such imaginative *speech* [my emphasis] evokes new sensitivities, invites people to hope, that is, to respond to social possibilities which the old administrative *language* [my emphasis] has declared unthinkable, unreasonable, and impossible.[2]

To illustrate his point, Brueggemann turns to what he calls "the passionate words" of Jeremiah 4:19-20:

O my bowels, my bowels! I writhe!
O walls of my heart!

My heart is in storm within me,
    I cannot be still.
You have heard, O my soul, the trumpet blast,
    The battle shout.
Disaster comes hard on disaster,
    All the land is laid waste.
Laid waste of a sudden my tents,
    In an instant my curtains. [AB]³

In his analysis of this poem—the term is his—he comments on a "tightness of language" that profoundly binds "*internal upset* and *external disarray* [his emphasis]." He says also: "*The words seem to rush and tumble in a visceral spree* [my emphasis]." The point of his analysis, he claims, is not "to study poetic style" or "to celebrate aesthetic qualities"; no, "the point is rather that Jeremiah the prophet is portrayed as a consummate artist, who uses his artistic gifts to *overthrow* [my emphasis] the deathly technique and unexamined ideology of his society."⁴ The forms of prophetic speech must shatter the forms of moral complacency: the prophetic word, like the satiric, must attack language itself and the forms of language because they shelter the customary and the complacent.

Ridicule here only intensifies this already volatile scene. The name-calling, the demeaning of what was familiar and even venerated, the guilt-by-association—all these devices and more hammer home the censure of morally reprehensible behavior. Its subverting viewpoint is a volatile force. Action hitherto unchallenged, reassuringly, confidently, even thoughtlessly repeated needs now to justify itself. What had been, before Hosea, fertility rites to Baal become now morally unspeakable viciousness that sacrifices children in a ritual to secure fruitfulness! The worshiped divinity here, insists Hosea, cannot be Yahweh. Even Baal is inadequate as a name. Call him rather Shame, Rival, Slayer (Hos 9:10, 13, AB). Hosea's perspective cannot be shaken off. The once unchallenged rite assumes a new, far less attractive form. The reality complacently and approvingly viewed appears differently in Hosea's ideal perspective. A satisfying and indulgent view of former action disappears, its dominating, unified, coherent, and unchallenged quality now shattered. It fights off a new, grotesque, ridiculed, and unseemly quality. Micah chastises the offering to Yahweh of "a blind victim, . . . a victim lame or distressed," a liturgy that looks back to Cain, of all people, for its exemplar (Mic 1:8, NEB). Such distorted forms reflect the moral grotesqueness of challenged behavior. Prophecy and satire are replete with the grotesque and the absurd because these are the images, the correlatives of their judgment. They are the external signs of an inward *dis*-grace, a reverse sacrament as it were, pointing in the grotesque to the absence in reprehensible behavior of any defensible principle of identity, humanity, unity, coherence, or purpose that could give attractive moral form to such unspeakable acts. These reprehensible forms of human misconduct are themselves ludicrous, formless parodies of moral vision and energy. The grotesque, often distorted rhetorical forms in which prophet and satirist speak become then the verbal counterpart of grotesque behavior. Prophecy and satire jumble form and content because the world they indict is a moral jumble. Either text is a disturbing potpourri of scenes and forms, a deliberate, ridiculing olio—to use Juvenal's image in the *First Satire*—that serves up for censure every human indecency:

> Whatever since that Golden Age was done,
> What humankind desires, and what they shun,
> Rage, passions, pleasures, impotence of will,
> Shall this satirical [or prophetic?] collection fill.[5]

The weird, grotesque, misshapen, half-shapen, parodied, borrowed, altered, and abused forms used by the prophets and the satirists embody the formless, anarchic, moral dysentery each chastises and exposes. The textual consequence is the generic mishmash frequent in, perhaps even integral to, both discourses, their external sign of the inward moral chaos. Once Amos parodies the call to worship at the Northern Kingdom's two principal shrines—

> Come to Bethel—and rebel!
> Come to Gilgal—and rebel the more! [Amos 4:4, NEB]

—can that call ever again sound with unequivocal, uncomplicated meaning? Will it not henceforward ever be a summons and a parody of itself at the same time? Who shall now venture

54

to Bethel or to Gilgal without some show of embarrassment?

For a comparable instance among the satirists of how the ideal vision of the critic undermines and distorts the complacent view of the real in a single image of moral grotesquerie, Evelyn Waugh provides a formally instructive incident near the end of the 1930 satire *Vile Bodies*, one of his earliest exercises in a career of unrelenting criticism of the Twentieth Century and its lack of values. The on-again, off-again engagement of Nina Blount and Adam Fenwick-Symes is, apparently, now permanently off. Nina is flying away with the Ginger she has decided to marry and whose child she is carrying. Their flight carries them over the England where the vacuous, tedium-inspired, and morally irresponsible action of the novel has been set. *Vile Bodies*—a 1930 novel, remember—will reel giddily towards World War. As Ginger looks out the plane, he shouts:

> "I say, Nina, . . . when you were young did you ever have to learn a thing out of a poetry book about: *'This scep-ter'd isle, this earth of majesty, this something or other Eden'?* D'you know what I mean? *'this happy breed of men, this little world, this precious stone set in the silver sea. . . .*
>
> "'*This blessed plot, this earth, this realm, this England This nurse, this teeming womb of royal kings Feared by their breed and famous by their birth . . . .'*
>
> "I forget how it goes on. Something about a stubborn Jew. But you know the thing I mean?"
>
> "It comes in a play."
>
> "No, a blue poetry book."
>
> "I acted in it."
>
> "Well, they may have put it into a play since. It was in a blue poetry book when I learned it. Anyway, you know what I mean?"
>
> "Yes, why?"
>
> "Well, I mean to say, don't you feel somehow, up in the air like this and looking down and seeing everything underneath. I mean, don't you have a sort of feeling rather like that, if you see what I mean?"
>
> Nina looked down and saw inclined at an odd angle a horizon of straggling red suburb; arterial roads dotted with little cars; factories, some of them working, others empty and decaying; a disused canal; some distant hills sown with bunga-

lows; wireless masts and overhead power cables; men and women were indiscernible except as tiny spots; they were marrying and shopping and making money and having children. The scene lurched and tilted again as the aeroplane struck a current of air.

"I think I'm going to be sick," said Nina.

"Poor little girl," said Ginger. "That's what the paper bags are for."[6]

Ginger and Nina are trying without success to remember a "sacred" text of sorts, John of Gaunt's speech in William Shakespeare's *Richard II*. True, John speaks of England as a select, hallowed place, a "demi-paradise," but neither Ginger nor Nina remembers that he goes on to indict that England "now bound in with shame," that England that has made "a shameful conquest of itself." It is a John of Gaunt expecting little of the near future who concludes: " . . . would the scandal vanish with my life, / How happy then were my ensuing death."[7]

Waugh's scene is a prophet's melange. A "sacred" text haunts the scene of contemporary viciousness and indicts it. Indeed, these two current defilers of England's "blessed plot" vaguely, uncomprehendingly, and inaccurately speak of a text that excoriates the desecration of a sacred place. Yet neither Nina nor Ginger remembers the indictment at all. John of Gaunt's mournful commentary has been transformed into the verbal chic of a travel agent's brochure. Neither, in fact, can locate the text accurately. The plane jumbles the perspective even more as it moves them on to other things. Nina sees the scene "at an odd angle," an urban-suburban amalgam little reminiscent of John's England: his is a moral vision, hers a layout of bricks, mortar, streets, and everyday business. Then, the scene "lurched and tilted again." Most fittingly, the narrator invites us to share, but wittingly, Nina's response: "I think I'm going to be sick." Her vomiting destroys any reassuring picture which she and Ginger seek to impose by partial and uncomprehending use of a familiar, "sacred" text. A defiled, vomited-on moral landscape emerges precisely because the narrator allows an ideal and ironically condemnatory image to peep through this vacuously cheap exercise in pseudo-pastoral nostalgia. John of Gaunt's speech is more timely than Ginger and Nina will ever know.

Waugh's blurred, multiple, jumbled image is here, as throughout prophecy and satire, a formally inescapable requirement of both as critical discourses, the generic mishmash that provides the formal equivalent or correlative of meaning. Forms are mixed, borrowed, and parodied. The mishmash of forms can be viewed as an ironically subtle but sympathetic parody and technique arising out of and expressing a significant theme in the first of the two Creation accounts in Genesis. The very opening of the Hebrew Scriptures draws attention to a before-time, characterized by formlessness, the *tohu wabohu*: "the earth was without form and void" (Gen 1:2, KJV). Word creates distinguishable forms: God's repeated utterances make distinct light and darkness, land and sea, earth and sky—all the many forms of creation. Here, the correspondence between word and form is perfect, because the form corresponds to God's intention in bringing it into being. Morally objectionable action, however, violates moral form, but seeks to escape that awareness by tricks of language whose real objective is not to distinguish and designate, but to disguise. The mishmash of forms, with their use of words in unconventional ways, shatters that illusion. The prophetic utterance, like the satiric, exposes such pseudo-creation that seeks to transform what is morally formless and void into acceptable human action.

Were the prophetic or satiric text a canvas—to steal Horace's image from the *Art of Poetry*—, we would be simultaneously aware of several superimposed images, each commenting on the others. Picasso's "The Old Guitarist" in The Art Institute of Chicago has never been the same for me since a friend made me aware of a second, but unbowed, head, visible under the pigment of the painting Picasso decided to put on that canvas instead. I will always see two heads there. Satire and prophecy deny and subvert the acceptable moral form which complacency imposes on human action. They jumble and disfigure that form by seeing it against the moral norm which motivates both discourses. Generic mixture is a formally inevitable consequence of that view.

a.

Unnumber'd Throngs on ev'ry side are seen
Of Bodies chang'd to various Forms by Spleen.
Alexander Pope, *The Rape of the Lock*

Critical analyses of satire and prophecy recurrently point to the mixture of speech forms as a major feature of both, a fertile field for the appearance of all sorts of forms, each a form of forms using and subverting the shape of language familiar from other discourse and from other walks of life. By very etymology, satire is a stew, a mixed dish: *satura*, the term itself Latin, denotes a yearly offering to the gods of various fruits, hence, a mixture or medley. Adverbially, *satura* denotes confusion, lack of discrimination, something done helter-skelter. The culinary component of *satura* leads Smith Palmer Bovie, in his translation of Horace's *Satires*, to explain the presence of "so much foodstuff" in the second book of the *Satires* as Horace's upholding "the customs of his ancestors" by providing the vicarious meals that parody and perfect "the archetypal pattern of this distinctively Roman literary genre, . . . meals with moral menus and a blackberry plenty of raisins."[8] Not only does Bovie point out how Horace's Roman successors Juvenal and Persius continue this culinary archetype. He reminds us as well that almost seventeen hundred years later John Dryden succinctly epitomized his preference between Horace and Juvenal by returning to the culinary component of *satura* itself: "The meat of Horace is more nourishing; but the cookery of Juvenal more exquisite."[9]

No such culinary component, of course, appears in the etymology of prophecy, in Hebrew, in Greek, or in English. But if, in the first place, the farrago character of satire draws attention to its subject matter as one of its essential components, Johannes Lindblom's recital of the widely varying content of prophetic revelation sounds a similar note: "sermons and admonitory addresses, announcements of doom and punishment, lyric poems, prayers, hymns, parables, dialogues, monologues, short oracles, didactic sentences, predictions, messages, letters, *etc.* [my emphasis]."[10] A literary critic might regard

58

most of these terms as formal as well as material elements of prophecy. Most revealing, in a way, is Lindblom's *etc.*, a useful, catchall abbreviation that also serves Joseph Blenkinsopp as he speaks of "the diatribes, mock laments, taunt songs, etc., against hostile nations [which] form a distinct compilation" in Ezekiel, viz., chapters 25-32, no insubstantial part of the prophecy as a whole, and a compilation, he notes, to be found, again substantially, in other prophecies, like Isaiah 13-23 and Jeremiah 46-51.[11] Etc. is no small component of Hebrew prophecy. Gene Tucker speaks of "the *maze* [my emphasis] of sayings and speeches and reports which simply run together in the prophetic books," in which, he later observes, "the list of genres, genre elements and formulas used by the prophets to express themselves is almost endless."[12] Lindblom himself mentions "a great many rhetorical and literary types . . . represented in the utterance of the prophets":

> There are exhortations to repentance, reproaches, announcements of judgement, threats against the apostates in Israel and against pagan nations, words of consolation and promises for the future. There are woe and satire, scorn and lamentation, hymns and prayers, monologues and dialogues, judicial debating, utterances formulated after a ritual pattern, descriptions of visions and auditions and confessions of personal experiences of different kinds. There are letters and messages, short oracles and extended sermons, historical retrospects, confessions of sin, decisions in cultic matters, parables and allegories, similes and sententious phrases of wisdom, lyric poetry of various kinds, and discussions of religious and moral problems.[13]

Lindblom's description of these as "rhetorical and literary types" is most useful for this comparative study of prophecy and satire. When Leon Guilhamet, for example, in pursuing the generic nature of satire, explains "the multitude of forms related to satire," he proffers a twofold explanation, as applicable to prophecy as to satire: "First," he insists, "satire is by its nature a borrower of forms. Second, these forms . . . are essentially rhetorical, a fact that accounts for a host of similarities between them."[14] Biblical scholarship repeatedly stress the oratorical nature of prophecy, prophecy as utterance, while literary critics just as often emphasize the rhetorical nature of satire, an art, like prophecy, of praise and blame. As he introduces his analysis of prophetic speech, for example, Tucker argues that "oral communication was the essential—if not the only—feature of [the prophets'] vocation and work." He singles out biblical scholar Hermann Gunkel for having "raised this observation to the level of methodological consciousness and made it the basis for finding a way through the literature to the speech genres."[15] Later in this book my analysis of the prophetic character constituted in the text also draws attention to the essentially spoken nature of prophetic discourse and to the fiction of utterance that appears in satire. If Horace is a representative example of conversational satire and Juvenal of declamatory satire, both forms convey speech, however fictional it might be in the case of satire.[16] The significant role of rhetorical forms and rhetorical borrowing in both prophecy and satire is, however, inescapable. Integrally related to a vision of the real, both critical discourses emerge in and comment on the history that gives them birth. Both seek to de-form, to use Guilhamet's term, the accepted view in which language has complacently couched the external. Hence, Guilhamet can insist that "this appropriation of other forms is unique to satire and is one of its chief identifying characteristics."[17]

More than any other forms of utterance, prophecy and satire, like the sermon, stand in uneasy and hostile relationship to the external world. To succeed in what they are about, they must subvert. So, as Walter Brueggemann admits of that call to Jeremiah "to *shatter* old worlds . . . and to *form* [his emphasis] and *evoke* new worlds," clearly "such a linguistic enterprise . . . is in fact subversive activity, and indeed may be the primal act of subversion."[18] Prophet and satirist utter the curse to destroy. To borrow the phrase Gerald Bruns uses of satire, prophecy too is "generically unstable."[19] What else, in such a rhetorically explosive landscape? Micah's epitome of prophetic function declares war in and against language: "to declare unto Jacob his transgression, and to Israel his sin" (3:8, KJV).

The confusion, however, is only an appearance of rhetorical chaos. The prophetic text, like the satiric, is the product of controlling imagination. As Guilhamet observes of its sibling: "the neglect of form in satire is more shadow than substance, more appearance than reality."[20] Prophecy and satire are morally shaped and controlled rhetorical chaos.

The madcap "most devoted servant of all modern forms," for example, insouciantly celebrating all the religious and intellectual lunacies of the modern age in Jonathan Swift's *Tale of a Tub* and meandering through title page and dedication, bibliography and allegory, digression and dedication, hiatus and preface, is, after all, a puppet, a creation, in the hands of Swift, pursuing a satirical course his delightfully nutty narrator has no idea of. Likewise, the prophetic text, however much it borrows and assimilates, parodies and evokes, never lets us lose sight of what strategies of prophetic language lead up to: "to declare unto Jacob his transgression, and to Israel his sin."

The prophetic text, most assuredly fashioned in times after the marvelously wrought irony of the J writer in the Pentateuch, does with language what that artist does with Yahweh's earlier dealing with his people. For the Yahwist, God is a supreme narrative or dramatic ironist, achieving results his human actors like Abraham and Jacob, Sarah or Rebecca, cannot even conceive, a God delivering scripts to a cast denied the whole play. So, the prophetic texts continue this well-established tradition of irony, but now turned towards language itself. The prophets use words and the forms of words as their original users could never have envisioned. The irony has the same purpose, however: to declare to Israel how the purposes of the LORD will be achieved despite what humankind does. That irony is of a much less delightful, indeed a far grimmer, kind, than the irony of the Yahwist. It is, nonetheless, an irony in the use of language itself and an indication that Yahweh's laughter in the Hebrew Scriptures is multi-faceted and not always reassuring.

b.

"... changeable as Proteus, capable of penetrating other genres"
Mikhail Bakhtin, *Problems of Dostoevsky's Poetics*

One particular mixture especially prominent in the longer prophetic texts is the combination of prose and poetry, seen, for example, in First Isaiah, Ezekiel, Jeremiah, or Amos. In their commentary on Hosea, Francis I. Andersen and David Noel Freedman not only point to the mixture of prose and poetry in the prophet, but also to the relationship between that mixture and the oratorical nature of prophecy itself. As they discuss the difference between Hosea 1-3 and the next eleven chapters (i.e., Hosea 4-14), Andersen and Freedman claim that

> what we have here is what Farrar . . . called the "intermediate style," partaking of both prose and verse, which has its roots in oratory. It also has affinities with spoken dialogue in epic narrative. This has already been discerned in part by Gordis . . . who said, "There is no iron curtain between prose and poetry in the ancient world." What is needed is the recognition of a distinct third category—rhetorical oratory.[21]

Now such a mix of prose and poetry appears in Menippean satire as well, a genre originating in the third century BC and taking the name of its supposed originator, the Cynic philosopher Menippus of Gadara, whose satire later influenced Varro and Lucian. What particularly prompts a comparison of Hebrew prophecy and the menippean form is the interest in the latter by the influential twentieth-century Russian critic Mikhail Bakhtin.[22]

Admittedly, Bakhtin's interest is based in his conviction that Menippean satire provides a most important development on the way to what Bakhtin calls the polyphony of Dostoevski's novels: the presence within them of many voices, none of which, not even the narrator's, are privileged. Although Bakhtin concedes that "the ancient menippea does not yet know *polyphony* [original emphasis],"[23] he finds them most important for their dialogic quality. Philip Holland succinctly distinguishes between the dialogic and the monologic in Bakhtin:

> . . . the seriocomic genres [like the menippea] are united not only from within but from without, through their common opposition to the serious genres . . . . [which are] monological, i.e., they presuppose (or impose) an integrated and stable universe of discourse. The seriocomic genres, by contrast, are dialogical; they deny the possibility, or more precisely, the experience of such integration. As tragedy and epic enclose,

Menippean forms open up, anatomize. The serious forms comprehend man; the Menippean forms are based on man's inability to know and contain his fate. To any vision of a completed system of truth, the menippea suggests some element outside the system. Seriocomic forms present a challenge, open or covert, to literary and intellectual orthodoxy, a challenge that is reflected not only in their philosophic content but also in their structure and language.[24]

At first glance, both the nature of Menippean satire as well as Bakhtin's view and use of it seem for two reasons to preclude any fruitful comparison with Hebrew prophecy. Menippean satire, first of all, is indirect satire. It delivers its judgment through narrative. Except for Jonah, narrative is at best incidental to the satire in Hebrew prophecy. Apart from very occasional parable or symbolic incident, Hebrew prophecy proceeds for the most part as direct, first-person statement. When the prophets are satiric, therefore, the satire is direct and explicit. When prophecy is ironic, the irony has little if anything to do with narrative technique. Any use of Menippean satire to illustrate satire in Hebrew prophecy is a loose adaptation, consequently, from essentially narrative satire.

Bakhtin himself, secondly, seems even more forcefully to deny any similarity. Even were prophecy viewed as dialogue— among Yahweh, the prophet, and Israel—Bakhtin explicitly denies dialogic quality to Biblical dialogue.[25] "Thus says the LORD" hardly introduces a mere exchange of views. On Bakhtinian grounds, prophecy and satire appear to be forms of those serious genres earlier described by Philip Holland as enclosed, as a "completed system of truth." Bakhtin also claims that "in rhetoric there are the unconditionally right and the unconditionally guilty."[26] The prophet thus works in a "high declamatory" genre, and the prophetic text is really a monologue which, of its nature, "pretends to be the *last word* [original emphasis]."[27]

A major ground, however, of Bakhtin's interest in the menippea is precisely in its subversive nature. The menippea stands outside the institution, even the literary institution,[28] as it poses its challenge to the monologic voice. Prophet and satirist likewise stand outside the accepted, the customary, the usual: they seek to subvert the closed system of the institution.

Bakhtin, however, seems wholly unaware of the subversive nature of prophecy or the threat it poses to reigning institutions and ideologies. While admitting, therefore, that prophecy, like Menippean satire, is not and perhaps cannot be dialogic or polyphonic, Bakhtinian premises allow for a very useful comparison with prophecy as a related instance of subversion, particularly because Bakhtin is so detailed about features of the menippea. If Bakhtin elsewhere can epitomize Rabelais' goal as an attempt "to destroy the official picture of events," surely prophet and satirist can also qualify.[29]

Bakhtin pursues this analysis in *Problems of Dostoevsky's Poetics*. As Menippean satire evolves out of the Socratic dialogs, the comic—I would say the satiric—increases its presence. As the next chapter shows, the wide variety of satire in the Hebrew prophets substantially and frequently subverts the official idolatry of Judah and Israel with sustained ridicule. When Bakhtin claims that "in all world literature, we could not find a genre more free than the menippea in its invention and use of the fantastic," he is formulating differently Northrop Frye's insistence on fantasy—the empirically improbable—as a constituent structural principle of satire. That fantasy is prominent in prophecy seems to go without saying. The purpose of this inventiveness, for Bakhtin, is "the provoking and testing of a philosophical idea, a discourse, a *truth* [original emphasis], embodied in the image of a wise man, the seeker of this truth . . . . The fantastic serves here . . . as a mode for searching after truth, provoking it, and, most important, *testing* [original emphasis]."[30] Menippea, says Bakhtin, combines "the free fantastic, the symbolic, at times even a mystical religious element [I do not see this in the prophets at all] with an extreme and crude *slum naturalism* [original emphasis]." Abraham Heschel says succinctly: "the prophets take us to the slums."[31] Unlike the menippea, however, they do not endorse the slums as healthful.

"The boldness of invention and the fantastic element" of the menippea combine, for Bakhtin, "with an extraordinary philosophic universalism and a capacity to contemplate the world on the broadest possible scale." Is it any wonder that an Isaiah introduced into the councils of the LORD can hardly behold either Assyria or Egypt without ridicule? A consequence of this universalism is the appearance in the menippea of what Bakhtin calls the three-planed construction of earth, Olympus, and the nether world. Isaiah, Ezekiel, and Jeremiah visit all three. Menippea features "observation from some unusual point of view, from on high, for example, which results in a radical change in the scale of the observed phenomena of life." How else could Jeremiah call the very Pharaoh of Egypt "Big Noise" (46:17, AB), speak of Yahweh picking clean "the land of Egypt like a shepherd picking lice from his clothing" (43:12, AB), or Isaiah picture God's summoning of the Assyrians as a man might whistle for his dog (5:26, NEB)? Why is it that Isaiah, as much at home in the councils of Israel as in the council of Yahweh, has nothing but contempt for the schemes of statecraft that Judah would substitute for trust in Yahweh?

Bakhtin continues:

> Very characteristic for the menippea are scandal scenes, eccentric behavior, inappropriate speeches and performances, that is, all sorts of violations of the generally accepted and customary course of events and the established norms of behavior and etiquette, including manners of speech.

Isaiah 28:7-22, for example, with its drunken priests and prophets and their cocky, raucous behavior surely qualifies as a "scandal scene." Much in the first few chapters of Isaiah as well as Ezekiel's long tour with an angel would qualify as "eccentric behavior." Where the prophetic text thus subverts, the sympathy is with the subversion. Menippean satire loves "sharp contrasts and oxymoronic combinations"; it plays "with abrupt transitions and shifts, ups and downs, rises and falls, unexpected comings together of distant and disunited things, mesalliances of all sorts." The stuff of prophetic consolation would seem to find a place in Bakhtin's observation that "the menippea often includes elements of *social utopia*," the promise of the restored Israel.

Bakhtin notes that the menippea provides "a wide use of inserted genres," and, characteristically, "a mixing of prose and poetic speech." This insertion of genres effects a "multi-styled and multi-toned nature" in the menippea. And, finally, there is

the concern of the menippea with "current and topical issues."
What Bakhtin stresses in concluding is "the organic unity of all
these seemingly very heterogeneous features, the deep internal
integrity of the genre."[32] In the prophets, however, one more
important distinction remains. Menippean satire is concerned
with intellectual folly; the prophets' emphasis is moral. I know of
no instance where a Hebrew prophet criticizes an idea as such.
However rhetorically diverse and even rhetorically playful, the
prophetic text for all its many elements proceeds integrally and
coherently to one aim: "to declare unto Jacob his transgression,
and to Israel his sin."

ii.

> " . . . behold, after above six months' warning, I
> cannot learn that my book hath produced one single
> effect according to mine intentions."
>   Captain Gulliver to His Cousin Sympson

Lemuel Gulliver's is a not uncharacteristic complaint of the
reformer-satirist: little evidence abounds of any improvement in
those to whom chastisement has been addressed. Swift's indis-
criminate celebrator of everything modern in the *Tale of a Tub*
goes even farther: he abjures any satirical objectives whatever
because "there is not, through all nature, another so callous
and insensible a member as the world's posteriors, whether you
apply to it the toe or the birch."[33] The implication is unmistakable: however forceful or pointed, satire leaves the world pretty
much as it finds it. When we leave the playfulness of the irony
coursing through these two admittedly fictional voices to the
voice of the satirist speaking in his own person, the pessimism
remains unchanged. No hope whatever appears in the note
Pope adds to the conclusion of *Dialogue II*, in effect, his very
last poem, except for the new *Dunciad*, published four years
later. This note did not appear when Pope first published the
poem; it appeared only in Warburton's edition of Pope's poems
seven years after the poet's death. At any rate, the impervious-
ness of society to reform is its clear theme:

> This was the last poem of the kind printed by our author, with
> a resolution to publish no more; but to enter thus, in the most

plain and solemn manner he could, a sort of PROTEST against that insuperable corruption and depravity of manners, which he had been so unhappy as to live to see. Could he have hoped to have amended any, he had continued those attacks; but bad men were grown so shameless and so powerful, that Ridicule was become as unsafe as it was ineffectual. The Poem raised him, as he knew it would, some enemies; but he had reason to be satisfied with the approbation of good men, and the testimony of his own conscience.[34]

After a quarter century as a leading critic of Walpole's England, Pope still finds "insuperable corruption and depravity of manners" and the ridicule of satire "ineffectual." No brave new world on the scene. Such an expectation occurs not in satire but in comedy and serves as a major difference between them.

As Northrop Frye points out in the *Anatomy of Criticism*, comedy moves towards a new society. Whatever obstacles have impeded the success and happiness of, usually, the young couple at the center of comedy, the conclusion sees the obstacles overcome, villains chastised and often confessing, and a brave new world ahead. Not infrequently, a wedding ends the comic work, an appropriate image of the attractive future ahead. Comedy tends to be inclusive. The convenient reappearance of the entire cast just moments before the conclusion of, say, any Gilbert and Sullivan operetta reminds us that the chorus is the most characteristic music sung to celebrate the end of the comic work. So, Frye can insist, "comedy usually moves toward a happy ending, and the normal response of the audience to a happy ending is 'this should be' . . . ."[35] Biblical critic David Robertson has defined comedy succinctly as "a work in which the hero is in the end incorporated into the society to which he properly belongs."[36] Within the comic work itself, then, whatever problems occur are finally resolved, and even villains, as Frye notes, "are more often reconciled or converted than simply repudiated." The movement of action within comedy inescapably points to the closed nature of comedy: no strings remain unraveled; "this should be."[37]

Comedy, however, also forgives and reconciles. Nowhere perhaps is the forgiveness at the center of comedy more beautifully and poignantly brought out than in the concluding scene of

Mozart's *Marriage of Figaro*. Having been tricked into seducing his own wife because he assumed her to be, in the darkened garden, her servant girl, Susanna, the Count falls before his wife to ask pardon: "Contessa, perdono." And when she has forgiven him, the entire cast concludes with a chorus urging that everyone celebrate this reconciliation with an appropriately public festivity: "Corriam tutti a festegiar."

Prophecy and satire do not forgive; they do not reconcile. Even if the prophecy ends, as so many do, with a consolation, even if the satire can detail, as Johnson's *Vanity of Human Wishes* does in its concluding paragraph, an ideal to be sought, neither prophecy nor satire celebrates a resolution achieved within the text. Reformation remains to be done. A strong sense of the unresolved and incomplete haunts the ending of prophecy and satire. The redemptive awareness shared one way or another by all the actors in the comic drama is precisely the awareness denied or rejected by many in the prophetic or satiric drama. Hence, opposition, exclusion, repudiation. The open-ended quality I find essential to prophecy and satire prompts us to respond and respond forcefully: "This should not be." The new society will come only at the cost of painful self-awareness. But little in the prophetic or satiric text provides the comfort or expectation of precisely such a conversion. Indeed, if the two are measured against the historical circumstances which seem tied to their origin, prophecy and satire are discourses about great moral failure. Prophets and satirists repeatedly complain about their ineffectiveness.

Notice how unresolved are the problems in satire. True, the last canto of Pope's *Rape of the Lock* presents sympathetically a speech by Clarissa that places earthly beauty in appropriate second place to concerns of the soul. But the Hampton Court set split asunder by the taking of sides over Belinda's shorn lock of hair repudiates that advice in the battle that follows. "So spoke the Dame," says Pope, when Clarissa finishes, "but no Applause ensued" (V, 35). Will the fictional Belinda heed Clarissa's warning? We do not know. *The Dunciad* ends in cosmic annihilation: should this be? A singularly unaware Gulliver, as blind as the self-satisfied Pharisee of Luke 18, announces himself as a chastiser of the human pride of which he is the most consummate example. Not only unreconciled with the humanity he claims to save, he is ludicrously unreconciled with his own wife and children. Should this be? Ask Mrs. Gulliver.[38] Are we delighted to see Winston expressing his love for Big Brother in *1984*, Tony Last reading Dickens ad infinitum to Mr. Todd in the Brazilian jungle (Evelyn Waugh's *Handful of Dust*), the recent Stoic convert Damasippus, unaware of the moral uselessness of his "wisdom" that everyone is foolish (Horace, *Satires*, II, iii)? The incomplete and the unresolved are of the essence of satire. Were they not, there would be no need for the satirist.

Prophecy presents the same open-endedness. It celebrates no achieved new society. Rather a powerful, blind, and wilful old order hears ceaseless, relentless, and threatening challenge. It makes little difference to a formal understanding of prophecy whether the consolations which appear there are from the prophet himself or from a later time.[39] In either case, the consolation as the celebration of a restored and new order describes a festivity of the future, not a celebration of the present. No prophecy is as unresolved as Jeremiah: the prophet simply disappears near the end of the text and is not heard from again. His shadow disappears while that of Babylon grows larger. Prophecy affords no immediate expectation whatever of reconciliation and forgiveness, of self-awareness and reform. Isaiah records the wilfulness and the imperceptiveness strenuously:

> You may listen and listen, but you will not understand.
> You may look and look again, but you will never know.
> This people's wits are dulled,
> their ears are deafened and their eyes blinded,
>> so that they cannot see with their eyes
>> nor listen with their ears
>> nor understand with their wits,
> so that they may turn and be healed. [Isa 6:9-10, NEB]

And when Isaiah asks, "How long, O LORD?" Yahweh's answer promises only destruction as the aftermath of impenetrability:

> Until cities fall in ruins and are deserted,
> houses are left without people,

and the land goes to ruin and lies waste,
until the LORD has sent all mankind far away,
and the whole country is one vast desolation.

[Isa 6:11-12, NEB]

The narrative conclusion to First Isaiah (chapters 36-39), drawn almost verbatim from 2 Kings, merely sets up the coming of the Babylonian Exile and Captivity, a century and a half after the career of the historical Isaiah. Within the prophetic text, the festivity of present reconciliation simply does not occur. The prophet's present is unending repudiation: unlike comedy, prophecy's internal dynamics do not move forward towards the triumphing of healthful, unillusory perception. In his analysis of the text of Jeremiah, for example, Joel Rosenberg effectively contrasts the secure, settled picture that emerges only from a distance with the maelstrom which is the immediacy of the prophetic text and situation itself:

> . . . the prophetic vocation is not a matter of steady augmentation of the prophet's doctrine or of increasing acceptance by his public, but rather one of continual reversal, deadlock, setback, and resurgence. The restlessness and apparent aimlessness of the prophet's career is thus captured in a unique and profound way. Patterns emerge in his ministry which are hard to see in the short run (for the reader as much as for the prophet or his contemporaries), but which, over the long run, show simultaneously a deep consistency of vision and an immense versatility of expression. The relativity of the historical hour, the alteration of preachment to context and circumstance, are stressed as the prophet is shown churning about in relentless movement—adapting, clashing, revising, retrenching, threatening, pleading, promising. Yet one thread of argument runs through this Heraclitean swirl of change. The only human power that transcends all circumstances, all nations and alliances, all empires and kings, is the power of repentance. It is this power alone that grants insight into history, for it is here shown as the force that shapes history. And behind all motions and changes is the voice of Jeremiah, whose book characteristically leaves us in the dark about where he spent his final days—a not untypical ending for prophetic cycles (consider Moses' unknown gravesite, Elijah's exit in a chariot of fire, Jonah's silent perplexity before a divine question).[40]

As assessment or sentence, prophecy's judgment admits of but one response: "This should not be."

iii.

> If so wretched a State of Things would allow it, methinks I could have a malicious Pleasure, after all the Warning I have in vain given the Publick . . . to see the Consequences and Events answering in every Particular. I pretend to no Sagacity: What I writ was little more than what I had discoursed to several Persons, who were generally of my Opinion. And it was obvious to every common Understanding, that such Effects must needs follow from such Causes . . . .
>
> Jonathan Swift, *Answer to a Memorial*

The consolation promised in prophecy, like the ideal to be recovered in satire, conveys a concern with the future. The supposedly predictive nature of prophecy, however, suggests that any comparison between the two falters badly when confronted with this apparently essential component. Indeed, as early as 1755, Samuel Johnson is offering prediction, or a declaration of something to come, as the only denotation of prophecy. Although modern dictionaries have expanded the denotation to include any utterance by a prophet, prediction still appears as an acceptable alternative denotation of the term. If prophecy thus delineates a future revealed in irrevocable quality by the divine, the rhetorical skills of the prophets seem designed to purposes far different from those of satirists. Satirists chastise living vice and folly. Prophets predict the future. What I propose here, however, is twofold: first, old news for biblical scholars, viz., that prediction is really an insignificant feature of Hebrew prophecy; and, secondly, that satire and prophecy are both concerned with the future and depict that future as morally conditioned by present action.

First of all, why is Hebrew prophecy even defined as prediction? Because principles of Christian hermeneutics, based in Christian faith, see the Hebrew Scriptures as the Old and thus

71

incomplete Testament providing types that find completion and fulfillment in the supposedly New Testament. Christian hermeneutics is the single most important cause of the predictive view of Hebrew prophecy. So while Northrop Frye, for example, insists that "'the Bible' has traditionally been read as a unity, and has influenced Western imagination as a unity," he likewise admits that central to his objective in *The Great Code*— discussing "a unified structure of narrative and imagery in the Bible, . . . the core" of the book—is an inescapable assumption: "the only possible form of the Bible that I can deal with is the Christian Bible."[41] However literary his interest, Frye recognizes that Christian belief, as a matter of cultural fact, has indelibly influenced the reading of both Scriptures, Christian and Hebrew, and has, as a matter of cultural fact, assimilated the earlier. Without that underpinning the supposedly predictive nature of Hebrew prophecy diminishes to a staggering degree. Little if any prediction is left.

Scripture scholar John Barton begins his *Oracles of God*, on the contrary, by celebrating the way in which, "within the mainstream of Christian thought in the West, 'prophecy' has come to mean something very close to what it means in critical Old Testament scholarship," that is, something said "that poses a challenge to a complacent world." Whatever "forebodings of disaster to come" might figure in such a challenge, however, they will not be "mere prognostications of the clairvoyant sort" but "understood as the inevitable consequences of present sin which a change of course could, at least in principle, avert." In short, "crystal-gazing is not what 'prophecy' means in biblical religion."[42]

a.

Men's curiosity searches past and future
And clings to that dimension.
T. S. Eliot, *Four Quartets*

Two very familiar texts from Isaiah exemplify the difficulty of viewing prophecy as primarily predicting the future. A third text, from Jeremiah, reveals that on the rare occasion when the prophet foretells the future, he is often quite mistaken.

The first example from Isaiah is the supposed prophecy-that-is-prediction of the birth of Jesus:

> "Behold, a virgin shall conceive, and bear a son, and shall call his name Immanuel." (7:14, KJV)

Without a Christian frame of reference, however, a foreseeing and promise of the birth of Jesus is impossible to see in the text. The context of Isaiah's remarks is very clear. King Ahaz of the southern kingdom, Judah, is being urged to avoid any foreign alliance as a means of withstanding the obvious threat of Assyria. Specifically, the prophet warns Ahaz against yielding to pressure from Israel (the Northern Kingdom) and Syria to league against the Assyrians. The prophet recognizes that such an alliance against so great a power will only exacerbate matters with the Assyrians. Instead of treaties, Isaiah firmly recommends trust in the LORD. Isaiah even assures the King that the pressure exerted against him by Israel and by Syria will disappear: the days of these kingdoms are numbered. How long? Sooner than it will take an infant born to a young woman today to reach an age of discriminating between right and wrong:

> "For before the child shall know to refuse the evil, and choose the good, the land that thou abhorrest shall be forsaken of both her kings." (7:16, KJV)

The Assyrians, in other words, will destroy Syria and Israel precisely because of their attempt to league against her. It will be a matter of at best a few years. In the chapter immediately following, Isaiah repeats this assurance and once again provides a similar comparison. Isaiah conceives a child through the prophetess who bears a son, named, by divine command, Maher-shalal-hash-baz (i.e., "speedy-spoiling-prompt-plundering"):[43]

> ". . . Before the child shall have knowledge to cry, My father, my mother, the riches of Damascus [i.e., the capital of Syria] and the spoil of Samaria [i.e., the Northern Kingdom] shall be taken away before the king of Assyria." (8:4, KJV)

Not only has Christian hermeneutics turned an analogy about the duration of time into a prediction of the birth of Jesus, it has, to the best of my knowledge, wholly ignored the second of these two comparisons. Yet Isaiah's point is exactly the same in both: not much time will pass before Assyria destroys Israel and Syria. Whatever the basis of Isaiah's assurance, a crystal-gazing interpretation of the text is indefensible on the basis of the text itself. It is really non-predictive. Isaiah has announced the likely consequence upon politically insignificant and powerless nations of a desperate attempt to league against one more powerful. In addition, the promise to Ahaz of a consolation some seven centuries later would be useless and perhaps even unintelligible.

The validity of the Christian reading of this text is not my concern here: I seek only to affirm that a predictive interpretation of the words is inescapably tied to a Christian frame of reference. Christianity makes the text predictive by a highly selective process of adaptation. The Hebrew text, for instance, does not use the available term for virgin in Isaiah 7:14 but speaks only of the mother as a young woman, with whose youth virginity is a likely though not necessary assumption. The Septuagint translation specifically narrowed the word to virgin. The second child, whose birth likewise suggests a short span of time, is clearly the product of usual human generation: Isaiah has intercourse with the prophetess. That text is hardly adaptable without violence to the prediction of the virgin birth of Jesus.

A second and very familiar instance of supposed prophetic prediction in the Hebrew Scriptures appears in Isaiah 52 and 53, verses often used in the liturgies of Good Friday. In Christian hermeneutics this passage (Isa 52:15-53:12) looks forward in some detail to the sufferings of Jesus. Here again, however, the process of adaptation is inescapable. Much in the text that is apparently not at all applicable to Jesus must be passed over in silence, particularly the insistence on a lifetime of despite and disregard from his fellows, a view of Jesus' early relationship with others that simply does not appear in any of the Christian Scriptures:

> He had no beauty nor honor; we saw him, and his appearance did not attract us.
> He was despised, the lowest of men: a man of pains, familiar with disease,

> One from whom men avert their gaze—despised, and we
> reckoned him as nothing. [Isa 53:2-3, AB]

Was Jesus, furthermore, "given a tomb with the wicked, with evildoers his sepulcher" (Isa 53:8, AB)? To see these verses as prediction is to recognize, as in the case of Isaiah 7:14, that sometimes the details fit and sometimes they don't. Again, and apart from a Christian frame of reference, one most important feature of a text supposedly predictive militates against such a view at all: Sheldon H. Blank has pointed out that in this passage "all the verbs . . . are in the past tense."[44] The sufferings have already taken place at the time Second Isaiah speaks of them in the time of the Babylonian captivity. They are history, not prediction.

Finally, one example from Jeremiah shows the prophet indeed foretelling the future, and this example, like others in the prophetic text, is intelligible without appeal to any frame of reference except that of the prophets themselves. The view of the future, however, is mistaken. The text of Jeremiah moves towards a rhetorically fitting climax in its violent denunciation of Babylon, the last of several oracles against foreign nations with which the prophecy concludes. The text anticipates the end of Babylon in bloody carnage

> That will leave her land a shambles
> With no one living there,
> Both man and beast having fled, having gone. [50:3, AB]

The devastation Jeremiah anticipates will be total:

> Through the wrath of Yahweh uninhabited,
> Wholly a waste shall she be;
> All who pass by Babylon shall whistle,
> Appalled at all her wounds. [50:13, AB]

John Bright argues that "it is . . . not to be wondered at that many a Jew came to look upon Babylon as the very arch-foe of the people of God, and that the prophecy [read here prediction] directed against that nation should exceed all the others both in volume and in the emotional intensity that informs it." However, he also notes that the actual fate of Babylon at the hands of Cyrus could scarcely have been more unlike the awful picture of slaughter and destruction that we see in these poems. Cyrus actually entered Babylon without a fight, refrained from harming it in any way, and treated its citizens with the utmost consideration.[45]

When the prophets make predictions in the sense of foretelling the future, they are often wrong.[46] Clearly, predictive accuracy had nothing to do with the preservation of the prophet's words.

Johannes Lindblom, furthermore, introduces a useful distinction about the prophets' view of the future: "ordinary prophetic predictions of the future" differ from "clairvoyance, telepathy, presentiment, and similar extraordinary powers" because "the contents of these [prophetic] predictions are always related to contemporary historical circumstances and may be explained as the result of *a normal faculty of observation combined with an intensified insight into the religious and moral situation of Israel* [my emphasis]." The prophets and those who preserved and collected their revelations "did not lay much stress upon the details of the predictions." What was constant was "the certainty of a coming judgement and the conviction of future salvation."[47] Nothing, in fact, more strongly underscores the insignificance of the predictive element in Hebrew prophecy than the inescapable fact that wrong predictions were preserved. The significance of Hebrew prophecy does not lie in its clairvoyance. If it did it would have a fairly sorry record indeed. Hence James Crenshaw can assert: ". . . prediction in the narrow sense occupies a minor role in ancient prophecy."[48]

b.

" 'Well, it's like this war that's coming . . . .' "
Evelyn Waugh, *Vile Bodies*

When Hebrew prophecy concerns itself with the future, as it often does, it shares with satire the conviction of a morally conditioned future: what will be depends on what now is. Thus, when the prophetic challenge includes, in John Barton's words, "forebodings of disaster to come, ... they will be understood as the inevitable consequences of present sin which a change of course could, at least in principle, avert."[49] What is wholly lacking in Hebrew prophecy is that gratuitous, arbitrary foretelling of the future characteristic of astrology charts: predictions of things to come that have no moral relationship to present behavior. The prophetic message, on the contrary, asserts: this will come *because* you act so now. The prophetic future, like that in satire, has a cause-effect relationship to the present. Prophet and satirist insist on the same cautionary theme: actions have consequences. The future each spells out is the elaboration of those consequences.[50] The future nevertheless is morally conditioned. At least through Ezekiel, the prophetic message is succinct: Israel and Judah will fall because Israel and Judah have sinned. Prophets do not predict; they announce consequences.[51]

Satire shares such a view of the future. Notice, first of all, how satire could be as easily dismissed for its predictive failure as prophecy were we to emphasize clairvoyance as its most important feature. Great satiric failures would include George Orwell's *1984* (at least outside Eastern Europe) or Alexander Pope's *Dunciad.*[52] Satire, however, no more compels because of its clairvoyance than prophecy. Satire compels because of its morally imaginative power to picture the consequences of irresponsible behavior that speak to and yet transcend the circumstances of their time. George Orwell's *1984* projects a totalitarian nightmare emerging out of amoral, irresponsible bureaucracy with fearful technological resources at its disposal. Like Swift's vision of the Flying Island and the Grand Academy of Lagado, the lunacies dominate society because amoral technological fascination is put to the service of political power. Pope's *Dunciad* is not a prediction but a prophet's warning: humankind cannot tamper with the impulses and principles of civilizing itself—that is, it cannot tamper with the Word in its fullest, richest signification—without finally destroying what Word itself brought into being, Creation as a whole. Kurt Vonnegut's *Cat's Cradle* is a cautionary tale about scientific amorality, again in the tradition of Part III of *Gulliver's Travels.* The World War that concludes Evelyn Waugh's 1930 *Vile*

Bodies is not a triumph of crystal-gazing, but a perceptive awareness, widely shared at the time, that Europe was moving towards war, that the absence of any driving moral purpose among the obviously incompetent, irresponsible leaders of society could, indeed, have but one obvious, catastrophic consequence. Satirists, like prophets, see these consequences in moral terms. The moral insight—not the happenstance of accurate prediction, if it appears at all—compels the interest in both discourses.

The frequent description of the satiric process as a *reductio ad absurdum* only offers a different verbalizing of how satire proceeds imaginatively and morally by extending into the future the likely consequences of present behavior or absurdity. Such projecting explains the frequency in satire of the dystopia, often a mordantly ironic commentary on highly touted expectations of a better life arising out of the practices and discoveries of the present. I suspect this is a major reason why many satires are much less fittingly seen as science-fiction. The list must surely include Part III of *Gulliver's Travels*, Aldous Huxley's *Brave New World*, George Orwell's *Animal Farm* and *1984*, Evelyn Waugh's *Love Among the Ruins*, subtitled *A Romance of the Near Future*, much of Kurt Vonnegut, including *Player Piano*, *Cat's Cradle*, and *Slaughterhouse-Five*, and virtually all of Stanislaw Lem. Even Swift's *Modest Proposal*, although not a dystopia, extends into the future a grisly and ironically devastating insight: since the Irish poor are being treated like animals, why not dispose of them as animals? Genocide, as the logical consequence of current neglect and maltreatment.[53] Such imaginative insight would certainly qualify as the equivalent in satire of what Johannes Lindblom earlier described in prophecy: "a normal faculty of observation combined with an intensified insight into the religious and moral situation of Israel."[54] The morally conditioned future that figures so prominently in prophecy and satire is one of their most striking similarities. As Jonathan Swift succinctly phrases it, "I pretend to no Sagacity . . . . such Effects must needs follow from such Causes."[55] Keen insight, not clairvoyance, is the key.

iv.

> But whoever stirs me up (better keep your distance,
> I'm telling you!) will be sorry; he'll become a thing of
> derision throughout the city.
>
> Horace, *Satires*, II, i, 45-46 (tr. Niall Rudd)

To whom and for whom are such proclamations of fearful consequences being spoken? The very first satire of Horace brings out inescapable ambiguity in answering the question. At face value, this program of Horatian satire sounds a note often repeated in the tradition: the satirist speaks to correct lives being misled by false values, in the case of Horace's first satire, to those destroying their tranquility by fruitless and groundless dissatisfaction with self because they envy others supposedly better off. When Horace again analyzes the sources of the satiric impulses, in the satire that opens Book II, his language is more aggressive, even military. Satire, he explains, is his "special way of fighting enemies."[56] For the first time, Horace must consider the possibility of danger in such proclamation: the enemy might respond with physical or legal attack. Such justification of the satiric impulse inescapably brings out the attack so central to satire. The satirist seeks to overcome an enemy, that is, to see the enemy change. Why does the satirist write? To change foolish and vicious behavior. So, at least, conventional wisdom has it.[57]

Yet these two poems, like other statements of satiric objective, raise questions. The opening of Horace's Book II, for example, not only entertains the possibility of legal action against the satirist; the anticipation of a court decision in the satirist's favor further implies unchanged behavior in the plaintiff. Suing your critic is hardly evidence of change. The much more aggressive Juvenal seems nowhere to expect or allow for change in the almost wholly corrupted individuals and institutions he assails through the satires. His friend Umbricius, for instance, spokesman for the attack on Rome in *Satire III*, has obviously given up the fight: he is leaving the city. As noted earlier, Pope gives up ridicule as ineffective and Swift expects disastrous consequences to follow inevitably. The situation with the prophets is comparable. When John Barton argues that the prophets' "forebodings of disaster" be "understood as the inevitable consequence of present sin," he carefully qualifies the possibility that changing behavior will change consequences as something that could "at least in principle" occur. Hans Walter Wolff, however, states categorically: "Nowhere at all can it be perceived that the prophet expects an alteration of circumstances through repentance of the people on the basis of his indictments."[58] Indeed, the very first prophetic text in the canon grimly announces that "the LORD of Hosts has a day of doom waiting" (Isa 2:12, NEB). So the conventional view that satire and prophecy are motivated by a desire to reform runs counter to a pervasive sense in both that no change will occur. Why speak to deaf ears? Why write for blind eyes?

The very texts, however, that speak of an impenetrable audience also make clear more sympathetic hearers. Horace, for example, is engaging in an internal monologue as he opens Book I. But addressing the musing to his patron, Macaenas, reveals Horace's security about the sympathy and understanding he anticipates from him. The kindred, admittedly not always perceptive, hearer in the opening of Book II is the lawyer friend, Trebatius, whose professional status adds no insignificant weight to the poem's concluding assurance that the satirist will go free in court, even if the plaintiff remains unconvinced. Although no auditor is specified in Juvenal's *Satire I*, his friend Persicus, in *Satire XI*, comes across as one who readily shares Juvenal's values. No satire of Juvenal is comprehensible, in fact, without the assumption of a sympathetic listener sharing the satirist's values and thus understanding the reasons of his disquiet. Yes, Umbricius is leaving Rome, but why does the Juvenal who hears his attack on the city remain behind to write satire? Has Hans Walter Wolff perhaps overstated the prophet's despairing anticipation of no change? The same apparently hopeless Isaiah nonetheless urges—likewise at the outset—a message of reform:

> Cease to do evil and learn to do right,
> pursue justice and champion the oppressed;
> given the orphan his rights, plead the widow's cause.
>
> [Isa 1:17, NEB]

To whom is he speaking? A later generation? And what about
Joel? The fearsome future—

> Great is the day of the LORD and terrible,
>   who can endure it? [Joel 2:11, NEB]

—is apparently not a determined future:

> And yet, the LORD says [Joel continues], even now
> turn back to me with your whole heart,
> fast, and weep, and beat your breasts.
> Rend your hearts and not your garments;
> turn back to the LORD your God;
> for he is gracious and compassionate,
>   long-suffering and ever constant,
> always ready to repent of the threatened evil.
> It may be he will turn back and repent
> and leave a blessing behind him,
>   blessing enough for grain-offering and drink-offering
> for the LORD your God. [Joel 2:12-14, NEB]

Satire and prophecy thus seek and despair of reform at the
same time, urge change yet expect none. They speak to those
in need of reform, some of whom will hear and some not. They
speak also, however, to a third group: those who share the
ideals and abhor the abuses that prompt the utterance, the
likeminded, in other words, who find self-validation in what
prophet or satirist attack and uphold. Robert R. Wilson, who
defines prophets as intermediaries, claims that they cannot be
"socially isolated" and that the popular view of prophecy as a
"personal process" is hardly convincing.[59] The prophet also
speaks, therefore, to and for those who encourage him and seek
expression of their values. The text of the classical prophets
provides little specific information about who such people were,
how large or small their number, or what their subsequent
fortunes. But Jeremiah had Baruch, and the kings of Judah and
Israel reveal both respect for as well as fear of the prophets.
Then, too, somebody preserved the prophet's message. In
prophecy and in satire, validation for the likeminded is not
limited to one's contemporaries. Satiric texts, of course, provide
a list as specific as it is long of those who stand by the satirist
and encourage him to write: Macaenas and Trebatius for Hor-

ace, Umbricius and Persicus for Juvenal, all whom Pope generously compliments and often addresses in his satires, the Swift
to whom *The Dunciad* is dedicated, and the Pope who under-
took for Swift in Dublin the publishing of his *Gulliver's Travels*
in London.

Considered then in terms of their audiences, prophecy and
satire are simultaneously persuasive and punitive, though in
degrees that vary from text to text and from one situation to
another. Each punishes, i.e., each holds up to ridicule and
humiliation those whose vice spurs the censure to begin with.
That shame certainly satisfies those who concur in the moral
norms underlying the ridicule. In this sense, prophecy and satire
punish one audience as they reinforce another. Prophecy and
satire also seek change; they are thus persuasive. The likeminded need no persuasion: they already agree.[60] The very
lack of illusion about the world which emerges in the prophetic
or satiric text cannot be divorced from either's hardheaded
awareness of how unlikely change will be. A later prophet and
storyteller put it this way. Some seeds fall along the path where
the birds devour them; some, on stony ground, where they
wither; some, among thorns, where they are choked. Some, of
course, fall on good ground where they produce grain. But as
any farmer, like Amos, knows, when you scatter seed, a lot of it
goes to waste.

To determine if punishment or persuasion predominates in
a given text is not really an urgent critical issue. Speaking to
those whose hearing is not likely to improve while uttering
judgments which those who encourage and support you share
is a context of utterance fraught with irresolvable tension. We
are brought back to the volatile, explosive landscape of censure.
Attack is needed and demanded; but attack will be repelled and
might fail. The origins of prophecy and satire in the curse might
put to rest any uneasiness about the impossibility of simply
answering the question of to whom and for whom do prophets
and satirists speak.

The story of Balaam illustrates the tensions well. The Moabites, we are told, "were sick with fear" at the sight of the
Israelites, whose march toward Canaan had so far been unim-

peded (Num 22:3, NEB). The likeminded king of the Moabites summons Balaam to curse the Israelites, a satisfying prospect that will put everyone's fears to rest. We know the rest of the story: at God's behest, Balaam blesses the Israelites instead. Balak, we are told, was "very angry with Balaam" (Num 24:10, NEB), not the last king in the Hebrew Scriptures to dislike what his prophet says. A curse, in other words, must be summoned by those likeminded in their conviction of what is evil. Balaam really doesn't speak on his own. He responds to a summons, to a need. As such he takes on a social function. Responding to one society, he is asked to attack another. The curse, of course, might not prove efficacious. Balaam's becomes a blessing, as later Moses' curses prove more powerful than those of Pharaoh's retainers. A curse always demands an enemy, those likeminded in their conviction of what constitutes an enemy, and the verbal manipulator who utters the curse. If the attack fails, the only resort is to curse again. As long as the efficacy of words commands belief, the prompting of the curse must always be punitive and persuasive, reassuring for some but challenging for others. When belief in the efficacy of the curse dies, prophets disappear and satirists put down their pens.

3

DIVINE
DERISION
AND SCORN:
SATIRE AND IRONY
IN THE
PROPHETS

Jesters do often prove prophets," so William Shakespeare says in the last act of *Lear*, in a remark Samuel Johnson uses to illustrate his definition of prophet in the *Dictionary*. This implied equivalence of jest and prophecy, of ridicule and preaching,[1] appears throughout the Hebrew Scriptures, where prophets do often prove jesters. They taunt, gibe, scoff, mock; indeed, modern literary criticism would affirm that prophets do often prove satirists. Elijah taunts the prophets of Baal to cry louder, for their god may be "deep in thought, or engaged, or on a journey" (1 Kgs 18:27, NEB). The urging to cry louder deliberately parodies pagan practices to bring rain, and *engaged* perhaps speaks euphemistically of Baal's attending to his own bodily needs and thus being unavailable for the needs of his priests.[2] In other words, Baal may be in the bathroom. Isaiah promises the people of Judah that after their pain, fears, and cruel slavery, they will sing a "song of derision over the king of Babylon" (Isa 14:4, NEB). Jeremiah calls the false gods of Judah "Lord Delusion," "Lord Useless" (Jer 2:5, 11, AB); the Pharaoh of Egypt, on whom Judah misguidedly leans for support, is "Big Noise" (Jer 46:17, AB); the idolatrous nation herself he describes as

> a swift she-camel
> Crisscrossing her tracks
> Snuffing the wind in her heat.
>   Who, in her rut, can restrain her?
> Males need not trouble to chase her;
>   In her month they will find her.
>   [Jer 2:23-24, AB]

Derision, scorn, and ridicule befall the enemies of righteousness and, on occasion, as Psalm 137 reminds us, intensify the sufferings of the just, taunted to sing songs of Zion in the alien land of captivity, humiliation, or disgrace. Often indistinguishable from the prophetic message itself, satire serves as a major weapon in the arsenal of the Hebrew prophets, whose careers and writings strongly buttress the Psalmist's confidence: "He that dwelleth in heaven shall laugh them to scorn; the LORD shall hold them in derision" (Ps 2:4).[3]

The nature and characteristics common to both prophecy and satire explain their frequent intermingling and shared identity. The message of biblical prophecy is pervasively and predominantly criticism, and criticism is always the content of satire. Things as they are profoundly dissatisfy prophet and satirist alike. From the time of Samuel, the greatest of the early prophets, these "critics and censors of the spiritual well-being of the worshiping community"[4] remain somewhat aloof from and independent of the political and even religious institutions, and from that vantage point censure the nation's straying from the paths of righteousness and justice, often under the direction of king and priest. Samuel publicly rebukes Saul for leaving unfulfilled the horrid demands of holy war against the Amalekites.[5] As so many prophets were later to do, Samuel reminds Saul that Yahweh is not "as pleased with holocausts and sacrifices as with obeying Yahweh's voice" (1 Sam 15:22, AB). With the indirection of a story—an exemplum, the rhetorician would call it—Nathan tricks David into condemning himself before announcing, "You are the man!" (2 Sam 12:7, NEB). Elijah chastises the foul idolatry of Ahab and Jezebel, and his successor in the prophetic mantle—Elisha—satisfyingly sees the temple of Baal reduced to a privy (2 Kgs 10:27). Their prophetic activity in the northern kingdom approximates in time that of Isaiah in the south, the censoriousness of whose Yahweh-sent message strikes out ominously from its opening verses: "I have sons whom I reared and brought up, but they have rebelled against me. The ox knows its owner, and the ass its master's stall; but Israel, my own people, has no knowledge, no discernment." Yahweh restates the priorities announced by Samuel:

> New moons and sabbaths and assemblies, sacred seasons and ceremonies, I cannot endure. I cannot tolerate your new moons and your festivals; they have become a burden to me, and I can put up with them no longer. . . . Cease to do evil and learn to do right, pursue justice and champion the oppressed; give the orphan his rights, plead the widow's cause.
>
> [Isa 1:2-3, 13-14, 17, NEB]

On the brink of her extinction, the surviving and supremely confident southern kingdom hears almost identically threatening and insulting messages from the prophetic near-contemporaries, Jeremiah and Ezekiel:

> On every high hill
> > Under every green tree, [Jeremiah accuses,]
> > > There you sprawled, a-whoring.
> A Sorek vine[6] I planted you,
> > Of wholly reliable stock.
> But what a foul-smelling thing you've become . . . .
>
> [Jer 2:20-21, AB]

Through Ezekiel, the LORD Yahweh threatens:

> I am coming at you, for my part;
> I will execute judgments in your midst in the sight of the nations,
> > Doing in you what I never did,
> > and the like of which I shall not do again
> > because of all your abominations.
> Surely parents will eat children in your midst,
> > and children shall eat their parents,
> I will work judgments in you
> > and scatter your survivors to every wind. [Ezek 5:8-10, AB]

Frequently contemptuous and shockingly insulting, criticism is at the core of the message of the Hebrew prophets.

In one essential quality, however, criticism as prophecy and criticism as satire diverge. "An object of attack," according to Northrop Frye, is only one of the "two things essential to satire." Satire also demands, in his words, "wit or humor founded on fantasy or a sense of the grotesque or absurd." Satire ranges through a wide spectrum bounded, on the one hand, by pure denunciation, "attack without humor," and by "the humor of pure fantasy," or romance, on the other.[7] Ordinarily, the prophet's message falls comfortably within the realm of pure denunciation, although prophets can prove very mordant commentators on Israel's expectations from the fantasy-land of false gods. But moral denunciation and invective, as Frye has pointed out, are "very close." As one of satire's devices, invective requires literary talent to be successful, a talent specifically described by Frye as including "a sense of rhythm, an unlimited vocabulary and a technical knowledge of the two subjects which ordinarily form the subject matter of swearing, one of which is theology."[8] The other, I assume, is anatomy or physiology, at least sexual and excremental. At any rate, the appearance of even this one satiric device in prophecy demonstrates how prophecy and satire comprise a common rhetorical market across whose borders the individual critic can easily and profitably pass. Whenever the prophet joins humor to his attack, whenever he ridicules as well as criticizes, the prophet dons the satirist's mantle.

i.

O sacred Weapon! left for Truth's defence,
Sole Dread of Folly, Vice, and Insolence!
To all but Heav'n-directed hands deny'd,
The Muse may give thee, but the Gods must guide,
Reverent I touch thee! but with honest zeal;
To rowze the Watchmen of the Publick Weal . . . .
Alexander Pope, *Dialogue II*

As critical fantasy, parodying romance's view of life, satire travels the wide spectrum between invective and romance and not infrequently shares this road with the prophets, whose criticism and complaint skillfully draw on the resources of art to fashion a less than flattering view of the subject. Prophetic invective, for example, often displays the tone, quality, and devices of satiric name-calling. When 2 Kings draws on prophetic legend to recount King Ahaziah's mission to a false god, the text states that the king "sent messengers to inquire of Baal-zebub the god of Ekron whether he would recover from his illness" (2 Kgs 1:2, NEB). The god's name, meaning "lord of the flies," is, according to the New English Bible, "a distorted, contemptuous alteration of Baal-zebul, 'Baal the Prince.'"[9] As elsewhere through the prophets, insulting and humorous wordplay is a central device of prophetic invective. Not surprisingly, contemptuous, denigrating images recur to describe the false gods wooing the Israelites and seducing their enemies. Hosea speaks ironically of the divinity being appealed to by a chief priest for advice:

> He makes inquiry of his Wood,
> And his Staff reports to him. [Hos 4:12, AB]

If the parallel nouns *Wood* and *Staff* are, indeed, synonyms for a penis, Hosea has conjured up the delightfully ludicrous picture of a man seeking counsel from two wooden phalluses![10] One of the woes Habakkuk directs against the traitor is a comparable scoffing about the uselessness of his idols:

> What use is an idol when its maker has shaped it?—
> it is only an image, a source of lies;
> or when the maker trusts what he has made?—
> he is only making dumb idols.
> Woe betide him who says to the wood, "Wake up,"
> to the dead stone, "Bestir yourself!"
> Why, it is firmly encased in gold and silver
> and has no breath in it. [Hab 2:18-19, NEB]

Jeremiah ridicules the false gods of the nations in this same scoffing vein:

> What the peoples believe in—pure delusion!
>> It's but wood chopped out of the forest,
> Graved by the artisan's hand,
>> And decked with silver and gold—
> . . . Fastened with hammer and nails
>> To keep them from wobbling.

> Like scarecrows are they in a cucumber patch—can't talk!
> Have to be carried—can't walk!
> Fear them not—they can do no harm,
> Still less is it in them to help. [Jer 10:3-5, AB]

Here, even in translation, the enhancing of insult with rhythm is inescapable. At Judah's hope that Egypt and her gods will provide succor against the king of Babylon, Jeremiah sneers that Yahweh "will pick clean the land of Egypt like a shepherd picking lice from his clothing" (Jer 43:12, AB).

The human accomplices in this perversion of faith receive no better rhetorical treatment. For Hosea, Israel is a "rebellious cow" (Hos 4:16, AB), this image of bovine immobility perfectly suited to convey the sense of a nation's stubborn, intransigent adherence to sinfulness. Ephraim, the northern kingdom, he calls "a cake half-baked" (Hos 7:8, NEB), so mixed in with the pagan nations and their practices as to be virtually indistinguishable from them.[11] In rhythmic, parallel accusation and insult, Isaiah calls shame upon priests and prophets, "mighty topers, valiant mixers of drink," who pervert justice (Isa 5:20-23, NEB); priests and prophets alike are drunkards (Isa 28:7-9), the same invective used later by Joel, prophet in the time of the Second Temple, who tells the indolent, lolling drunken elders:

> Wake up, you drunkards, and lament your fate;
> mourn for the fresh wine, all you wine-drinkers,
> because it is lost to you. [Joel 1:5, NEB]

A lament for coming abstinence! For Amos, the complacent, morally insensitive wealthy women of Samaria are "the cows of Bashan" (4:1, NEB), oppressing the poor and crushing the destitute.

Whatever intensity the prophetic text conveys, unmistakable traces of artfulness also appear, signs of that careful attention to the ordering of language which suggest that the prophetic text, like the satiric, is not so much emotion as emotion recollected in tranquility. Here, for instance, is Nahum's powerful description of the fall of Nineveh, a passage admittedly devoid of humor, but graphic, carefully balanced, and, at the end, momentarily exploiting the resources of figurative language to explain why Nineveh has fallen:

Ah! blood-stained city, steeped in deceit,
full of pillage, never empty of prey!
   Hark to the crack of the whip,
the rattle of wheels and the stamping of horses,
bounding chariots, chargers rearing,
   swords gleaming, flash of spears!
The dead are past counting, their bodies lie in heaps,
corpses innumerable, men stumbling over corpses—
all for a wanton's monstrous wantonness [he explains],
   fair-seeming, a mistress of sorcery,
who beguiled nations and tribes
   by her wantonness and her sorceries. [Nah 3:1-4, NEB]

Was Nahum actually there? Irrelevant, claims the New English Bible: "We need not suppose that Nahum was present; an active imagination is enough."[12] Precisely. In the Hebrew prophets, as the text of their message has come down to us, is a shaping artistic imagination working together with powerful moral purpose. The arts of language working coherently with moral aim provide the detachment necessary to render criticism satiric and to support the claim that prophecy is often satire. Here, in Northrop Frye's phrase, is that "impersonal level . . . that commits the attacker, if only by implication, to a moral standard." So the prophet, like the satirist, "commonly takes a high moral line."[13] Prophetic invective often satisfies the requirements set down by David Worcester in his *Art of Satire* to render invective satiric: "detachment, indirection, and complexity in the author's attitude."[14] Since satire, again quoting Worcester, is "the most rhetorical of all the kinds of literature,"[15] it is not surprising that the devices of the comparably rhetorical art which is prophecy should so often prove satiric. Scripture scholar Samuel Sandmel, after all, urges us "to think of a prophet more as an orator than as an essayist."[16] Ezekiel, in fact, complains to Yahweh that the prophet's message is ignored because his audience considers him only a crafter of words and stories: "They say of me," Ezekiel laments, "'He deals only in parables'" (Ezek 20:49, NEB). So clearly do the prophets reveal their skill in language that their very wordcraft is held against them.

   Amos, one of the first of the Hebrew prophets, is a master verbal craftsman.[17] Take, for example, the series of dooms which begin the prophecy (Amos 1:3-2:16). This series works like a progressively chilling, ironic thriller in which the ultimate and principal victim, disarmingly satisfied and rendered complacent by the misfortune of others, comes slowly and fearfully to realize that she has been witnessing an irresistible movement towards her own destruction. Amos moves geographically from the farthest peripheries of the northern kingdom in Damascus and Gaza, Tyre and Edom, to the very eastern and southern borders of the kingdom—Ammon, Moab, and Judah—until, ironically, only Israel is left, to receive not words of encouragement but rather the longest of the oracles of doom. Amos parodies the priest's call to worship, as he sarcastically dismisses the value of the ritual performed at Bethel and Gilgal, the two principal shrines of the north:

> Come to Bethel—and rebel [he jeers]!
> Come to Gilgal—and rebel the more!
> Bring your sacrifices for the mornings,
> your tithes within three days.
> Burn your thank-offering without leaven;
> announce, proclaim your freewill offerings;
> for you love to do what is proper, you men of Israel!
>
> [Amos 4:4-5, NEB]

Drawing on the hated role of Egypt and the despised place of Sodom and Gomorrah in their history, Amos, ironically, has Israel play the role of these three despised nations in experiencing like them the ineffectual chastisement of the LORD and soon to experience like them the doom of the LORD (Amos 4:10-11).[18] Israel is the new Egypt, the new Sodom and Gomorrah. He anticipates Isaiah's scorn of the false security derived from ritual observance: "Spare me the sound of your songs," he cries; "I cannot endure the music of your lutes" (Amos 5:23, NEB). He contemptuously conveys the indolent, moral insouciance of the privileged, oppressing classes and looks forward to their reversal of fortune:

> Shame on you who live at ease in Zion,
> and you, untroubled on the hill of Samaria . . . .
> You who loll on beds inlaid with ivory
> and sprawl over your couches,

> feasting on lambs from the flock and fatted calves,
> you who pluck the strings of the lute
> and invent musical instruments like David [!],
> you who drink wine by the bowlful
> and lard yourselves with the richest of oils,
> but are not grieved at the ruin of Joseph—
> now, therefore,
> you shall head the column of exiles;
>   that will be the end of sprawling and revelry. [Amos 6:1, 4-7, NEB]

With intense sarcasm, Amos poses a series of rhetorical questions that wonderingly compare Israel's prostitution of justice with physically miraculous and Herculean achievements:

> Can horses gallop over rocks?
> Can the sea be ploughed with oxen?
> Yet you have turned into venom *the process of the law*
>   and justice itself into poison. [Amos 6:12, NEB; my emphasis][19]

He projects himself imaginatively into the irritation and impatience of a criminal professional class, restless during ritual because the demands of liturgy are cutting into the time available for dishonest money-making:

> When will the new moon be over so that we may sell corn?
> When will the sabbath be past so that we may open our wheat
> again, giving short measure in the bushel and taking over-
> weight in silver, tilting the scales fraudulently, and selling the
> dust of the wheat; that we may buy the poor for silver and the
> destitute for a pair of shoes? [Amos 8:5-7, NEB]

An almost Dickensian picture of what is really going on in Uriah Heep's mind as he publicly proclaims his humble submissiveness. Or, if you prefer, a Blake-like scene: these are the godly in Amos' *Songs of Experience*.

Amos, indeed, demonstrates that the satiric weaponry of the prophets is not limited to their consignment of invective. His parody of the priest's call to worship, like Elijah's parody of the rain-making practices of the priests of Baal, exemplifies another satiric device in the prophets, the ironic use of established, traditional, or recognizable forms. When a supposedly or conventionally serious subject or form receives demeaning treatment in the prophets, we have that specific kind of parody known as low burlesque—what Byron does, for example, in *Don Juan*, when he ludicrously recalls the convention of epic invocation with his "Hail, Muse, etcetera!"

In *Myth, Legend, and Custom in the Old Testament*, in fact, Theodor Gaster argues that it is possible "to discern in many a prophetic utterance (particularly in the Twelve Minor Prophets) pointed jibes at standard pagan rites and ceremonies and to recognize *satire* [his emphasis] as a cardinal element of the prophetic technique."[20] Hosea he regards "as a sustained satire on pagan seasonal festivals" and offers for consideration there eight of what he calls only "the more arresting instances" in that prophet.[21] "The prophecies of Amos," he claims, "appear to be studded with jibes at pagan seasonal practices, suggesting that they may have been delivered at festive assemblies." He offers eight specific instances from Amos' text and includes the observation that Amos' famous statement—"Let justice roll on like a river, and righteousness like an ever-flowing stream" (Amos 5:24, NEB)—"assumes added force if it is read as a satire on the rite of pouring water as a rain-charm."[22] According to Gaster, the opening words of the prophecy of Zephaniah "parody the standard descriptions of the languishing earth in myths connected with the 'vanished and returning' (or 'dying and reviving') deities of fertility . . . ."[23]

Gaster finds comparable parody of form in the major prophets. The vision in Ezekiel 7, for example, draws "metaphors from the familiar symbols of the heathen cult" and gives "to each a particular homiletic twist." Ezekiel's harvest festival will reap doom, not fruit; tumult, rather than joy, will sound in the hills. His rites of the autumnal harvest of God's judgment include as well, according to Gaster, "a pointed jibe at the gaudy raiment and the parade of statuettes . . . which characterized the pagan ceremonies":

> They shall fling their silver into the streets;
>   their gold shall be as an unclean thing
>   [an allusion to menstrual uncleanness].[24]
> Their silver and gold shall be powerless to save them
>   on the day of YHWH's rage.

> They shall not satisfy their hunger,
>   nor their bellies [with it],
> For it was their stumbling-block of iniquity.
> Their beautiful adornment in which they took pride—out of it
> they made images of their abominable loathsome things: there
> I will turn it into an unclean thing for them. [Ezek 7:19-20,AB]

In the conclusion of Ezekiel's vision Gaster sees a sly allusion "to the pagan seasonal ceremony of seeking the lost or ousted god of fertility. . . ." In this parody-procession, incidentally, the knees of all the marchers "shall run with water" (7:17), in other words, passing urine in their fright—a touch that would be very much at home in Alexander Pope's *Dunciad*.[25]

In the prophets as well, mock funeral song or dirge occasionally celebrates the demise of enemy kingdoms, like Egypt and Babylon. A sizeable chunk of the text of Ezekiel, chapters twenty-five through thirty-two, for instance, prominently features mock lamentations on the demise of some of Israel's pagan neighbors and traditional enemies. Isaiah, too, parodies the form in that "song of derision over the king of Babylon" (Isa 14:4, NEB) which, he promises, the returning exiles will sing as they return to Judah. This later interpolation—the historical Isaiah was concerned with the Assyrian, not the Babylonian threat—is "a taunt song or a mocking song" applicable to "the downfall of [any] tyrant."[26] The song's opening ironically contrasts the stillness of a "frenzy ceased" with the rage, anger, and persecution so markedly a feature of the tyrant's life:

> See how the oppressor has met his end
>   and his frenzy ceased!
> The LORD has broken the rod of the wicked,
> the sceptre of the ruler
> who struck down peoples in his rage with unerring blows,
> who crushed nations in anger
> and persecuted them unceasingly. [Isa 14:4-6, NEB]

Even the stillnesses contrast, however, for while the oppressor lies low in Sheol, "the whole world has rest and is at peace" (14:7). As the cosmos breaks into cries of joys and exultation, the murmurs of mock expectation from below reveal the hustle and bustle of Sheol for the great arrival:

> Sheol below was all astir
>> to meet you at your coming;
> she roused the ancient dead to meet you,
>> all who had been leaders on earth;
>> she made all who had been kings of the nations
>> rise from their throne. [14:9]

The shades of the once glorious dead greet the tyrant with mock astonishment and evident satisfaction at their common fate, the low burlesque of destiny that one so great should be brought so low:

> So you too are weak as we are,
>> and have become one of us!
> Your pride and all the music of your lutes
>> have been brought down to Sheol . . . . [14:10-11]

Mock accoutrements deck the tyrant's bier:

> maggots are the pallet beneath you,
>> and worms your coverlet. [14:11]

In a manner very comparable to Juvenal's skill in depicting the satisfaction of the less great at the fall of the greater and the wild, tumultuous change from weal to woe, the shades mockingly review the tyrant's pretensions and his final doom:

> How you have fallen from heaven, bright morning star,
> felled to the earth, sprawling helpless across nations!
>> You thought in your own mind,
>>> I will scale the heavens;
>> I will set my throne high above the stars of God,
>> I will sit on the mountain where the gods meet
>>> in the far recesses of the north.
>> I will rise high above the cloud-banks
>>> and make myself like the Most High.
>> Yet you shall be brought down to Sheol,
>>> to the depths of the abyss.
>> Those who see you will stare at you,
>>> they will look at you and ponder:
> Is this, they will say, the man who shook the earth,
>> who made the kingdoms quake,
> who turned the world into a desert
>> and laid its cities in ruins,

who never let his prisoners go free to their homes,
the kings of every land? [14:12-18]

The final indignity in this mock lamentation is the tyrant's
dishonoring lack of burial and the slaughter of his sons. For
while "the kings of every land" who had once been his prisoners now "lie all of them in honour" and "each in his last
home," you, the tyrant,

> have been flung out unburied,
> mere loathsome carrion,
> a companion to the slain pierced by the sword
> who have gone down to the stony abyss.
> And you, a corpse trampled underfoot,
> shall not share burial with them,
> for you have ruined your land and slaughtered your people.
> Such a brood of evildoers shall never be seen again.
> Make the shambles ready for his sons
> butchered for their fathers' sin;
> they shall not rise up and possess the world
> nor cover the face of the earth with cities. [14:18-21]

The prophecy of Isaiah, which provides this marvelously
ironic use of the funeral lament, whose contempt for the oppressor glides through these verses with serpentine ease, is also
the source of a satiric catalog on female ornament. This device
reduces a subject to absurdity by an ever-growing accretion of
detail or predication whose cumulative effect is to ridicule. In
the last part of *Gulliver's Travels*, for instance, Jonathan Swift
breaks into this form of verbal exuberance several times in order
to satirize the differences of opinion that lead to war, the
attractions of war as a spectator sport, the advantages of luxuri-
ous living as a spur to criminal behavior, and the sources of
medicines.[27] Isaiah begins his catalog by first mimicking the
demeanor, look, and gait of the grand dames of Jerusalem,
whose heads shall shortly display the customary external signs
of exile and defeat:

> Because the women of Zion hold themselves high
> and walk with necks outstretched and wanton glances,
> moving with mincing gait
> and jingling feet,

> the LORD will give the women of Zion bald heads,
> the LORD will strip the hair from their foreheads. [Isa 3:16-17, NEB]

Then, in a detailing of elaborate finery and its ornaments, Isaiah fashions a ludicrous image of a society matron staggering under the weight of fashionable gewgaws, which the LORD will strip away in the day of exile:

> In that day [Isaiah says] the LORD will take away all finery: anklets, discs, crescents, pendants, bangles, coronets, head-bands, armlets, necklaces, lockets, charms, signets, nose-rings, fine dresses, mantles, cloaks, flounced skirts, scarves of gauze, kerchiefs of linen, turbans, and flowing veils. [3:18-23]

The LORD, however, has an exchange in mind for this treasured pile of fashionable dross:

> So instead of perfume you shall have the stench of decay,
>   and a rope in place of a girdle,
> baldness instead of hair elegantly coiled,
> a loin-cloth of sacking instead of a mantle,
> and branding instead of beauty. [3:24]

Isaiah's conclusion completes the stripping away from layers of bric-a-brac to nakedness, a progress from the vanity of carefree ornamentation to the shame of exile:

> Your men shall fall by the sword,
>   and your warriors in battle;
> then Zion's gates shall mourn and lament,
> and she shall sit on the ground stripped bare. [3:25]

Theodor Gaster notes that one of the items listed by Isaiah can be a "house of the soul," perhaps a bottle of scent or perfume—frequently translated as such--the smelling of whose contents would be reminiscent of the breath which is life.[28] If this interpretation is plausible, the presence of such a potentially serious item among those ornamental and ornamenting trinkets registers the same levelling of values apparent in the objects on Belinda's dressing table in Alexander Pope's *The Rape of the Lock*: "Puffs, Patches, Powders, Bibles, Billet-doux" (I, 138). Scripture's ornamental value wins it a place at Belinda's toilet.

ii.

And all your Courtly Civet-Cats can vent,
Perfume to you, to me is Excrement.

Alexander Pope, *Dialogue II*

For Northrop Frye, this passage in Isaiah, which he calls "a
satire on female ornament," is one of the earliest displays of
that "creative exuberance" one of whose "most typical and
obvious" signs is "the verbal tempest, the tremendous outpour-
ing of words in catalogues, abusive epithets and erudite tech-
nicalities" especially apparent in that satire which strips away
customary associations necessary to the maintaining of human
dignity.[29] Nowhere do satire and prophecy prove more outrageously shocking and more outrageously funny than in their use
of the ordinarily tabooed subjects of sex and excretion, whose
use as images can prove wondrously effective medicine for
shocking satiric and prophetic victims into a healthier, albeit
diminished, view of themselves. Swift and Juvenal, Pope and
even Horace, Ezekiel and Jeremiah deliberately flaunt dignity-
preserving conventions that require us to think of one another,
as Frye says, "apart from excretion, copulation, and similar
embarrassments." Hence, Frye concludes, "Genius seems to
have led practically every great satirist"--and every great prophet as well, I would add—"to become what the world calls
obscene."[30]

Jeremiah's compelling figure of a Judah hot for idolatry as
a rutting she-camel, "restlessly pacing to and fro in her
heat,"[31] vividly exemplifies the satiric power of prophetic
imagery. In Jeremiah, Judah becomes a streetwalker, seeking
out whatever passersby appear, ironically, unaware that all the
street traffic despises her and seeks her life:

> And you—[he challenges] what mean you
>   Dressing in scarlet,
> Binding on bangles of gold,
>   Smearing your eyes with paint?
> In vain do you primp!
>   They loathe you who accost you,
>   It's your life that they seek. [Jer 4:30, AB]

In their unrelenting, yet disquieting thirst for idolatry, the sinning Judahites resemble opportunists lingering at a brothel, stallions eyeing a nearby mare:

> Why should I forgive you? [Yahweh asks through Jeremiah,]
>> Your people have left me
>>> And sworn by no-gods.
> Though I gave them their fill, they whored!
>> At the harlot's house they tarried.
> Stallions, sleek and lusty, they,
>> Whinnying each for his neighbor's wife. [5:7-8, AB]

In Yahweh's voice, Jeremiah recalls the exposure of Judah's sinfulness and his impatience with her lack of repentance:

> It was I myself who snatched
>> Your skirt up over your face,
>>> Exposing your shame.
> Your whoring! Your rutting!
>> Your wanton affairs!
> On the hills, in the fields,
>> I have seen your indecencies. . . .
>> Will you never be clean? [13:26-27, AB]

The fornication or adultery which is Judah's idolatry, her ill-advised attempt to seek in foreign nations security against the king of Babylon, is grossly pictured in Jeremiah as the behavior of an adulterous wife, insatiable in her quest for lovers:

> Yes, you who have whored with hosts of lovers
> [Yahweh incredulously asks]—
>> You would return to me? . . .
> Look up to the high, bare hills, and see!
>> Where have you not been tumbled?
> By the roads you sat waiting for them
>> Like an Arab in the desert
>> [i.e., "waiting to waylay a caravan"[32]].
> You've polluted the land
>> With your whorish depravity. [3:1-2, AB]

That pollution, in Jeremiah, takes on the anatomically graphic, ludicrous, and indelible picture of "committing adultery with stones and trees" (3:9, AB)!

The bowdlerizing of satiric texts that has silently or euphemistically passed over sections of Juvenal and Swift, or Horace and Pope, has made its presence felt even in modern versions of Scripture, where divine verbal armament has, on occasion, been safely and innocuously defused. One striking instance in the prophets occurs in Third Isaiah's psalm of lamentation, as translator John McKenzie calls it, where the prophet, as spokesman for the community, acknowledges its sinfulness and rebellion: "We have become like one unclean," he admits, "and all our righteous deeds like the rag of a menstruous woman" (Isa 64:5, AB). A "somewhat crude image," McKenzie comments, with language admittedly "unusual."[33] The King James and Revised Standard versions both admit to something foul in the cloth, but judiciously refrain from specificity: "all our righteousnesses are as filthy rags," laments the Authorized Version, while its more contemporary counterpart admits that "all our righteous deeds are like a polluted garment," phraseology appropriate to a warning from the Environmental Protection Agency. The Jerusalem Bible evokes images of All-Temperature Cheer when it speaks of "all that integrity of ours like filthy clothing," but at least it cross-references the mention of menstrual uncleanness in Leviticus 15:19. Ronald Knox somewhat hesitantly approaches the specificity of the Hebrew when he translates the passage, "no better than the clout a woman casts away."

Although not in the prophets, a second example, from the Books of Kings—which do draw on prophetic legends—, shows how delicacy triumphs over accuracy even in modern scholarly versions. 1 Kings 16 narrates the assassination of Elah, a king of Israel and son of Baasha, by his servant Zimri. To secure his claim to the violently won throne, Zimri sees to it that no male of Elah's family or kin survives. 1 Kings vividly expresses this complete extermination of any possible male claimant, vividly at least in the King James: Zimri so thoroughly slew the entire house of Baasha that "he left him not one that pisseth against a wall, neither of his kinsfolks, nor of his friends" (16:11, KJV), a refreshingly direct and accurate rendering. The Revised Standard affirms only that Zimri "did not leave him a single male of his kinsmen or his friends"; the New English Bible assures us that Zimri "left not a single mother's son alive"; and

Knox, comparably, speaks of Zimri's "leaving no male among them alive." The pictorially vulgar, debasing, and funny form of the idiom disappears in these more socially acceptable euphemisms.[34]

At the core of the debasing sexual language and imagery of the prophets—basically, their repetitions of and variations on the motif that Israel is a whore—is an ironic inversion, an ironic reversal of the traditional, highly complimentary figuring of the relationship between Yahweh and Israel as that of a husband and wife. In his commentary on Ezekiel, Moshe Greenberg observes that this figure of Israel as the wife of Yahweh

> derives from the cardinal commitment that Israel worship YHWH alone. To that demand of exclusive fidelity, the obligation of a wife to her husband offered a parallel. . . . The prophetic development of this figure is built upon this early foundation.[35]

Hosea's denunciation of the northern kingdom, in the eighth century, constitutes "the first recorded use" of the uncomplimentary side of this image. Intriguingly enough, private disappointment may have provided additional prompting for Hosea to find a suitable image of Israel's apostasy in the uncomplimentary inversion of the husband-wife figure. In the very outset of his prophecy, Hosea recounts God's instruction that he marry a woman who will become a prostitute and beget children by her. In their translation and commentary on Hosea, Francis Andersen and David Noel Freedman offer the following interpretation:

> The history of [Hosea's] marriage and children became a continuing source of insight into and understanding of the story of God and his people. . . . In the case of Hosea it seems clear that the theological imagery arises out of his personal tribulation. . . . If the relationship between God and Israel was to be compared to that between Hosea and his faithless wife, then the consequences were clear, and the message could not be in doubt. Israel would reap the same reward for its conduct that a straying wife deserved. . . . [In Hosea then, as in the later prophets,] promiscuity and idolatry are interchangeable terms. . . .[36] For the eighth century this imagery is unique to Hosea, but it exerted a powerful influence in subsequent thought and speech on the subject, and we find Israel as the

faithless partner of Yahweh central in the proclamations of Jeremiah and Ezekiel. . . . [Hosea's] private tragedy is a paradigm for that of Israel.[37]

Like a canvas by Bosch or the Brueghels, the prophets' portrait of Israel teems with an obscene, disfigured mob: Pharaoh Big-Noise, Lord Delusion, Lord Useless—these leering down approvingly on the Vanity Fair of Jerusalem the streetwalker, the sexually alert stallions whinnying for their neighbors' wives, the human sacrifices, the sexual exhibitionists on public platforms, and the bent figures seeking oracular pronouncement from a wooden phallus. This prophetic cacophony jumbles the noises of ritual observance, sexual invitation, restless murmuring about dishonest profit, and the auctioning of the poor and the destitute into slavery. Only the clamor of the oppressing privileged class rises above this din, as the well-to-do stubbornly claim prerogative, oblivious to any easily overwhelmed voice warning that such hideous abuse of the nation's very institutions must and will fall of its own horrid weight. Yahweh will remember and bring it all down. These Messalinas, Flying Islands, and Yahoos of prophetic satire move towards that fantasy which provides, as Frye notes, "a high degree of the ridiculous" in satire. These fantastic creatures, however, lack the unchallenging innocuousness of romance because of that "powerful undertow" which Frye describes as "the implicit reference to experience in the perception of the incongruous."[38] These are not the monsters, giants, and strange creatures of romance. These are the nightmares of the satirist's—and the prophet's— reality, in Scripture, that wide disparity between Israel's complacent, flattering view of herself and the monstrous thing the prophets see there.

That prophecy employs the fantastic is implied in the very denotations of unusual vision or sight frequently included in various definitions of the term. Isaiah's call in the temple, when he sees the high and exalted LORD surrounded by six-winged seraphim, ceaselessly singing to one another a song of the LORD's holiness (Isa 6); Ezekiel's vision in a plain full of bones, where the ossified remains come to life, just as the LORD has promised (Ezekiel 37); his vision of the four living creatures in human form in the midst of a fire (Ezekiel 1)—these incidents reveal prophecy's capacity to draw on the fantastic, on the empirically improbable material of romance, as an integral part of prophetic utterance. Prophets, however, can employ fantasy satirically as well. Perhaps no single text in Hebrew prophecy demonstrates better the prophet's skill in fashioning the critical fantasy which is satire than the account of Jerusalem the ubiquitous harlot in Ezekiel 16. If Ezekiel's Jerusalem does not approach the cosmic prostitution of John's Whore of Babylon in the Book of Revelation, she has certainly done enough sleeping around in the Near East to pose a formidable challenge to Messalina, Juvenal's Olympic gold medalist in sex. Indeed, Ezekiel's account of the whoring Jerusalem, according to Moshe Greenberg, "may be the earliest instance of what became a motif of hypersexuality in erotic literature."[39]

This single longest unit in Ezekiel's prophecy—sixty-three verses—allegorizes Israel's history from her remotest origins, through her deliverance from the Egyptians and her political triumph, to the threshold and beyond of her extinction by and in Babylon.[40] In Ezekiel's allegory the ongoing flirtation of Israel with the powers and divinities of her enemies—a millennium of prostitution with the Egyptians, Philistines, Assyrians, and Chaldeans—becomes a most prominent feature in his story of the marriage of Yahweh and Israel. In this rags-to-riches tale, however, the rescued Cinderella repeatedly cheats on her prince and proves at the end, to her shame, no better than her wicked stepsisters.

Ezekiel's is a circular account, beginning and ending in Jerusalem's shame. At the very outset, in an ethnographic insult, Yahweh pointedly reminds Jerusalem of her pagan, not her patriarchal, origins: "Your origin and your birth were in the land of the Canaanite: your father was an Amorite, your mother Hittite" (Ezek 16:3, AB). At the end Jerusalem is saved only along with her sisters, Samaria and Sodom. She who had long considered these siblings bywords of wickedness will "bear the disgrace of having justified them," of making them "look righteous in comparison!" (16:52). Jerusalem will be restored to her former state only when her "sister Sodom and her daughters" and her sister "Samaria and her daughters are restored to their former state" (16:55). "So you will remember," Yahweh concludes, "and be ashamed and not be able to open your mouth again because of your disgrace" (16:63). Jerusalem returns to the disgrace from which she came.

What will Yahweh have Jerusalem remember? First, the unregarded and unassisted nakedness of her birth, a nakedness of vulnerability in the child, but ironically foreshadowing the exposed nakedness of Jerusalem, later the practicing and revealed harlot, and the nakedness in which her punishing lovers shall leave her after "they demolish [her] platform and tear down [her] heights" (16:39). Here the cycle and circle of Jerusalem's nakedness moves from her guiltless abandonment as a child, to her guilty abandon as a whore, and, finally, to the contemptuous abandonment of her by her now sated and loathing former lovers. But in her infancy and in her puberty, her nakedness draws the loving attention of her destined husband: "Left to die in the field," the naked, infant Jerusalem drew Yahweh's loving attention; he made her "flourish like the plants of the field" (16:5,7). Let Jerusalem recall as well that when she arrived at "the age of love-making," Yahweh regarded her nakedness again—"your breasts" . . . well formed and your hair . . . sprouted"—and covered her with a garment, as Boaz covered Ruth, and pledged himself to her: "you became mine," he recalls, of her who became everyone else's (16:7,8). Touchingly, the old man has fallen in love with his young ward, a January-May marriage, with the customary results. "I washed you with water and rinsed your blood off you and anointed you with oil" (16:9); Yahweh gave her precisely those marks of attention that had been denied her as an infant, for on the day she was born, Yahweh recalls: "your navel-string was not cut, you were not washed smooth with water, you were not rubbed with salt or swaddled. No one cared enough about you," says Yahweh, "to do any of these things for you out of pity for you" (16:4-5). All sorts of ornament now enhanced her nubile beauty: "You were very, very beautiful, fit to be a queen," and since Yahweh had set on her head "a glorious crown," a queen she, in fact, became (16:13,12). But then let Jerusalem remember

104

that, like Claudius' empress Messalina, Queen Jerusalem became an imperial whore.

These powerful memories of Yahweh, initially a compassionate and loving recollection, now turn contemptuously to Jerusalem's career as a married prostitute with sarcastic astonishment at the quality, extent, and ever-to-be-outdone outrageousness of her sinful excesses. "You were mine," Yahweh had recalled. Now, "it was his," anyone's that passed by. "Confident of your beauty, you harloted on your fame" (16:15). The specification of Jerusalem's increasingly insatiable nymphomania employs the Juvenalian technique of surpassing one outrage with an ever greater to a climax in an outrage or reversal that bathetically undercuts the others. First, Jerusalem prostitutes the gifts of her husband: "You took some of your clothes and made gaily-colored shrines and harloted on them" (16:16). That was not enough: "You took your glorious articles, of my gold and my silver that I gave you, and made yourself male images and harloted with them," covering them with embroidered clothes and setting before them oil, incense, and food, "the fine flour, oil and honey that I fed you" (16:17-19). Like the morally fetid infanticidal matrons of Juvenal's *Satire VI*, Queen Jerusalem did not recoil from offering her own children as food for her new lover-gods:

> You took your sons and daughters that you bore me and sacrificed them to them for food. . . . You slaughtered my sons as an offering and delivered them over to them! And with all your abominations and your harlotry you did not remember the time of your youth when you were stark naked, wallowing in your blood. [16:20-22]

Queen Jerusalem becomes the Juvenalian exhibitionist:

> After all your evil . . . you built yourself a platform and made yourself a height in every square. At every crossroad you built your height and you made your beauty abominable by opening your legs to anyone who passed by. [16:23-25]

This gross picture of wanton sexual display yields to an even grosser: "Increasing your harlotry," Yahweh recalls, "you harloted with the Egyptians, your big-membered neighbors"

(16:26). So the Egyptian is recommended to Queen Jerusalem for the same reason that Proculeius or Gillo, in Juvenal's *Satire I*, comes to the service of "some rich old bag": "the size of his tool."[41] One ironic triumph of this depravity, Yahweh recalls, was how it shocked the women of the Philistines, "who were ashamed of your depraved way" (16:27). In his *Satire VI* Juvenal tells how Eppia, the wife of a Roman senator, deserted her husband, her children, and the theatre to run off with a superannuated, one-armed gladiator to that moral cesspool Alexandria, where she found the Alexandrians morally outraged at her conduct. In self-infatuation the saucy wife turns on her husband in ceaseless, relentless sexual viciousness: "you increased your harlotry to vex me" (16:26). She pursues an Assyrian and Chaldean clientele, a veritable smorgasbord of Near Eastern erotic delights (16:28-29). And, finally, the contemptuous wonder of Yahweh at the ultimate, bathetic outrage:

> Nor were you like other harlots, in that you scorned hire. . . .
> Every harlot receives gifts, but you gave your gifts to all your
> lovers, paying them to come to you from all around . . . you
> paid hire, no hire being paid to you. [16:31, 33-34]

Wonder of wonders, Jerusalem is the prostitute who pays her customers!

Here are all the touches of Juvenal's notorious pictures of perverted sexuality in a scene as carefully elaborated and vividly pictorial as any semi-dramatic vignette in the work of that Roman master: the ever-increasing outrages, the bathetic climax, the graphic images, the explicit diction—including the reference to vaginal secretion—[42] the contemptuous astonishment, the satisfaction in the downfall of such wickedness, and even the Juvenalian conviction that perverted sexuality attracts a host of manipulating partners and retainers who rush at the opportunity—as Jerusalem's lovers do—to strip bare that same carcass now, not for pleasure, but for gain and vindictive satisfaction. This is Ezekiel's counterpart to the erotic gymnastics of the Empress Messalina, in Juvenal's *Satire VI*, working all night in disguise as a prostitute, with her back to the grindstone, taking on all comers, and, ironically, returning to the palace at dawn sexually unsatisfied. Like Juvenal, Ezekiel makes vividly and dynamically clear the really erotic core of the religious rites that attract the stately young matron Jerusalem as they were later to attract the stately matrons of Rome. In Ezekiel, as in Juvenal, this is the shame of the married woman. Like Juvenal, Ezekiel can quip about the tradition of foulness such conduct reveals: "Like mother like daughter," Yahweh sarcastically remarks (16:44). This daughter of a Hittite mother, who shocked even the women of Philistia by her immorality, scandalizes even her legendarily immoral sisters, Sodom and Samaria. How disgraced will she be to secure her former state only in company with them! The ethnographic insult that opens the account nicely closes it as well: Jerusalem, who springs from the Canaanite, the Amorite, and the Hittite, proves at the end morally indistinguishable from, perhaps morally inferior to, the Samaritan and the Sodomite. For Jerusalem, Queen of Sinners, a future of silence, so disgraced that she will not be able to open her mouth again. For Yahweh, whom this unfaithful wife sought to vex, the silence of a calm and satisfaction brought on by the marvelously cathartic effect of his derision and scorn: "I will spend my fury against you and my rage at you shall subside; I will grow calm and not be vexed any more" (16:42).

iii.

Can't you see he's thinking of the days when he was happy . . . . *Memoria praeteritorum bonorum*—that must be unpleasant.

Samuel Beckett, *Waiting for Godot*

Ezekiel's hypererotic fable about Judah's worldwide career of prostitution and infidelity provides an intense instance of that satire of the high norm whose essential characteristic Northrop Frye isolates as the breaking down of "customary associations" like the social convention which demands that "the dignity of some men and the beauty of some women should be thought of apart from excretion, copulation, and similar embarrassments."[43] This kind or phase of satire is very characteristic of the Hebrew prophets when they engage in that direct, ridiculing criticism indistinguishable from satire, a ridicule notable for the intensity and savagery of its attack. The particularly vehement anti-feminine quality so integral to Ezekiel 16 has counterparts in Swift's scatological poetry as well as in Juvenal, particularly in the unrelenting attack on married women in *Satire VI*.

Frye's paradigm, however, is also useful for indicating the kinds or phases of satire not found in the prophets. Little appears, for instance, of that satire of the low norm, characterized by a willingness to use and even manipulate the conventions and norms of society, but to use them more sensibly and productively than most.[44] Such is the satire of Jane Austen and of Horace, each confidently arguing a street-savvy of sorts, manifested in discretion, prudence, and timing so that the more perceptive can live comfortably within the admittedly limited customs and institutions of the social order. While many of the cautions of Qoheleth qualify, none of the remarks of the Hebrew prophets do. No prophet seeks a modus vivendi with the established order, because each roundly challenges and excoriates the guiding assumptions of religious and political practice in Israel and Judah. No prophet wants a way of living with ritual human sacrifice. The quieter, low-key voice so pervasive in Austen or Horace is conspicuously lacking in the prophets.

As satire moves into its second phase, the very conventions of the social order are exposed as bootless. Here, appealing to experience over theory, the satirist shows that theories do not work.[45] The wild, exuberant, but violent and savage travels and trials of Candide well illustrate such satire. Some prophetic utterance likewise qualifies. As the likes of Hosea, Jeremiah, and Isaiah point to the conventions or schemes in which their societies seek refuge—alliances, fertility rites involving human sacrifice, syncretistic religious practice—they point with a sometimes Voltaire-like power to the disastrous consequences of these customary devices of safety and security.

In the wisdom books, Qoheleth, of course, repeatedly takes this tack. One most notable instance occurs when he directly challenges the theological premise that the wicked are punished. Appealing to experience over theory, he says it simply isn't so: "there are anomalies in life" (8:14, AB). Job's misfortunes lead him to abandon the exact same theological premise which his supposedly comforting friends still cling to. But while second-phase satire occasionally appears in the prophets, satire of the high norm, third-phase satire, most characterizes their ridicule. Customarily respectful, thoughtful, and discreet associations are repeatedly set aside with scatological or sexual insult. The prophets shatter and bespatter with their words. Ezekiel 16 is only one such instance.

But what of irony in the Hebrew prophets? Satire, says Frye, appears when norms are explicit and direct. When attitude is shaded in ambiguity, when no explicit statement of principle appears, then satire shades into irony, in three kinds or phases roughly parallel to those of satire.[46] If first-phase irony, such as one finds in Austen or Horace, brings out the avoidability of human folly and stresses the humanity of its characters, little if any such irony appears in the prophets. They do not extenuate the faults they chastise; they do not, in Frye's terms, supply "social and psychological explanations for catastrophe."[47] Jane Austen's Elizabeth Bennet, for instance, comes to see that much of the pain she suffers is the result of her own wilfully indulged biases. Horace discusses the ease with which adulterous relationships or excessive concern with money can be avoided by sensible, hardheaded insights into a situation.[48] Such processes of self-discovery, with their calm reassurance about more beneficial possibilities, do not appear in prophecy. The prophets urge no thoughtful dialog where two points of view can meet to arrive at a better. Catastrophe comes not for social or psychological reasons, but because of wilful, flagrant, and insensitive violation of the Covenant.

Second-phase irony, "in which the main emphasis is on the natural cycle, the steady unbroken turning of the wheel of fate or fortune," seems virtually absent in the prophets.[49] Such irony well describes the puzzlement of Qoheleth or his classic statement in Ecclesiastes 3 of the déjà-vu quality of human experience. Only the prophets' reminders of how their contemporaries repeat the obtuseness of their forebears might exemplify second-phase irony, somewhat resigned comments in Jeremiah and Isaiah, for instance, on the unvarying immorality of Judah and Israel despite warning after warning. Such prophetic statement is "stoical and resigned," to use Frye's terms, and if biblical scholars correctly argue that little hope appears in the prophets, that lack of confidence, along with the characteristic and stereotypical designation of Israel and Judah as the new Sodom and Gomorrah, underscores the sense of inevitability in prophetic utterance.

What of the last phase of irony, however, that ironic counterpart of high-norm satire where irony presents human life "in terms of largely unrelieved bondage," where parodies of religious symbols are not uncommon, where, according to Frye, one experiences, as in Kafka's *In the Penal Colony*, "the humiliation of being constantly watched by a hostile or *derisive* [my emphasis] eye"? Such irony is the point of "demonic epiphany, the dark tower and prison of endless pain, the city of dreadful night in the desert, or . . . the goal of the quest that isn't there."[50] This is the irony of Hosea, with a God capable of disturbing laughter and satisfaction, as in Ezekiel 16, cathartic for the divine, as if such laughter were relieving intense disgust at viciously criminal behavior. Hosea's is an obscene, nightmarish fantasy, replete with sexual and scatological insult, that nowhere makes explicit its terrifying warning: Yahweh is revoking a centuries' old assurance of support. I AM will become I AM NOT. As James Ackerman observes, "Biblical literature is . . . capable of highly sophisticated irony."[51] Hosea's is not only sophisticated, but deeply disturbing as well.

A few reminders, first, about the basic assumptions and workings of irony. Central to the notion of irony as non-literal statement is the twofold audience: one, accepting the statement at face value, misunderstands and misinterprets it, is frequently puzzled by it; the other recognizes its real, intended meaning. Irony is thus ambiguously interpreted statement, discourse that puzzles, bewilders, or surpasses the comprehension of some while a supposedly more sophisticated, perceptive, and smaller group fathoms what is really meant. From its earliest manifestations, the Hebrew Scriptures often present ironic situations. A religious faith like the faith of Israel, I would argue, in asserting the incomprehensibility to humans of God's purposes, implicitly establishes irony not as a mere device or trick of style but as the inevitable mode of human experience. The believer lives in irony. Unless privy to the inner councils of God—like the prophet—the believer cannot fully comprehend God's way. *Irony* may not appear in the Hebrew lexicon, but irony is a necessary mode in the faith of Israel. And from the Yahwist in the ninth or eighth century BC to Qoheleth several centuries later, irony frequently appears in the sacred writings of Israel.

For Qoheleth, as noted before, the irony of life itself puzzles. Nowhere does he exhibit the prophet-like assurance that comes from the full perception of human action which admission into God's own councils provides. Whatever the purposes of the God whose existence Qoheleth never doubts, Qoheleth also affirms categorically that humans have no intelligible or systematic way of fathoming God's purposes. No Pangloss he, proclaiming that we live in the best of all possible worlds. Irony is the believer's necessary mode of being. The much earlier irony of the Yahwist, however, expresses repeated delight at the workings of Yahweh, for the Yahwist, unlike the characters in his story, knows how things will work out, how God's designs will finally be effected. Be it the story of Abraham or Jacob or Joseph, the Yahwist gives us a divinity achieving its objectives despite the incomprehension, resistance, and scepticism of the human actors. The Yahwist's is a comic irony, close to romance. The individual stories and adventures come to happy endings despite complications, reversals, setbacks, and all the other familiar devices of comedy. As is characteristic of the comic mode, the human actors find themselves satisfied at the last, aware how the master manipulator of the comedy, Yahweh, has all along been directing the plot, in which they have played not wholly comprehending parts. Qoheleth's is hardly comic irony. If God has a script, Qoheleth neither sees it nor expects to. Critical and unresolved as are his reflections, his ironic viewpoint exposes the limits of human awareness and human cocksureness and challenges those who, like Job's friends, confidently assert they know how God works. Anyone familiar with Samuel Johnson's *Rasselas*, a work much influenced by Ecclesiastes, can see the parallel in mood. The title of Johnson's last chapter—"The Conclusion in Which Nothing Is Concluded"— would have served Qoheleth well (better, perhaps, than the editorial addition [12:9-14] designed to tug the text safely into the harbor of orthodoxy).

With Hosea we enter an ironic world like Samuel Beckett's *Waiting for Godot* or Waugh's *Vile Bodies*. The text itself is a jumble of form and content, almost that very parody of form, of fragmented, incomplete utterance which accidentally or deliberately appears repeatedly in the tradition of satire and irony.[52] Andersen and Freedman claim that Hosea "competes with Job for the distinction of containing more unintelligible passages than any other book in the Hebrew Bible," "maddeningly difficult to grasp, no matter how we approach it."[53] As in *Godot* or *Vile Bodies*, furthermore, or Pope's *Dunciad* (where many of the echoes are scriptural and specifically apocalyptic), the Book of Hosea ceaselessly echoes, but reverses, earlier familiar and reassuring texts. The Creation account or the Exodus narrative figure as disturbing subtexts in a message already disturbing in itself. Hosea's language, say Andersen and Freedman, is "rich with connotations of the covenant, . . . an elaborate *recapitulatio* of the Exodus, . . . [at times] a pastiche of deuteronomic phrases."[54] Hosea uses this language to subvert its original meaning and assurance, an overturning capable of apparently blasphemous dimension not only in sexual and scatological insult but even more so in parodying the very name of God. The Ehyeh (I AM) of Exodus 3:14 becomes in Hosea 1:9 Lo-Ehyeh (I AM NOT). Yahweh promises not his presence, but his absence.[55] Hosea has a variant narrative of Yahweh's wooing of Israel: not the gentle, delightful courtship that leads to a land flowing with milk and honey, despite the incomprehension of Abraham, the resistance and fear of Jacob, or the dangers of Joseph. No, Hosea's is a tale of adultery and murderous child abuse. The future promises the withdrawal of God, the abolition of the covenant, the loss of land, and the slaughter of posterity. The Yahweh who sears the text of Hosea proclaims himself as I AM NOT. You will look for me and you will not find me because I will withdraw to my place. You are not my People; I am not your God. Hosea's is the irony of the void.[56]

Many echoes, first of all, sound ironically in Hosea's very language. The opening three-chapter account of the prophet's marriage to Gomer is, according to Andersen and Freedman, "pervaded by memories of Israel's past." They point out other instances of echo as well: the "abundant references to animals, plants, and cosmic powers [in 2:16-25] take us . . . at least back to the creation stories"; "the listing of wild beasts, birds, and reptiles is like that in Genesis 1 in sequence and vocabulary," the irony of which allusion is reinforced, I believe, in the fact that the reference here is not to "cultivated land [a garden?] but [to] the untamed wild"; the verb used at 3:1—which they translate "turning to other gods"—"figures in the Deuteronomic vocabulary, where it designates apostasy"; at 5:2, the use "of the same verb to describe Abraham's sacrifice of Isaac (Gen 22:10)" underscores the dreadful, ironic contrast with the human sacrifice now part of the worship of Yahweh; the image of Yahweh as healer (11:3) goes back to Exodus.[57] Hans Walter Wolff notes "how thoroughly Israel's history is embedded in Hosea's proclamation," and specifies the murdering of kings and the usurping of thrones in the decade preceding Hosea's mid-eighth-century ministry; the crimes of the Jehu dynasty, whose founder "became king in a bloody revolt at Jezreel" that led to the wiping out of the house of Ahab[58]—even in English the similarity in sound between Israel and Jezreel is unmistakable; the beginnings of the kingship under Saul; the conquest; the deliverance from Egypt. Against this background Hosea chastises the apostasy of the Baal-worship and argues Yahweh's case against the wife-turned-whore in a proceeding which recasts the old covenant formula "as a formula of divorce" and in "sayings which threaten Israel's return to Egypt, whereby the gift of land is taken back."[59] Yahweh succinctly proclaims the irony of Israel's history: "I will reverse myself" (2:11, AB).

These shocking about-faces enter the Book of Hosea immediately with the account of the prophet's morally scabrous marriage to the wife who will prove repeatedly unfaithful, her infidelity the promiscuous involvement in sex rites to Baal, worshipped as if he were Yahweh, Baal, indeed, an anti-Yahweh. If Gomer is unfaithful, whose are her children, Yahweh's or Baal's? The fourfold appearance of the root *zny*, for Andersen and Freedman, announces whoredom as the subject of this first prophecy. Yahweh's urging that Gomer "remove her promiscuity from her face / and her adultery from between her breasts" (2:4, AB) could be "a dramatic and vivid way of advising her to abandon her conduct" or could suggest "something more physical, something which identified her as available and whose removal would signify her rejection of such a status." Uncovering her nakedness (2:11) "is a euphemism for genitals." Gomer's promiscuity is indistinguishable from idolatry. That equivalence explains the repeated association in Hosea between Israel's apostasy and sexually irregular behavior. As Andersen and Freeman point out, these first three chapters of the Book of Hosea deal

> with two matters at once—his wife's infidelity and the nation's apostasy. The two are virtually indistinguishable because Gomer's activity is more than a paradigm of Israel's disloyalty; it was a specific instance of the heresy. It was not just that promiscuity was a sin against Yahweh as well as a wrong done to her husband; the form of her promiscuity involved her in the Baal cult. The same activity was at once promiscuity and idolatry. There was also an ingredient of sorcery. The same themes continue in Hos 4:1 - 5:7, and many of the key words of cc 1-3 continue to be used. Although the remainder of the book is in a different mode from it, these chapters are the seed bed of the exposition that follows. Hos 4:1 -5:7 is dominated by a cluster of words based on the root zny, which occurs twelve times. It is almost as though the passage were a commentary on Yahweh's first word to Hosea (1:2), in which this root appears four times.[60]

The indecency Hosea predicates of Israel's behavior is equally "the seed bed" of derisive, insulting language which describes the nation's cult, its false gods, and their devotees. In the uncompromising, unextenuating quality so characteristic of the third or final phases of satire and irony, I note Andersen and Freedman's comment: "The prophets in general found nothing whatever in Canaanite religion that could be considered so reasonable or attractive as to make the choice between Yahweh and Baal a difficult one. They suggest rather that Canaanite religion appealed to everything that was vile in human beings." Hosea, specifically, they speculate, hints "at base motives, rather than conversion to a rival theology that could be stated in sophisticated terms."[61] The use of the name Baal, for instance, is a rare biblical example of denominating a false god by its name, and "even that was often replaced with insulting substitutes and parodies, of which several are found in Hosea." The name given Baal in 4:7, *qalon*, expresses "disgust." In 9:11 and 10:5 Hosea calls him not Glory, but Shame. Although Andersen and Freedman more decorously translate as "Filth" the god persistently sought by Israel (5:11), they admit that "a four-letter word is needed to bring out the associations of this term (however read)." *Shit* does the trick nicely for the Hebrew *sh't*.[62]

In this context, a comment of Wolff's underscores the satiric and ironic power of the Book of Hosea: not only does the text "use new, extremely bold expressions in referring to [Yahweh]." But because the prophet uses as well "impudent, modernistic language, some of [his] similes must have sounded almost flippant to his audience." Wolff specifies Hosea's description of Yahweh as "pus to Ephraim" (5:12), the context in which Yahweh also compares himself to vermin on the open sores of Israel.[63] Yahweh derisively laughs at an Israel that turns to a Lo-El, a No-God (7:16, AB), a punning parody on Yahweh's own name or title that underscores the vacuity which is Baal. Yahweh derides as well the Canaanite rites in this worship (7:13-14). The *ônîm* of 9:14, which Andersen and Freedman translate as "idols," might be "another of Hosea's artificial plurals designed to imitate *elohim*."[64] Such scatological, sexual, and irreverent punning and insult pervades the Book of Hosea.

When Jonathan Swift takes on, in *A Tale of a Tub*, the lunacies of modern religious practice, his climactic discussion of the wind-worshiping Aeolists in Sections VIII and IX uses a comparable technique of frequently sexual insult. Swift's infatuated narrator speaks of the Aeolist's worship of wind as the ultimate cause of all things, hence "of BELCHING, . . . the noblest act of a rational creature"; of Aeolist priests gaping into the wind to become as wind-filled as possible and to pass on their windy achievements to their panting disciples; and, in stunning and shocking suggestion of oral-genital sex, to

> female officers, whose organs were understood to be better
> disposed for the admission of those oracular gusts, and enter-
> ing and passing up through a receptacle of greater capacity,
> and causing also a pruriency by the way, such as with due
> management hath been refined from a carnal into a spiritual
> ecstasy[!][65]

Similarly, in the Book of Hosea, cult prostitutes lie with the priests "under oaks, poplars, and terebinths, whose shade is good" because its provides a cooler location for noontide sex rites, the Samarian Siesta that Hosea everywhere makes fun of and denounces. Hosea's is "bitter parody" of the spirit in their midst, of the Aeolists of his time.[66] Major instruments of this depravity are the priests themselves, goons of the shrine, lying in wait, as if they were "gangs of priests" (6:9, AB), to commit murder, wilfully assassinating "defenseless people for spoil"![67]

The Book of Hosea thus satisfies Frye's requirements for irony of the void, with its view of human life as largely unrelieved bondage, its parody of religious symbols, its disturbing note of being watched constantly by a hostile eye, its abundance of sinister parental or authority figures, its revelation of a demonic epiphany. In Hosea, this irony finds expression repeatedly in the reversal of the past language of assurance: Ehyeh is Lo-Ehyeh (1:9, 5:6-7), Yahweh's People are no longer his (1:9); Israel returns to Egypt and to the wilderness, hungry, not fed (5:10), thirsty, not slaked (2:5), wandering, not settled (9:17), deprived of children, not spared the last and worst of the plagues that humbled Egypt (9:16). These, after all, are Israelites slaughtering their own children in fertility rites. Yahweh reverses himself indeed. The Psalmist surely speaks perceptively when he sings: "He that dwelleth in heaven shall laugh them to scorn; the LORD shall hold them in derision."

PART II

THE MESSENGER

4

PROPHETS
OR
PROJECTORS?
CHALLENGES
TO
CREDIBILITY

The need for a rhetoric of credibility in the Hebrew prophets, the subject of this chapter,[1] draws attention to two more important parallels between prophecy and satire: first, that the Hebrew prophets are most often in conflict with other prophets claiming to speak for Yahweh; in other words, that Hebrew prophecy, like much satire, records an intrafraternal conflict, particularly strident in Jeremiah and Ezekiel, that poses a need for a rhetoric of credibility and a problem of authority admitted in the Hebrew Scriptures themselves; and, secondly, that the opposition to the Hebrew prophets employs accusations frequently levelled in later times against satirists: that the prophets are mad, malignly motivated, and treasonably subversive of the public order. Having concerned myself in the first three chapters with the message of prophecy and satire, I turn in these two chapters to the messenger.

i.

"Who hath believed our report?" (Isa 53:1, KJV)

The military imagery almost necessarily present in discussions of satire, which evolved from times which believed that words can kill,[2] appears casually, but with ironic predictive accuracy, in Alexander Pope's comment, in the *Preface* to his 1717 *Works*, that "the life of a wit is a warfare upon earth." Assaulting as they do "every sort of rebellion against right reason and good taste,"[3] Pope's literary forays very often assail other users of the word. The life of a wit is often a warfare against other wits. Word fights word. Satirists not only use words as weapons, but make the very use of the word the subject of their assault. "Laugh at yourself" becomes satire's parodic inversion of the Delphic injunction.

Already hoary by Pope's time, this emphasis lays bare the very self-referential quality of satire as a use of language. Horace, first of the formal satirists, provides evidence of it in his opening satire, where his mild-mannered amusement at the folly people make of their lives concludes with a parting shot at "a verbose Stoic writer," Crispinus, whom he despises. Persius quickly makes fun of the writing in "regular metre" of "a prodigious work" that leaves "the mighty sons of Rome in a dither" as a poet "with a clear preparatory warble" and "eyes swooning in ecstasy" declaims the stuff Persius knows will be preferred to his satires. Juvenal enters the satiric coliseum inveighing against writers whose theme and whose practice is business-as-usual. As often as he graphically limns the Gross National Product that Rome has become he just as often chastises the frivolous, obtuse writers who satisfy an equally frivolous audience.[4] By 1717 the life of many a wit has already been a warfare upon earth.

With equal justice, however, Jeremiah might counter that the life of a prophet is a warfare upon earth and that the prophet often finds himself in combat against other prophets. From the earliest times of the classical prophets in the eighth century—Amos, Hosea, Micah, and Isaiah—to the catastrophic times of the early sixth century—Jeremiah and Ezekiel—, Hebrew prophecy castigates not only a panorama of viciousness that includes human sacrifice, religious syncretism, gross social injustice, and equally gross sexual excess wearing the garb of religious worship, but also other prophets. Like satire, prophecy is also very self-referential. Prophetic Word counters Prophetic

Word. In imagery kindred to Swift's in *A Tale of a Tub* or the *Discourse Concerning the Mechanical Operation of the Spirit*, the Hebrew prophets jeer at the ranting and raving of false prophets, at prophetic obstetrics that deliver only wind, at illusory, self-serving assurances that all is well when disaster is imminent. In the trying times that witnessed finally the successful threat of first the Assyrian and later the Babylonian empire, the religious and political institutions of Israel and Judah did not lack a personnel of temple prophets speaking reassurance and confidence, perhaps with the utmost sincerity. Every Hebrew Bufo had his Bavius still, while the Hebrew Virgils fought for a hearing. Jeremiah was probably at odds with no other single class as much as with his fellow prophets. And the Hebrew term for prophet was, in fact, in so much disrepute during the time of the classical prophets that none of them designate themselves by that term.[5] Such an apparently trivial instance of designation reveals a Hebrew prophecy not insensitive to the connotations of language in countering the claims of other prophecy to speak for Yahweh.

In the shadow of the Assyrian and Babylonian threats, in particular, that is, between the eighth and sixth centuries BC, the need to establish one's prophetic credibility is much more intensely urgent than in the times before prophecy assumes written form. In those times, among earlier prophets, the commonest confrontation pitted prophet of Yahweh against prophet of Baal or any other foreign, presumably false, always convenient, and, God help us, luridly inviting god or goddess. From the standpoint of the Hebrew Scriptures little need for establishing credibility appears here. Like the instant villainy conferred in satire where association affords conclusive evidence of guilt—"*Qui Bavium non odit*"—, where the company one keeps does condemn a person, so a prophet's allegiance to any one of these false, foreign deities brings instant guilt and sentencing for wrongdoing. So when Elijah confronts the prophets of Baal (1 Kings 18) or Moses the magicians of Pharaoh (Exodus 6:28-12:36), the Hebrew Scriptures leave no doubt about the truth or falsity of prophecy at the time. Allegiance, wonderworking, and effect verify belief. Suspense cannot be integral to such narrative: the outcome is a foregone conclusion.[6]

When one prophet speaking in the name of Yahweh, however, challenges another prophet making the same claim, what principle of choice emerges? Historical verification and predictive accuracy are useless for the prophets' contemporary audience, and preternatural wonders are conspicuously absent in the narratives about the "written" prophets. Inescapably, the great prophets had to sell themselves, had to convey a character more compelling, more believable than that of the prophets they roundly condemned as false or speciously reassuring. Such condemnation appears in Hosea, Micah, and Isaiah in the eighth century, in Zephaniah in the seventh, in Jeremiah and Ezekiel in the sixth, and as late as Deutero-Zechariah, dated by some scholars as late as the third century. The intrafraternal conflict among Yahweh-prophets, in other words, recurs as a motif in Hebrew prophecy throughout the entire span of the history of "written" prophecy in Israel. Particularly frequent in Jeremiah and Ezekiel, a number of these attacks appear as diatribes, heavily satiric in quality, while others take on the cast of the semi-dramatic vignettes, the exemplifying mini-scenes, so characteristic of Juvenal's development of a theme.

With perhaps a specific but unnamed prophet in mind, for example, Hosea confronts an also unnamed priest with the challenging word of Yahweh:

> My contention is indeed with you, priest.
> You will stumble by day
>   and the prophet will stumble with you by night. [Hos 4:4-5, AB]

The unnamed prophet here, like his sacerdotal colleague, is presumably a high official in the cult.[7] Micah uses a "sarcastic word for prophecy," *rant*,[8] when he dismisses the oracles of false prophets spinning out their flimsy webs like Swift's notorious spider in *The Battle of the Books*:

> How they rant! They may say, "Do not rant";
> but this ranting is all their own,
> these insults are their own invention. [Mic 2:6, NEB]

For these people, willing to hear only the pleasant, a drunk "would be as good a preacher as any":[9] "If anyone had gone about in a spirit of falsehood and lies, saying, 'I will rant to you of wine and strong drink,' his ranting would be what this people like" (Mic 2:11, NEB). Isaiah ridicules the consoling prophetic message that believes alliance with Egypt against Assyria has become "a treaty with [i.e., against] Death" and "a pact with Sheol" to enable Judah to stand securely "when the raging flood sweeps by." This "refuge of lies," Isaiah counters, shall be swept away by hail, "and flood waters [shall] carry away your shelter" of falsehood (Isa 28:15, 17, NEB). Concisely, for Zephaniah, Israel's prophets are "reckless, no true prophets" (Zeph 3:4, NEB). Punning like Swift on the root and ambiguous senses of inspiration as a breathing into—the Hebrew word is *ruah*—Jeremiah charges:

> The prophets—they're full of wind!
> The word is not in them. [Jer 5:13, AB]

In contrast to this oral flatulence, Yahweh's word in Jeremiah is "a fire" that will consume a people like "a pile of wood" (Jer 5:14, AB). He accuses all of fraud, "from prophet on up to priest." The fraud is their peddling of verbal nostrums. They are religious quacks soothingly hawking "It is well! It is well!" "But it is not well!" Jeremiah insists (Jer 8:11, AB). For Deutero-Zechariah, the diviners see "false signs"; "they tell lying dreams and talk raving nonsense" (Zech 10:2, NEB).

The brevity of the denunciations just cited in no way implies that charges against rival prophets are a theme of only passing interest in Hebrew prophecy. In Jeremiah and Ezekiel in particular, as stated earlier, the "head-on collision"[10] of prophet with prophet recurs as a major motif in the text very much like the important concerns of Juvenalian satire to which the Roman poet returns several times within the confines of one poem. The Babylonian menace to the now sole-surviving Southern Kingdom obviously exacerbated the tension among Judah's prophets to a pitch previously unknown. One could, after all, believe on religious grounds that the Northern Kingdom's fall at the hands of Assyria in the late eighth century reflected Yahweh's chastising sentence on the impure, syncretistic bastardizing of Yahwistic faith in the North. But how could a supposedly unconditional promise of divine support for the Davidic kingdom and dynasty in the South be even challenged by men claiming to speak for that same divine authority? The prophetic text attributed to Jeremiah and to Ezekiel offers several diatribe-like castigations of fellow prophets, in theme and development very much like the satire of religious self-deception in Swift and Blake. The texts afford as well several semi-dramatic vignettes, again very Juvenalian in quality, which graphically, satirically, and even ironically portray the conflict between Jeremiah and Ezekiel and their prophetic contemporaries. I want to discuss first Jeremiah 23:9-40, particularly with reference to Swift and Blake, and Ezekiel 13. Then, I will take up the semi-dramatic vignettes that appear in Ezekiel 14 and in two incidents from the life of Jeremiah (Jeremiah 29, 27-28). A peripheral but by no means incidental concern in this analysis is the satirical quality of these texts, apparent even in translation, texts which emphatically point out how this severe intrafraternal conflict among the Hebrew prophets intensifies the need for a rhetoric of credibility in the prophets.

Like Juvenal's *Satire I* or Pope's *Arbuthnot*, Jeremiah 23:9-40 begins with an impression of the spontaneous overflowing of powerful emotion, which, in the rhetoric of prophecy, as in satire, often appears as the immediate prelude to judgment: *facit indignatio vaticinium.*

> My reason is staggered within me,
> My bones all give way;
> I've become like a man who is drunk,
> Like a person besotted with wine,
> Because of Yahweh—
> Because of his holy words. [23:9, AB]

This internal monologue of sorts, like those in Juvenal, quickly and vividly singles out its targets and their conduct: "prophet and priest alike are godless," a godlessness discovered by Yahweh in his "very own house" (11). In a characteristic feature of prophetic denigration, very common in Amos, for example, Jeremiah ironically charges that the self-assuredly morally superior Judah reveals conduct morally inferior to her despised Samaria: however "offensive" the false, Baal-inspired prophecy of the North, the conduct "in Jerusalem's prophets" is "a shocking thing," morally comparable to that of Sodom and Gomorrah (13-14). Jeremiah levels the Swiftian charge that the vision of Judah's false prophets is "a self-induced vision" (16): prophets not sent by Yahweh run to proclaim their vacuity; prophets who have heard only silence claim to pass on Yahweh's word (21). Excitedly scurrying about and proclaiming, "I've had a dream! I've had a dream!" they preach lies (25). Like Swift's Aeolists receiving rudimentary inspiration from a bellows at one end to expel it on panting disciples at the other, Jeremiah's Aeolists, "through their dreams which they tell to one another," transform this self-assuring, self-aggrandizing repetition of what other prophets declare into genuine divine inspiration.[11] Frequency of utterance in the self-contained circle of repeated prophets' dreams assumes epistemological status. The oftener heard and oftener repeated, the truer the message. But Yahweh stands against "the prophets who preach fraudulent dreams . . . and who, by repeating them, mislead [his] people with their mendacious claptrap" (32).

Jeremiah concludes this attack with extended punning on *massa*, a word denoting both a message or utterance and a heavy weight or burden.[12] Those interested in the utterance of Yahweh, in His *massa*, are told that Yahweh's message is that His people are a *massa*, a burden. He means to cast off this burden, this *massa*, because His people have turned their backs on the ominous, judgmental quality of Yahweh's utterance (*massa*). Its burden (*massa*) they refuse to accept (33-40).[13]

A rhetoric of credibility is implicitly demanded in a message so at odds with institutional authority and the confidence it assumes in its exercise and proclamation. The later section of this chapter, on the rhetoric of opposition to the Hebrew prophets, demonstrates how the institution and its representatives denounced these prophetic challenges to themselves. However urgently a passage like Jeremiah's underscores the need for winning over an audience, it also, like so many of these attacks on rival prophets, displays clear satiric quality, often with patterns of theme and imagery common in the two great satirists of religious delusion and of the arrogant confidence of orthodoxy: Jonathan Swift and William Blake.

Swift's *Tale of a Tub* in particular, or Blake's *Marriage of Heaven and Hell*, for a second, trenchantly expose a spiritual deception not unlike that challenged in the prophets. Isaiah, to whose prophecy Blake explicitly refers in the very opening of the *Marriage*, provides a satiric description of the perception that simply doesn't see: "the prophetic vision" that has now become "a sealed book" (Isa 29:11, NEB). A spiritually illiterate people, misled by prophet and priest, cannot read the primer of Yahweh's judgment. "While their hearts are far from me," Yahweh complains, "they approach with their mouths and honor me with their lips" (13). Like the shallow, insubstantial clichés that lend specious light to Blake's World of Innocence, the religion of this people is "but a precept of men, learnt by rote" (13). "The wisdom of their wise men shall vanish," Yahweh warns, "and the discernment of the discerning shall be lost" (14). When the ruthless and arrogant, however, "shall cease to be," when "those who are quick to see mischief, those who charge others with sin and lay traps for him who brings the wrongdoer into court or by falsehood deny justice to the righteous"—when "these shall be exterminated," then, promises Isaiah in his own prophetic contraries, the deaf will hear and "the eyes of the blind shall see out of impenetrable darkness" (20-21, 18). The reassurance of false prophets cannot withstand, delay, or even shorten the inexorable coming of exile, the destructive World of Experience that shall painfully reveal the hollowness of "All is well! all is well!" The prophets of Isaiah's *Songs of Innocence* have no greater perception than Blake's, and the *Songs of Experience* that await both are darkly and forbiddingly ineluctable.

Particularly in the *Tale* Jonathan Swift brings out the individual self-deception that sees divine revelation in self-induced vision, often of sexually ambiguous origin, or in trivial, airy, meaningless, but finally destructive dream vision in the worst sense of the term. Jeremiah and Ezekiel particularly dismiss the happiness and optimism peddled by prophets of consolation as a perpetual possession of being well-deceived, the groundless assurance that Judah can escape calamity.

Whatever divinity possesses them in such proclamation, it is not Yahweh. As Jeremiah readily admits, such a specious proclamation of weal wins its audience easily:

> The prophets—they prophesy falsely,
>   And the priests—they lord it beside them:
> And my people—they love it that way . . . . [Jer. 5:31, AB]

The self-flattering, unchallenging consolations of Israel's self-professed prophets exercise the secret, attractive sympathy that wins adherents like Jack's popular message in the *Tale*: the prophets' fascination with repeating the dreams of other prophets and transubstantiating them into divine communication. Showing the flaws and imperfections of false prophecy becomes a blasphemy against Yahweh. The blunt, caustic Jeremiah can easily be imagined in a momentary pose of satisfied naivety: "Last week I saw a prophet flayed, and you can hardly imagine how it altered his appearance for the worse!" Like Blake and Swift, Jeremiah occasionally exposes the personally licentious behavior that undercuts any claim to true prophetic status. When, as earlier, false prophecy spoke in the name of Baal or of a religious syncretism that permitted sexual excess to masquerade as religious worship, the attack on false prophecy included the sexual innuendo and explicit accusation that appear in Swift's *Tale*, in the early Blake, and also in Juvenal: the self-deception that transforms unbridled eroticism into divine worship. In the Hebrew prophets' censure of the false prophets of Yahweh, this falsehood figures as the air, breath, or wind of insubstantiality, a pejorative use earlier even than the written form of Ecclesiastes whose classic expression of this uncomplimentary use of breath or air is perhaps more familiar to literary criticism than its much older use in the Hebrew prophets. Indeed, except in pejorative senses, *ruah* as breath, inspiration, or moving force virtually disappears from classical prophecy between Amos and Ezekiel. The *ruah* of the Hebrew prophets is the *enthusiasm* of the eighteenth-century satirists, an always pejorative term defined by Johnson as a "vain belief of private revelation, a vain confidence of divine favour or communication."[14]

This same pejorative use of *ruah* appears in a second,

lengthy condemnation of false prophets of Yahweh, this one by Jeremiah's younger contemporary, Ezekiel, who lashes out against the

> villainous prophets
> who follow their own whims [*ruah*]
> without having seen a thing. [Ezek 13:3, AB][15]

"Like jackals among ruins," these prophets "have spoken idle things / and uttered false visions" (4, 8). Indeed, *idle* and *false* recur as verbal motifs (6-9 *passim*) in an accusation picturing these prophets as substituting whitewash for the more substantive repair on a wall that must, thereby, necessarily fail to withstand the driving force of the punishment Yahweh will direct against it (10-16). The "tempestuous wind" (13) of his fury will more than match the airy whims of these prophets "who prophesy out of their own hearts" and "utter visions of 'All is well' for [Jerusalem] / when nothing is well" (17, 16). The attack on lying prophetesses which follows arraigns them for discouraging the righteous with lies and confirming the wicked in their ways. Their vatic trinkets become the woefully inept gewgaws of superstition, available, of course, for a price (17-23). The prophetesses thus join the assembly of prophetic jackals profiting on the calamity of others.[16]

The incident of an elders' visit to Ezekiel's house (14) and two accounts of conflicts involving Jeremiah (29, 27-28) differ qualitatively from the diatribes, however satiric, in Jeremiah 23 or Ezekiel 13. Those texts, neither narrative nor dramatic, present none of the features of play or story that even concrete historical incidents afford. Like much Juvenalian satire, Jeremiah 23 and Ezekiel 13 appear as unsituated, generalized satire, evoking no specific settings or scenes. Assuredly, they reinforce an awareness of the Hebrew prophets' need for a rhetoric of credibility, but the three incidents that follow, as they likewise reinforce this need, do so within the context of semi-dramatic vignettes that even more powerfully underscore the opposition among prophets. Here, a different feature of Juvenalian satire emerges: the self-contained, graphically illustrated, and narratively or dramatically complete episode that exemplifies an important theme. That theme, for Jeremiah and Ezekiel, is the astonishing obtuseness and willfulness of the leaders of the religious community, and especially its priests and prophets.

A Blake-like irony pervades the incident in Ezekiel 14, which, in the overall structure of the prophecy, most fittingly follows the prophet's account of the rationalizations that dismiss true prophecy (12:21-28) and his own castigation of false prophets and prophetesses (13:1-23). Ezekiel recalls that "some men of the elders of Israel came to me and sat down before me" (14:1, AB). They hope to secure an oracle from the LORD. The Yahweh who can penetrate into the idolatrous mentality they display before him sarcastically and angrily asks his prophet: "Am I supposed to respond to their inquiry?" (3).[17] The presumption and obtuseness of the elders outrage Yahweh. That each elder approaches Yahweh while raising "idols in his thoughts" and "setting his stumbling-block of iniquity before his face" (14:4, AB) disturbingly highlights the dangerously differing conceptions of religious holiness that separate Yahweh and these elders. Like Blake's "wise guardians of the poor" in the first of the "Holy Thursday" poems, these elders are wholly insensitive to the worthlessness of their religious venture. The frightening dimensions of Yahweh's anger at this self-assured blindness appear in the LORD's sarcastically phrased willingness to "oblige [every idolatrously-minded inquirer among the elders] with an answer":

> I will set my face against that man; I will make of him a sign and a byword and cut him off from among my people Israel; and you shall know that I am YHWH. And if a prophet is so misled as to speak in an oracle, I YHWH have misled that prophet. I will stretch out my hand against him and destroy him from among my people Israel. Both shall suffer the same punishment . . . . [14:8-11, AB]

Yahweh's terrifying oracle is that there will be no oracle. His word promises no word. The doom of the inquirer "will serve as a warning for all who would force themselves on God," while the illegitimate prophet himself will be "a victim and a sign of God's fury."[18] A tempest of divine and prophetic outrage has confronted the vacuous confidence of false, airy prophetic assurance, but here the obtuse, presumptuous sycophant meets in God an angry, outraged patron. Defining idolmindedness as "the people's unregenerateness," Ezekiel scholar Moshe Greenberg trenchantly epitomizes this charged drama of wilful, obtuse unrepentance as exhibiting in the elders a frame of mind "nourished by misguided assurances of God's favor given them by the prophets denounced here and in prior oracles. But the prophets and laity who force themselves upon God, oblivious of their condemned status, will be destroyed."[19]

The abundant biographical and historical material in Jeremiah, however, much more extensive than any in Ezekiel or, for that matter, in any other of the prophets, most strikingly witnesses the conflict among the prophets of Yahweh. Two incidents in particular highlight the urgent problem of credibility which prophets like Jeremiah, in the rhetoric of their self-presentation, seek to resolve. The first incident concerns Jeremiah's message for those already in exile; the second involves his confrontation with a fellow prophet in Jerusalem, an encounter, furthermore, that illustrates an awareness of the problem of credibility at least as old as the text itself. Both incidents occur in 594 BC, an unusually perilous time for the Jews in Babylon and in Jerusalem because reassuring prophets are bringing the Jewish community to the brink of open revolt against Babylonian power.[20]

The illusory promise of a short exile—Babylon did not fall until 539—brings out with grim humor the intractable obtuseness of the well-saying prophets. Having earlier assured Judah that she would withstand the Babylonian assault, the sightless visionaries were now compensating with equally specious promises of a brief sojourn in the land of the conqueror. This particular vacuity is the subject of Jeremiah's letter to the exiles, which tells them:

> Build houses and settle down. Plant gardens, and eat their produce. Marry, beget sons and daughters; take wives for your sons and give your daughters in marriage, that they too may have sons and daughters, in order that you may increase in number there, rather than decrease. [Jer 29:5-6, AB]

And Jeremiah passes on Yahweh's warning:

> Do not let the prophets of yours who are in your midst, or
> your diviners, deceive you. Pay no heed to the dreams that
> they are always dreaming. It's a lie that they are preaching to
> you in my name! I did not send them—Yahweh's word. [8-9][21]

In that community of exiles, however—which would have
included Ezekiel and Second Isaiah—,[22] the letter prompts a
very angry response in Shemaiah the Nehelamite. On his own
initiative he writes to the priest in Jerusalem, Zephaniah ben
Maaseiah, to urge disciplinary action against Jeremiah:

> Yahweh has appointed you priest . . . to be overseer in Yah-
> weh's house to put any crazy fellow who takes himself for a
> prophet in the stocks and collar. Now then, why have you not
> disciplined Jeremiah of Anathoth, who takes it on himself to
> prophesy to you? [Jer 29:26-27, AB]

Ironically, blind and truculent obtuseness, impervious to the
very fact of the exile in which it finds itself, imperiously instructs
religious authority to act upon the confidence of its own judgment. Jeremiah responds with Yahweh's own denunciation and
curse of Shemaiah as a lying prophet: "He shall have no one
left among you to see the good things that I am going to do for
you—Yahweh's word—for he has preached rebellion against
Yahweh" (32, AB).[23]

However bitter that exchange, the conflict in Jerusalem
between Jeremiah and his fellow prophet Hananiah reveals
much more explosively than the situation in Babylon the tension
between warring prophetic messages and the difficulty for the
sincerely motivated to discern the truth in conflicting claims. The
ox-yoke God commands Jeremiah to fashion and to wear—the
incident is the concern of chapters 27 and 28 in the prophecy—becomes a dramatic symbol in this episode, a recurring
motif in the challenge and counter-challenge of prophet versus
prophet, almost, indeed, a weapon with which each vatic seeks
to subdue the other. First, for the ambassadors of the foreign
kings arriving in Jerusalem to consider what collective action
might achieve against Babylon, this yoke represents "the power
of Nebuchadnezzar, king of Babylon" (27:6ff., AB) "under
whose yoke" all these nations shall fall. The visiting dignitaries
are warned that any optimistic message from their own prophets

is a lie: "the people that brings its neck under the yoke of the king of Babylon and is subject to him, I will leave on its own land—Yahweh's word—to till it and to live there" (11). Opposition will bring only sword, famine, and plague. Jeremiah delivers this same message, secondly, to King Zedekiah: "Bring your neck under the yoke of the king of Babylon and be subject to him and his people, that you may live" (12). He too is warned against the prophets urging him to refuse submission. The cost of heeding them is high: "I will drive you out and you will perish, you and the prophets who have been prophesying to you" (15). To the priests and to all the people, thirdly— appropriately to the priests, since much of the third charge concerns the furnishings of the temple—, Jeremiah specifically challenges the expectation that "the furnishings of Yahweh's house are going very shortly to be brought back from Babylon" (16). "Submit to the king of Babylon, and live!" urges Jeremiah rather, in speech easy to consider both blasphemy and treason (That Jerusalem should fall!). Jeremiah poses a challenge to prophetic optimism: if the furnishings in Babylon are shortly to return, let these prophets intercede with Yahweh to keep in Jerusalem the furnishings now in the temple, the palace, and elsewhere in the city.

Jeremiah's message provokes the prophet Hananiah to reply. Using the formulas of prophecy—"This is what Yahweh . . . has said," for example (28:2)—Hananiah thrusts back at Jeremiah his own yoke image and insists rather that Yahweh has broken "the yoke of the king of Babylon," that "within two years' time [the LORD will] bring back to this place all the furnishings of Yahweh's house which Nebuchadnezzar, king of Babylon, took from this place and carried to Babylon" (3). In fact, the king (Jeconiah) and all the exiles already there will return: "I will break the yoke of the king of Babylon" (4). Indicative perhaps of a generous conviction on Jeremiah's part that Yahweh will speak through whomever he chooses—"the spirit bloweth where it listeth"—and more significantly revealing in Jeremiah nothing of the willful obtuseness, blindness, and truculence of the reassuring prophets, Jeremiah with apparent sincerity hopes that Yahweh may confirm "the truth of what you have prophesied" (6). He does, however, remind Hananiah that "the prophets who were of old . . . prophesied against many countries and great kingdoms of war, of disaster, and plague" (8). If Yahweh's word now is well-being rather than woe, "well," says Jeremiah, "when that prophet's word comes to pass, then it can be acknowledged that he is the prophet whom Yahweh has really sent" (9). However conciliatory and thoughtful Jeremiah's response, however indicative of his conviction that he must speak not his own word but Yahweh's, however sensitive Jeremiah is to the unusually optimistic quality of a supposedly Yahweh-sent oracle, Hananiah's response is brutally, dramatically, and symbolically dismissive:

> Then the Prophet Hananiah snatched the yoke from Prophet Jeremiah's neck, and broke it. And Hananiah spoke in the presence of all the people as follows: "This is what Yahweh has said: Just so will I break the yoke of Nebuchadnezzar, king of Babylon, off the neck of all the nations—within two years' time." [Jer 29:10-11, AB]

His message having been symbolically destroyed, "Prophet Jeremiah went away."

The final word in this confrontation of yoke versus yoke comes from Yahweh. First, an iron yoke, more durable as symbol, more potent as weapon, is flung back at Hananiah as if Yahweh dares the prophet to repeat with this yoke the self-assured violence with which he destroyed the earlier: "An iron yoke have I placed on the neck of all these nations, namely, to be the subjects of Nebuchadnezzar, king of Babylon. And they shall be his subjects" (14). Confronting Prophet Hananiah now with assurance, Prophet Jeremiah, secondly, conveys to him God's grisly punning about being "sent":

> Listen, Hananiah! Yahweh never sent you! And you—you have led this people to trust in a lie! . . . Believe me, I am going to "send" you—right off the face of the earth! This very year you are going to die, because you have uttered rebellion against Yahweh. [15-16]

The Hananiah who predicted deliverance in two years dies in two months.[24] Prophesying falsely in the name of Yahweh,

Hananiah has been sentenced to death by Jeremiah's curse. Like his fellow optimist in Babylon, the only word that Hananiah really does hear is the word that kills, the curse.

A very significant textual difference between the Hebrew and the Greek texts of this account underscores the severe, almost insoluble problem of belief posed for the contemporaries of these two prophets who had to choose. Jeremiah scholar John Bright notes that the

> Hebrew throughout [chapter 28] designates each of these men as "the prophet" whenever their names occur; [the Septuagint] consistently omits [it]. . . . It may be that the writer wished with utmost emphasis—and irony—to point up the fact that prophet was contradicting prophet, and in the name of Yahweh.

As Bright later observes: "one can imagine the puzzlement of the hearers."[25]

ii.

"What did this crazy fellow want with you?" 2 Kgs 9:11 (NEB)

If Hananiah's confrontation with Jeremiah, however dramatic, provides only a representative instance of the intrafraternal conflict among the Hebrew prophets, it underscores, like the other comments and incidents mentioned, the claim that a rhetoric of credibility in the now canonical prophets is neither superfluous nor surprising. Such a rhetoric is not carrying salt to the Dead Sea. That warfare among the prophets, furthermore, strikingly resembles the war of the wits alluded to by Alexander Pope, that war where *wit* itself, like *prophet*, and *enthusiasm*, like *ruah*, convey instantly ambiguous and suspicious suggestions. The prophets' warfare, however, differs significantly from that of the wits in at least one important feature. Whereas textual evidence provides abundant sources for securing the wits' opinions of one another—what Shadwell thinks of Dryden or Cibber of Pope—the false prophets of Yahweh, as the tradition eventually came to judge them, are denied their own voice in the Hebrew Scriptures. What we know of them, of how they presented and defended their prophecies of consolation, of

134

how they attacked the now canonical prophets—all this appears only in the texts of their "enemies." Only through these canonical filters do the opponents of the true prophets assume any shape, for no independent attacks of theirs on the likes of Hosea or Jeremiah have been uncovered—if any did exist—nor have any such attacks been incorporated wholly or in part into the Hebrew Scriptures. Indeed, the apparently speedy disrepute into which the false prophets of Yahweh fell would have militated strongly against preserving anything of what they said. Such attacks would undoubtedly reveal the ubiquitous presence of satire on both sides of this dispute, very much like the ridicule and counterridicule in the dialogs of Job and his three friends. What we know, then, of the charges against the canonical prophets we know only through the texts that present them as great, finally vindicated heroes in the long, checkered history of Israel's dealings with its God. However filtered these attacks, three major allegations are directed against the canonical prophets: that they are mad, malignly motivated, and subversive of the public order. Verbal contours from the landscape of satire appear once again.

As numerous studies of satire in this century have shown—and not all of them disapproving—the rhetoric of opposition to satire affords a voluminous treasure of insults to the satirist's personality, much of it variations on the one charge that the satirist's is a diseased and disordered character, that evidence of much mental instability and malign motivation appears everywhere in the satiric text.[26] From the reassuring final insanity of Swift, through the embittered closing years of Twain, to the publicly disturbing and insulting character of Waugh, the alleged mental unsoundness of the satirist has been since ages past a refuge for those caught in the stormy blast of his criticism.

The evidence of the Hebrew Scriptures suggests that madness, apparently, is also the oldest of the charges levelled against the Hebrew prophets, a charge that originates in the ecstatic behavior so often characteristic of the earliest prophets appearing in the Hebrew Bible.[27] Bystanders witnessing their ecstatic behavior unsympathetically dismissed them simply as "crazy fellows" (e.g., 2 Kgs 9:11, NEB). Johannes Lindblom's brief listing of the "accessory phenomena of a psychophysical nature," which he describes as "strongly diverging from the behaviour of ordinary man," graphically demonstrates why the effects of ecstasy could so easily foster this impression. Bystanders witnessed

> an abnormally intensified activity in the form of violent body movements, dancing, jumping, leaping, shouting, etc., or symptoms of unnatural passivity: paralysis, anaesthesia, torpor, etc. [In these cases, he continues,] the balance of the mental life is disturbed and self-control has been lost. Bodily or mental impulses have been disengaged. Now automatisms of several kinds set in, the organizing and controlling forces of every sound soul being made ineffective.

Now although the classical prophets of the eighth century and later display characteristics markedly different from their earlier ecstatic forebears Lindblom does point out that "many characteristics are common to both groups" of prophets.[28] A hostility less interested in accuracy than in ammunition could easily gloss over the distinctions—as it did—to see in the classical prophets and some of their immediate predecessors the suspiciously mad behavior with which their ancestors had dismissed the earlier ecstatics.

However limited ecstatic behavior may have been in the Hebrew prophets and in those who opposed them, enough vestiges and actual instances of such behavior occur near and during the time of classical Hebrew prophecy to explain why the supposed madness of prophecy serves as a convenient reason for dismissing it. In their contest with Elijah, for example, during the ninth-century reign of Ahab and Jezebel in the Northern Kingdom, the prophets of Baal rant and rave deliberately to bring on ecstasy (1 Kgs 18:25-29). Deutero-Zechariah's satire on prophecy (Zech 13:2-6), which I discuss in detail at the conclusion of this chapter, directs particular ridicule at the self-mutilation prophetic frenzy often led to. In this long, several-centuries interval between Elijah and Deutero-Zechariah, enough curious, strange prophetic behavior occurs to justify the suspicion, especially in the minds of those looking to discredit prophecy, that prophecy and mental instability go hand in hand. In fact as in legend those who live by the word give evidence of bizarre conduct. The most important of these strange acts are the symbolic gestures occasionally performed by the prophets. Isaiah goes naked for three years to witness in his body the coming slavery of Israel (Isa 20:2-4); Jeremiah fashions and wears a yoke, first of wood, then of iron, to make concrete Yahweh's threat of inevitable exile, captivity, and servitude (Jer 27:2-28:17). Ezekiel, however, is most given to symbolic action. The short span of little more than a chapter provides a quick succession of these strange acts: he shuts himself up in his house to remain speechless except when the word of Yahweh impels him to talk; he is to enact the siege of Jerusalem; he is to lie, first on his left side, then on his right, for 390 days—a number somehow revealing the length of the exile; during this time, Ezekiel is to feed himself from barley cakes baked on a bed of human excrement (until Yahweh relents and allows him to use animal excrement as a base for the cooking fire); Ezekiel is to pass a razor over his head and beard and then burn a third of the cuttings, cut a second third, and scatter the remaining portion to the winds (Ezek 3:22-5:17). However clear the symbolic import of these activities, all interpreted in the same place in the text, an assumedly friendly later Judaism did find these Yahweh-ordered activities embarrassing. The third-century Rabbi Abbahu encounters, probably, a Christian for whom the command to Ezekiel to lie on his left and then on his right side proves that "God is a joker"! The scandalized medieval Maimonides insists that "God is too exalted than that He should turn his prophets into a laughing stock and a mockery for fools by ordering them to carry out *such crazy actions* [my emphasis]." Maimonides eliminates the difficulty by claiming that these actions are merely visionary and thus provides a welcome, less embarrassing path for medieval and even later commentators.[29]

If such symbolic acts by the prophets raise questions about their mental stability, the occasionally intense emotional quality of their language can corroborate such a perception. Like a Juvenal no longer capable of restraint, Micah, for instance, claims a compulsion to utter profoundly shocking and disturbing words:

> . . . I must howl and wail [he announces],
> go naked and distraught;
> I must howl like a wolf, mourn like a desert owl. [Mic 1:8, NEB]

Ezekiel's tone is similar: transported to the exiles at Tel Abib, by the Chebar canal, the prophet arrives "bitter, my spirit raging, overpowered by the hand of YHWH" (3:14, AB).[30]

The claim that the Hebrew prophets are crazy is not only one of which they are themselves aware, but also one already traditional by the time of Hosea, the first of the so-called "written" prophets, functioning in the mid-eighth century sometime after ecstatic prophecy has been the prevailing mode in Israel. Hosea observes:

> (They say) "The prophet is a fool,
> the man of the Spirit is insane,
> because your iniquity is great,
> and your hostility is great." [9:7, AB]

Whether Hosea is attacking false prophecy here or recording the hostility with which he was himself rejected, an incident from the times of Elisha makes clear that such taunting of the prophets had a long-standing, ready-made vocabulary.[31] Acting on orders from Elisha, the prophet Ahijah comes to inform Jehu secretly that the royal house of Ahab is doomed, that he, Jehu, will become king in Ahab's place. In fact, Ahijah anoints Jehu king over Israel. When Ahijah had arrived at Ramoth-gilead, however, he had found Jehu sitting in the company of his fellow officers and had to ask him to come apart from them so that the two could converse privately. Not surprisingly, Jehu's fellow officers are curious about the prophet's mission. When Jehu rejoins them after the prophet has left, they insultingly inquire: "What did this crazy fellow want with you?" (2 Kgs 9:1-13, NEB). When Shemaiah the Nehelamite later calls Jeremiah "a crazy fellow who takes himself for a prophet," he is working in an already long-established tradition, several centuries old, of denigrating the prophets as madmen (Jer 29:26, AB).

Furthermore, as the bitterness and rage of Ezekiel or the highly rhetorical, very melodramatic self-presentation of Micah can imply, hostility to the canonical prophets can easily see in a supposedly malign motivation one particular symptom of the prophet's diseased personality. Even Jeremiah reminds Hananiah that his promise of coming weal, of a quick end to the Exile, sharply contrasts with a long-standing tradition of prophecy invariably announcing coming woe (Jer 28:8-9). The predictability of such an ominous proclamation in the prophets leads Jeremiah scholar John Bright to suggest that the prophet has used Terror-all-Around so often as the epitome of his message "that it was becoming a nickname" for Jeremiah. Bright adds this vignette, rich with Hogarthian possibilities: "One can imagine one man in the crowd nudging another as Jeremiah passed, and whispering, 'there goes old [Terror-all-Around].' "[32]

In another instance, the ninth-century King Ahab admits his reluctance to allow the hated prophet Micaiah into his presence: "I hate the man," Ahab admits, "because he prophesies no good for me; never anything but evil" (1 Kgs 22:8, NEB). Although the messenger sent to fetch the prophet tells him that all the other prophets "had with one voice given the king a favourable answer"—"And mind you agree with them," he adds— Micaiah prophesies true to expectation and denounces the king's prophets as liars. One of them, Zedekaiah, strikes the prophet in the face, while Ahab orders Micaiah to be arrested and placed in custody. "Did I not tell you," the king angrily complains, "that he never prophesies good for me, nothing but evil?"[33] (13-28, NEB).

For those inclined to impugn the prophets with malign motivation, Jeremiah's stunning outburst against those who have plotted against his life can vie with Archilochus for deep-bite language, the dog's black bite, the wasp-like sting—for all the evidence, in short, of a poisonous tongue which the earliest Greek tradition found in the legendary inventor of satire. As in Archilochus' famous curse, here too is a sense of personal injury, a frighteningly intense desire for revenge and vindication, and even, perhaps, a hint of satisfaction at the prospect of evil overtaking one's enemies. Uttered at a time that believed in the efficacy of words, Jeremiah's curse easily matches the fearful imprecations of Archilochus:

So—hand their sons over to starvation [Jeremiah beseeches]!
    Spill them out to the power of the sword!
Let their wives be childless and widowed!
    Let their men be victims of plague!
        And their youths cut down by the sword in battle!
Let a cry be heard from their homes
    When, sudden, thou bringest marauders upon them!
For they've dug a pit to take me,
    And traps have set for my feet.
But thou, Yahweh, does know
    All their plotting against me to kill me.
Forgive not their crimes,
    Nor blot out their sin from thy sight!
But let them be hurled down before thee—
    Deal with them whilst thou art angry! [Jer 18:20-23, AB]

Whatever imputations of madness or malign motivation curses like Jeremiah's might occasion, any such charges are much more directly aimed at discrediting the prophet's character rather than reflecting concern about his threat to public order. The allegation of treasonable and blasphemous utterance, on the other hand, questions the prophet's loyalty to the political and religious institutions of his time. That it is a much more dangerous charge appears clearly in the frequently expressed prophetic fear of physical abuse and the simple fact of such abuse in the case of prophets like Jeremiah. Like madness and malign motivation, nonetheless, the charge of disloyalty is an almost necessary consequence of the deeply critical attitude the prophets adopt towards the ruling institutions of their time. Messengers carrying unwelcome news, the prophets, like the satirists, find their characters impugned and their message freighted with the burden of disloyalty.

Such hostility to the prophets recognizes and fears the subversive quality of what the prophets often proclaim. Some of the prophets active in the days of the Divided Monarchy that followed the death of Solomon around the beginning of the ninth century—prophets like Elijah and Amos, later Jeremiah—severely chastised the reigning institutions of both the Northern and Southern Kingdoms. Indeed, the strong anti-monarchical bias in 1 Samuel's account of the Israelite's desire for a king (1 Sam 8:1-22), a desire expressed in the eleventh century, most likely reflects a ninth-century hostility towards monarchy that may have originated in the Northern Kingdom not long after the death of Solomon.[34] Such ideological anachronism reflects well the hostility towards social injustice which prophets like Amos see as a consequence of the despotic accumulation of wealth and power in the hands of a court-centered few, an injustice which the prophets relentlessly inveigh against. John Bright's summary of conditions in the eighth century reveals not only the degree of decay, especially in the Northern Kingdom, but also the degradation of the prophetic order as a whole. It had degenerated into a collection of sycophantic court retainers understandably threatened by the fearless, isolated, and charismatic prophetic figures who threatened their livelihood in challenging their judgment and their integrity. Bright points out that although the mid-eighth century witnessed great prosperity and military strength in Israel and Judah (soon to be eclipsed by Assyria's westward advance), the period

> also saw the northern state, at least, in an advanced state of social and moral decay. Unethical practices, the heartless oppression of the weak, highhanded infractions of covenant law, were common (Amos). The rich, through means both legal and illegal, took every advantage of the poor and robbed them of their property, and the state did nothing to prevent it; indeed, the leaders of the state were deeply implicated. At the same time, the national religion had been corrupted by the infiltration of pagan practices (Hosea), particularly the practice of the fertility cult with its immoral rites, to such a degree that, in some of its manifestations at least, it was scarcely recognizable as Yahwism. Yet to all this the prophets as a group seem to have uttered no effective protest. No doubt there were sincere men among them. But if we may trust such allusions to them as we find in the prophetic books of the Bible (and there is no reason why we may not), we must conclude that as a group they had become mere professionals, hangers-on at court and shrine, many of them timeservers interested chiefly in their fees (e.g., Mic 3:5, 11), who felt no impulse to criticize the state and the society of which they were a part.[35]

Ahab's denunciation of Elijah as a "troubler of Israel" (1 Kgs 18:17, NEB) and his dissatisfaction to the point of violence with the prophet Micaiah, whom he admits he hates, whose never-encouraging message he finds insolently predictable, and whom, finally, he arrests and imprisons (22:1-28), constitute perhaps the first instances in the Hebrew Bible where a prophet's loyalty to his native institutions is questioned. Amos' confrontations in the Northern Kingdom in the eighth century and Jeremiah's problems at the time of the Exile also bring out the menacing hostility towards the prophets which the last refuge of court and temple scoundrels mask as religion and patriotism. As an outsider, "one of the sheepfarmers of Tekoa" in the South (1:1), Amos has a greater degree of vulnerability as an unwelcome messenger in the North. Amaziah, high priest at the Northern Kingdom's chief shrine, Bethel, tells this outsider from the Southern Kingdom: "Off with you to Judah . . . . do your prophesying there!" Ironically, Amaziah's dismissal blindly assumes that prophecy is primarily a means of livelihood: "you can earn your living in Judah!" The priest, however, has already warned King Jeroboam that "Amos is conspiring against you in Israel; the country cannot tolerate what he is saying." Amos is undermining morale by telling the Israelites: "Jeroboam shall die by the sword, and Israel shall be deported far from their native land," that is, to Assyria. This "drivelling on," as Amaziah characterizes it, is the politically unwelcome news Amos is instructed not to monger (7:10-17, NEB).

The terms of this accusation appear almost verbatim nearly two centuries later, but now in the Southern Kingdom as one of its own, Jeremiah, warns his people that nothing can withstand the coming lengthy exile in Babylon. In one instance, the princes of Judah beseech the easily intimidated and vacillating King Zedekiah to put Jeremiah to death:

> "We ask that this man be put to death, for he is weakening the morale of all the soldiers remaining in this city, as well as that of all the people, by saying such things to them. Indeed [they continue], the fellow does not desire the welfare of this people at all, but rather their hurt. [Jer 38:4, AB]

(In the first account of this incident, the princes had boldly challenged Jeremiah: "You are deserting to the Chaldeans!" a charge Jeremiah denounces as a lie. In their rage, nevertheless, the princes have the prophet beaten and confined in a house that has been transformed into a prison, in fact, placed "in one of the vaults of the cistern house and left there for some time" [37:11-16, AB].) Challenged by his eunuch for what he has done to the prophet, the wishy-washy Zedekiah orders him removed from the cistern but detained "in the court of the guard" (38:7-13, AB). Zedekiah cannot restrain his deep interest in the prophet's message although he sternly instructs Jeremiah to keep the fact and nature of their subsequent conversation private (38:14-28).

Less than a decade earlier, when Zedekiah's father Jehoiakim ruled as Babylon's puppet-king over Judah, the prophet had been similarly accused (26:1-24, AB). Seized by the priests and the prophets, Jeremiah is threatened: "For this you must die! Why have you been prophesying in Yahweh's name, saying that this house will be destroyed just as Shiloh was [a chief sanctuary of the Northern Kingdom], and this city left an uninhabited ruin?" The priests and prophets appeal to the princes: "A death sentence for this man! For he has prophesied against this city, as you have heard with your own ears" (8-11). But on this earlier occasion the princes and the people appeal successfully to the example of the prophet Micah whose oracles of doom in the days of King Hezekiah (seventh century) were no less ominous and who, nonetheless, was spared (16-24). The narrative of this incident, however, concludes with a unique reference to a third prophet, Uriah ben Shemaiah, who "prophesied against this city and this country exactly as Jeremiah had done," who fled "in terror" to Egypt to escape Jehoiakim's wrath, and who was extradited by the Egyptians to be executed and dishonorably buried at Jehoiakim's orders. Obviously, putting a prophet to death for alleged treason was no mere possibility for the puppet-king (20-23). It was, after all, Jehoiakim who destroyed the scroll of Jeremiah's prophecy as it was being read to him by Baruch and who ordered the arrest of both the prophet and his scribe (Jeremiah 36). The paranoias of nationalistic and religious frenzy cannot welcome Jeremiah's explosive and dangerous message of conquest and exile and his truculent recommendation of surrender. At a time when devotion to the nation was deeply and inextricably interwoven with religious belief, Jeremiah's proclamation that it was better to be alive in Babylon than dead in Judah must have occasioned an astonishing degree of offense.[36]

Louis Ginzberg's *The Legends of the Jews*, drawn from the sources of Jewish legends, strongly corroborates the Biblical picture of a Jeremiah accused of and persecuted for treason. Jeremiah, in fact, is supposedly born of a prophet-father fleeing "the persecution of Jezebel, murderess of the prophets," when his son is born. The legends make unequivocally clear Jeremiah's advocacy of surrender and his enemies' view of this as treason. One of the legends revealingly embellishes the story of Jeremiah's leaving Jerusalem for Anathoth to settle a family claim to land (Jeremiah 32). The watchman at the city gate accuses the departing prophet of "desiring to desert to the enemy." The watchman knows that his is "a trumped-up charge," but since he is the grandson of Jeremiah's prophet-enemy Hananiah, he seeks "to vent an old family grudge." Later, while confined in the cistern, Jeremiah is mocked by his jailer, Jonathan, who jeeringly calls down to the prophet from the edge of the pit: "Do but rest thy head on the mud and take a little sleep, Jeremiah"![37] Scriptural and extra-scriptural sources concur in their picture of a Jeremiah severely threatened, chastised, and abused for supposedly disloyal utterance.

A most important caution, however. No evidence supports the view that any of the canonical prophets seek an overthrow of the monarchical and religious institutions of their time. As deeply censorious as they are of their kings, priests, and prophets, no prophet calls for the overthrow of any of those orders. They question not the legitimacy of the institution, but its practice. The prophet's charismatic authority, based in a quality of individual personality, conflicts repeatedly with an institutional authority resting in tradition, social confirmation and legitimacy, and even bureaucracy. The necessarily unpredictable prophetic charisma—I think of Samuel Johnson's disparaging comment in the Highlands about "a poet by inheritance"—, which cannot be institutionalized, challenges the workings of the institution, not its legitimacy or desirability.[38] Prophetic criticism springs from a deeply held conviction about how king, priest, and prophet in Israel are most morally and fruitfully to function.[39] Prophetic judgment, in other words, seeks a better institution, not a world without one.

iii.

> ". . . happiness . . . is a perpetual possession
> of being well deceived."
>
> (Jonathan Swift, *A Tale of a Tub*)

Perhaps amidst the actual devastation that was Jerusalem in 587 BC—when the Temple fell—the poet of the Book of Lamentations, the *Wasteland* of the Hebrew Scriptures, provides the earliest extra-prophetic evidence of the conviction that led to canonical status for the classical Hebrew prophets and denied a place in the sacred writings to those whose never-ending assurances had proven so catastrophically wrong. The sadness of Hebrew elegy begins to echo the warnings of Hebrew prophecy.[40] Significantly, the second of these five lamentations uses Ezekiel's image of whitewash (Ezek 13:10ff.) to describe the message of the prophets now patently proved false:

> Your prophets saw visions for you [he laments] that were mere whitewash. They did not lay bare your sin, to make things better again, But they saw for you oracles that were empty deceptions. [Lam 2:14, AB][41]

In the depth and scope of this attack, Lamentations but reinforces the growing disrepute into which prophecy fell and chasteningly reminds us that the classical Hebrew prophets sought a hearing at a time when the institution of prophecy itself and the inspiration it claimed became more and more suspect. By the time of Deutero-Zechariah, prophecy is bracketed with idolatry as an evil that Yahweh will rid from the land. This particular passage (Zech 13:2-6, NEB), "the last mention in the canonical writings of prophets actually engaged in prophetic activity—not a very flattering reference as it happens—,"[42] presents a semi-dramatic vignette, Juvenalian in its texture of wild, outrageous hyperbole and inversion—e.g., parents against their own child—and an opening juxtaposition of apparent contraries worthy of the wit of Pope or Gibbon. The oracle assumes the form of a witty, satiric cross-examination in which the pseudo-prophet, caught with his hand in the prophetic cookie jar, seeks desperately but unconvincingly to defend himself against the prosecuting interrogation of first his parents and then the community. In the day of Jerusalem's deliverance, Yahweh begins, "I will erase the names of the idols from the land . . . ; I will also remove the prophets and the spirit of uncleanness from the land." Horror-stricken at having a son claim the prophet's office, parents will exclaim: "You shall live no longer, for you have spoken falsely in the name of the LORD." To rid themselves of this blaspheming embarrassment, "His own father and mother will pierce him through because he has prophesied"! Now although Deuteronomy 18:20 enjoins death for the false prophet, it neither requires nor specifies that the parents execute their falsely prophesying offspring in an ironic inversion of Euthyphro's piety! Because the shame of even being thought a prophet extends to the would-be seer himself, he studiously denies the possible prophetic association in any external thing about him: "On that day every prophet shall be ashamed of his vision when he prophesies, nor shall he wear a robe of coarse-hair," Elijah-like, "to deceive." Ironically inverting Amos' disclaimer of prophetic role (Amos 7:14), the pseudo-prophet insists: "I am no prophet, I am a tiller of the soil who has been schooled in lust from boyhood." Better the reputation of a lecher than of a prophet. But what of those marks on his body? Can these scars be the ecstasy-induced self-mutilation characteristic of earlier prophets? Oh no, the entrapped seer will counter: "I got them in the house of my [homosexual] lovers"! Better sodomy than prophecy![43] By the time of Deutero-Zechariah, the prophet is for Israel what the projector is for the eighteenth-century satirist.

Ironically, this last reference in the Hebrew Scriptures to practicing prophets is a prophet's satire on prophecy itself. This less than flattering climax to a tradition that includes some of Israel's greatest heroes thus nicely epitomizes the need for a rhetoric of credibility in the Hebrew prophets which this study bases in the similarities between prophecy and satire as essentially critical discourse. In the warfare among the prophets, as among the wits, principal sources of opposition come from within. Secondly, this infrafraternal conflict severely heightens the need for credibility because a peripheral consequence of the in-fighting, as the passage from Deutero-Zechariah shows, is to discredit prophecy itself. Finally, the self-defensively motivated opposition to both contents and justifies itself by dismissing either as mentally unsound, malignly motivated, or a threat to political and religious order. For prophet and satirist alike, a rhetoric of credibility is an inescapable need of self-presentation.

5

THE
PROPHET
IN THE
SATIRIST'S
MASK

The "writings" of the Hebrew prophets disguise moments of speech whose shape as text follows the prophetic act itself. Although each prophecy begins within a narrative framework or more properly with a title—which a modern ear might construe or misconstrue as the promise of history or biography or some form spatially and temporally locatable—the promise of a narrative frame vanishes almost instantly, within a verse or two in fact.[1] Suddenly a voice sounds—the prophet's or Yahweh's or a not always or easily distinguishable fusion between the two. The prophetic text proceeds as utterance. Just as suddenly the voice later stops and no narrative frame encloses it.[2] The prophetic text records what has been said; what has been said, however, does not record a text.

When satirists speak in their own voice, for all their uttered commitment to writing, the text likewise embodies a speaking which, in the fiction, precedes and anticipates the text.[3] Like prophetic writing, the satiric text witnesses utterance rather than script. In the *Verses* he fancifully fashions on his own death, Swift explicitly writes that he can "hear [his 'special friends'] speak." His elegy upon himself, indeed, is a conversational pastiche in which many voices utter parts in the *Verses on the Death of Dr. Swift*. The speech act is primary in such satires. Horace *tells*

Trebatius he will write. Amos is the word Yahweh speaks to the prophet to speak. A fiction, a deception dominates both: a speechless, silent text, as noiseless as Keats' urn, records sounds. The impression of actual utterance is an illusion. We seem to hear, but we hear nothing except perhaps the sound of our own voices reading a written text. The prophet and the satirist are "voices within a text."[4] Prophecy is the word, the *dabar*, of Yahweh. Satire, as Horace knows, is the *sermo*. Both are the word.[5]

Either voice, furthermore, the prophetic or the satiric, knows it is unwelcome. Each admits, only to counter it if it can, the louder, ubiquitous, and reassuring voice of Business-as-Usual, finally every critic's enemy. However muted, genial, or strident its judgment, the critical voice betrays anxiety and anger about not being well-received. "Who will read this?" Persius is asked. "Why, no one," he admits. Too much Literature-as-Usual around.[6] The voice excuses itself by pleading a compulsion to speak. Who willingly brings bad news? Who would admit to such a willingness? Some irresistible inner need impels the voice to break in upon the customary. Who will willingly hear Micah "howl and wail, go naked and distraught . . ., howl like a wolf, mourn like a desert owl" (Micah 1:8, NEB) when other prophets abound "who promise prosperity in return for a morsel of food," but "proclaim a holy war"—what mock-heroic piety!—against anyone careless enough to "put nothing into [these prophets'] mouths" (3:5, NEB)? Sweeten our mouths, say Micah's enemies in prophecy, and our mouths will utter sweets for you. Whereas the "little cakes" of Horace's first satire attractively disguise a hardier fare to come, the prophetic pap denounced by Micah remains insubstantial from start to finish.[7] No kernel of truth to crack the teeth here.

Even when the voice consoles—as Second Isaiah's "Comfort ye, comfort ye my people" (40:1, KJV) at the very outset—, the consolation almost at once links with the chastening reminder that Jerusalem "hath received of the LORD's hand double for all her sins" (40:2, KJV). Does a Jerusalem in exile need to hear that "all flesh is grass, and all the godliness thereof is as the flower of the field" (40:6, KJV)?[8] "The grass withereth," Second Isaiah continues, "the flower fadeth: because the spirit of the LORD bloweth upon it: surely the people is grass" (40:7,

KJV). The breath, the *ruah* of Yahweh—not the vacuous *ruah* of the reassuring prophets—has only recently withered this people. The *ruah* Jeremiah felt scarcely a generation before seared this people with unwelcome but fulfilled warnings. So now, even as Second Isaiah reassures, his voice betrays echoes of terrifying utterance. Consolation and affirmation have exacted a fearful price. Paul Fussell observes of the concluding verse paragraph of *The Vanity of Human Wishes* that

> we are brought to a kind of peace in these last lines, but we will not forget that we have arrived there through a devastated and ghostly landscape of shattered bodies, ruined fortresses, camouflaged enemies, and betrayed and deserted outposts.[9]

The commentary serves as perceptive postscript on much prophecy as well. Satiric and prophetic voices must speak; they will not be silenced; their commitment is aggressive,[10] their language hostile, their resolution exacting. Such sacred, morally motivated utterance makes audible a spontaneous overflow of powerful dissatisfaction. It denies ease, comfort. Unlike the sweet sounds of Keats' silent urn, this unheard melody disquiets. It does not tease out of thought; it jolts out of a darkness so habitual as to be comforting, out of a blindness so hoary as to be secure.[11]

The voice of satirist and prophet alike, however, makes clear the critic's uneasiness with himself. The word which burdens others lays a heavy load on itself.[12] So Moses, who in Jeremiah's lifetime is being shaped in Deuteronomic writing into the greatest of Israel's prophets, cries in desperation to Yahweh:

> Why hast thou brought trouble on thy servant? How have I displeased the LORD that I am burdened with the care of this whole people? Am I their mother? Have I brought them into the world, and am I called upon to carry them in my bosom, like a nurse with her babies, to the land promised by thee on oath to their fathers? Where am I to find meat to give them all? They pester me with their wailing and their "Give us meat to eat." This whole people is a burden too heavy for me; I cannot carry it alone. If that is thy purpose for me, then kill me outright. But if I have won thy favour let me suffer this trouble at thy hands no longer. [Num 11:10-15, NEB][13]

Cabin fever, but out in a desert crammed with the perceptively titled "children of Israel" whose infernally ceaseless question is "When are we going to get there?"

The frustration of a call to speak to the unheeding wells up intensely in Jeremiah, in graphic imagery of physical discomfort and convulsion. Like a boomerang, the disquieting utterance returns to discomfit only the prophet, who satisfies himself by directing against his people the sarcastic invective of the LORD:

> O my bowels, my bowels! I writhe [howls Jeremiah]!
>   O walls of my heart!
> My heart is in storm within me,
>   I cannot be still.
> You have heard, O my soul, the trumpet blast,
>   The battle shout.
> Disaster comes hard on disaster,
>   All the land is laid waste.
> Laid waste of a sudden my tents,
>   In an instant my curtains.
> How long must I see the [approaching enemy's] standard,
>   Hear the blast of the horn?
> "Ah, but my people are fools!
>   *Me* [AB emphasis] they know not.
> Stupid sons are they,
>   Senseless-they.
> Clever are they to do wrong,
>   To do right—they don't know how!" [Jer 4:19-22, AB]

For all its anger or insistence on its own unworthiness, the reluctance in and of the voice hints betrayal, a suspicion of the consequences that make the critical voice its own victim. What sin dipped me in speech? the prophet asks. Was I born for nothing but to speak? The calling thus rendered less attractive explicitly alleges the implied seduction. So Jeremiah, in terms explicitly sexual, reproaches Yahweh:

> You have enticed me, YHWH, and I've been had:
> You have overwhelmed me and prevailed . . . . [Jer 20:7][14]

Rape, perhaps with complicity? With Yahweh as the aggressor? But what has happened to the afterglow? For the prophet, what was the attraction? Practicing the arts of seducing his listeners, the prophet falls victim to the greater craft of the voice that impels him to speak. The prophet has been tricked into a thankless career. The more intense the sense of betrayal the less likely that the prophet will express any thanks for the insight or any enthusiasm for the call.[15] He curses the spite that called him to set right the out-of-joint time. He can hint, perhaps unaware, at a malevolence in the prompting that makes him, finally, a victim of his own calling.

The prophetic voice, it seems safe to say, apparently offends every canon, every desirable and justifiable ploy, of winning an audience: terrifying, yet terrified; impelling, yet impelled; charging unworthiness, yet pleading its own impurity; chastising arrogance, while claiming to speak for Yahweh. Uneasy with itself, disquieting its hearers, a tangle of contradictions, the voice nonetheless seeks a hearing. It has no other reason for being: it does not seek to be a tree falling in an empty forest. What strategy does the prophetic voice adopt, particularly when the internally troubling features of its utterance encounter the charges a hostile audience has devised to justify putting this sound out of earshot: namely, that the prophet is mad, malignly motivated, and subverting religious and political order?

i.

The Bishop said, it appeared from Horace's writings that he was a cheerful contented man. JOHNSON. "We have no reason to believe that, my Lord. Are we to think Pope was happy, because he says so in his writings? We see in his writings what he wished the state of his mind to appear."

James Boswell, *The Life of Johnson*, 9 April 1778

My study of satire in the Hebrew prophets has sought not only to point out the extent and variety of satire in those texts but also to speculate on why prophecy and satire so often intersect. The basic methodology for pursuing these objectives involves applying to the text of the prophets paradigms and other critical paraphernalia familiar from the literary criticism of satire, and demonstrating how approaches in the biblical criticism of prophecy offer fruitful possibilities for insights into satire. This chapter focusses on the strategies apparent in the text of the prophets for establishing credibility and countering the charges of mental instability or suspect possession, malign motivation, and subversion.[16] I seek in particular to show how the fashioning of the prophet's persona resembles the creating of a satirist's mask. The strategy of attractive self-presentation is of the essence of many of the first-person satires which literary criticism throws into the grab-bag of satiric apologias or program satires. There, often in response to the concern of a friend actually present in the text, or at least implied, the satirist defends his choice of career in comments less reliable for their autobiographical authenticity than for their role in constructing a favorable image of himself. To a considerable extent, the satiric apologia is an exercise in public relations—I use the phrase with no pejorative suggestions. The apologia seeks to render the satirist and his message attractive, no small task given the essentially critical nature of satiric content. The apologia, I would argue further, focusses relentlessly and exclusively on the satirist and his satire. Controversies, friendships, enmities and rivalries, education, parents, and patrons, compliments, help, and hindrance—whatever enters the apologia appears there only to throw a vocational light on the satirist. Nothing vocationally irrelevant intrudes. In the apologia-like self-presentation of Juvenal's *Satire XI*, for example, the simple, healthful way of the satirist's life detailed for his friend Persicus and the solid, traditional quality of the literature Juvenal enjoys sharply contrast in their detail with the noxious, malignant quality of Roman life in *Satire I*—where Juvenal vigorously commits himself to satire—and the banal literature that Rome enjoys. Horace's comments on his father—in the fourth and sixth satires of Book I—are an integral component of his satiric "personality." The material in the satiric apologia enters only to answer who the satirist is and why he writes. The apologia thus is the satirist as his own exemplum, his own illustration. He appears in and through his career, his calling, and that career and vocation illustrate who he is in the text. The opening of Horace's second book of *Satires* embodies both his motivation and skill as it fashions for Trebatius the very argument Horace's lawyer-friend can take into court to vindicate the satirist.

This vocational focus likewise determines the nature of first-person commentary in the prophetic text. Ezekiel says succinctly: "I spoke to the people in the morning, and that very evening my wife died" (24:18, NEB). The incident, however, is incorporated into the text only as an exemplary comparison for the Judahites. In the loss of their beloved Jerusalem, they are to avoid mourning and despair, to do, in other words, "as [Ezekiel] has done" (24:24, NEB). An equally astonishing subordination of apparently biographical detail to illustration appears in the opening three chapters of Hosea, where the prophet recounts what happens after Yahweh instructs him to marry the woman who will turn prostitute. Verisimilitude—were it relevant—would ask of the text some creative awareness and use of the at least near three years implied in three pregnancies brought to term, some exploration of the prophet's inner feelings about this strange order. Neither the narratively elaborated nor the personally revelatory intrude into the account, however. In fact, these three chapters in Hosea are very likely a parable, an exemplum,[17] all of whose details are controlled by and subsumed to the point being illustrated: Yahweh's on-going, on-again-off-again relationship with his faithless wife, Israel. The three children born of this marriage—whose names mean God Shall Sow (disaster, of course), Not Loved, and Not My People—enter the story only to be puns, the meaning of whose names is salvifically reversed.[18]

The literary critic recognizes familiar terrain here. The prophetic "I" only obliquely renders the actual prophet. The "I" appears in that construct which is the text, and only the most literal or fundamentalist of critics avers that the "I" of the text is the authentic "I" of history. What is denied is not necessarily a connection but an equation. A. R. Diamond traces major stages in modern scholarship on the so-called Confessions of Jeremiah,[19] a prophet about whom, he claims, "we have more biographical information . . . than on any other prophet."[20] These stages in biblical interpretation parallel literary criticism's movement from the confidently asserted authenticity of the "I" not uncommon in late nineteenth and early twentieth-century critics, particularly those who, taking their cue from Freud, read literature as an index to personality.[21]

In the first major period of modern Jeremiah studies, says Diamond, "with few exceptions the confessions are taken as primary sources of psychological and biographical data for the construction of a 'life' of the prophet." A second stage of interpretation considered the relationship of these Confessions "to the psalm genre—lament . . . . The prophet is understood to have availed himself of a longstanding genre and adopted it to express his own uniquely prophetic experiences." The third and latest development placed "greater emphasis upon a theological assessment of the prophet's sufferings in relation to the prophetic office." The resulting question is obvious: "how is it legitimate to read these highly stylized and stereotypical expressions as direct psychological transcripts and as 'confessions' in the true sense of that literary genre—i.e., as spiritual [auto-]biography?"[22] Both later developments relinquish "a direct contact with the inner experiences and personality of the prophet." Diamond's central question thus becomes: "how is a valid reading of these problematic passages to be achieved?"[23] Diamond concludes his study by arguing:

> It is not the personal experience of the prophet in the context of his mission per se and its value for the depiction of Jeremiah as an exemplary spiritual figure which lie at the heart of the editorial interest. Instead, the portrayal of the prophetic mission represents an element in the theodicy theme and is subordinate to it.[24]

Succinctly put, that theodicy theme is "the hopelessness" of Judah's situation which is

> crystallized by the nation's response of obdurate rejection and opposition to Jeremiah's mission. The desperate nature of the national sinfulness . . . required a merciless, unavoidable judgment mirrored and presaged in the manner of the prophetic mission itself—i.e., as Yahweh's representative the prophet is permitted only the posture of combatant toward the nation as a sign of Yahweh's resolute intention to judge.[25]

The shaping of the text of Jeremiah, so Diamond claims, subordinates all its elements to the presentation of this theme. Intermingling with the principal theological concern, however, are three subthemes: "prophetic conflict, prophetic iconoclasm, and prophetic paradigm," which Diamond thus explains:

> In terms of prophetic conflict, Jeremiah is vindicated as a model of righteousness in contrast to the nation's corrupt leadership . . . which promotes the nation in its wicked apostasy. The vindication of the prophet also adds support to the manner in which his message included an iconoclastic element in relation to popular religion. And, finally, Yahweh's destruction of his people is shown to have been an unavoidable necessity by the exposure of the nation's desperate wickedness through their unjustified persecution of the exemplary Jeremiah.[26]

Yet Diamond, who faults "an exclusively paradigmatic reading of the confessions" because such a reading "continues to treat the confessions as . . . a type of spiritual biography," nevertheless concedes that "a firm conclusion concerning the authenticity problem [of the confessions] is hard to reach," that "authentic material" was incorporated and reshaped into a prophetic text to serve theological purposes, and that Jeremiah himself "must have perceived wider significance in these prayers in order to account for their preservation within the tradition."[27] The thrust of the analysis is clear: the text has not been preserved to provide autobiographical material that is its own justification for being. As preserved in the text, the prophetic persona, like that of the satirist, seeks purposes other than autobiographical authenticity. The "I" appears in a construct and takes its shape and purpose in that construct. Yet only foolhardiness denies that no authenticity whatever emerges from the "I" of the text.

Were a literary critical fantasy to permit the first voice of Juvenal's *Satire III* to assume the role of a redactor preserving and shaping the words of Umbricius, a fairly specific parallel to Diamond's argument about the biblical text's Jeremiah appears. Juvenal the Redactor seeks to inveigh against Rome. In Umbricius, he remembers an honest Roman brought into interminable conflict with the wealthy, the powerful, and all those who court them. The iconoclasm of Umbricius' declamation searingly sketches the debasement of the Roman aristocracy, the abandonment of the old, virtuous Roman ways, and the amoral self-seeking of the foreign arrivistes. Umbricius' sufferings, indignity, and poverty are a paradigm of what a once worthy Rome has experienced. Virtuous old Rome will abandon the capital along with this virtuous old Roman. He does not go into exile alone.[28]

The conclusions affirmed by A. R. Diamond pique the curiosity of a literary criticism of satire that often evaluates the satirist's self-portrait in a work and in a body of works whose content is always criticism. Jeremiah as critic subordinates his self-presentation to a wider, morally significant theme. The growth of the prophet's mind, like that of the satirist, appears in his engagement with the world outside that mind and particularly in the moral judgment he fashions against it. Prophetic self-revelation, like satiric self-portraiture, comes only in service to a cause greater than the self. The power and craft of the text is subordinated to an ethical good. Indeed, Ezekiel complains that he is dismissed as a mere crafter of stories, as if agreeable technique were his ultimate aim, as if he were a pied piper with no interest in the danger posed by the rats (Ezek 20:49): "You are no more to them than a singer of fine songs with a lovely voice, or a clever harpist" (33:32, NEB). Satirist and prophet alike, on the contrary, are held in thrall by a cause, and each defines himself in relationship to it. The righteousness that contrasts with a wicked but responsible ruling class is like Pope's claim that, unlike Sporus, if he pleased, he pleased by manly ways. Since the customary is often the enemy of prophet and satirist, iconoclasm is each critic's fate and danger. And to persecute the prophet or the satirist is to be reminded that a society is judged not only by its successes—Jane Austen's insight—but also by its victims, the perhaps more discomforting awareness of Swift.

Timothy Polk's earlier 1984 study of the prophetic persona in Jeremiah, however, even more fruitfully pursues a critical tack that can illuminate the shaping of the satirist's persona, particularly by considering these prophetic confessions and their effect as vocational autobiography.[29] First of all, Polk recognizes the "patently poetic" nature of Jeremiah's confessions: "Poetic form, metaphor, the language of the heart, self-constituting behavior, the representation of a paradigm—all are closely interwoven there, just as in other first-person speeches of the prophet." While not seeking to deny a connection between the "Jeremiah of history" and the "Jeremiah of the text," Polk insists that it is "hermeneutically irrelevant if the 'original' circumstances were other than what the text describes."[30] So what, Maynard Mack contends, if Pope was fifty when, in the first dialog of the *Epilogue to the Satires*, he asks to be forgiven "the Prejudice of Youth."[31] Similarly, Polk continues:

> it matters not whether the compositions are the product of the historical Jeremiah himself or later redactors. In my opinion, it violates the integrity of the text, *qua* poetry, to replace the given literary context with the conjectured historical occasion of the writing process and so to construe the text as referring to authorial circumstances rather than to the subject as it is literarily defined.[32]

Although few if any problems emerge about the authorship of satiric apologias, Polk's emphasis cannot be gainsaid: what the satirist says of himself, he says through poetry, through art. And "the more comprehensive a system of internal relationships, references, and allusions the text becomes, the more it regulates the *way* it refers and the *terms* of its referentiality [Polk's emphasis]." Polk further recognizes the ambiguities of word and personae—a blurring of distinctions between God and the prophet—that contribute "to the book's depiction of the prophet as a theological paradigm."[33]

A most important passage follows in which Polk vigorously defends the use of literary terminology like persona or ambiguity in the analysis of a biblical text. In citing this defense here, I make no claim to high theological import in satire. But the satirist does claim to speak in defense of principle, chastises, however gently, departures from the norm, and does present himself as at least an attempt to live healthfully. Etymologically, salvation has family ties with health. Polk avers:

> The poetic, metaphoric qualities of our material are clear evidence that the book of Jeremiah is a work of the imagination. This is not to say that it is fanciful, unreal, or untrue. Nor

is it even to say that it is dominated by an aesthetic interest. Quite to the contrary, the aesthetic labors in the service of the religious [as satire claims that its art serves the ethical], and the book is clearly engaged in making truth-claims—about the world, about the prophet, and about God—though scarcely in propositional form. The point is that the kind of truth claimed . . . is of a special sort, one that cannot be expressed apart from the imaginatively charged language it employs.

Such truth has to do with matters of the deepest import which a purely discursive language can scarcely hope to express. The rule of thumb is that the more denotative (discursive) the language becomes, the less it is capable of conveying that sense of import. Trying to tell the deep truth of Jeremiah's life, to communicate his significance as an expression of the purpose and pathos of God and at the same time as an expression of the predicament and dread and hope of his people, required an imaginative re-presentation of the highest order. That is why a criticism concerned with elucidating the text's theological significance should not be misled into thinking it must first reduce the text to a historically assured minimum, or restrict the "authentic" Jeremiah to the *ipsissima verba*, or regard the text primarily as a source for fuller historical reconstructions. This can only result in missing precisely what the text wants to say, and replacing that with something else.[34]

The Jeremiah who emerges in the text uses "an action language": "he does not so much discuss attitudes, feelings, and the like as express them," and the exercise of this language gives "the self form and definition, depth and breadth." But

while exercising the self, the language targets something outside the self, namely the particular object and/or grounds of the emotion . . . . the primary interest is not in the self *per se* . . . but in what he or she represents, signifies, and points to. The self in this sort of writing is a medium for the message.[35]

Polk can just as easily be discussing the "Horace" or the "Pope" of the satires. "Horace" is a moral paradigm in his poems, an exemplar who leaves the truth "dramatically indicated,"[36] embodied in his way of living. "Pope" is

the detached observer, somewhat removed from City, town, and court, the centers of corruption [and seldom the preferred hangouts of the Hebrew prophets]; he is the friend of virtuous men, whose friendship for him testifies to his integrity; he is fond of peace, country life [like Amos or Juvenal], the arts, morality, and truth, and he detests their opposites which flourish in the great world [which the prophets roundly and repeatedly ridicule and attack].[37]

If the prophet is a theological paradigm at times, the satirist can occasionally shape himself into an ethical pattern. When Polk observes that "Jeremiah functions as an example, a model for imitation by believers who follow him," the hermeneutics of satire recognizes a kinship: Horace knows exactly what he is about when, in the *Art of Poetry*, he tells the writer to study "Socrates' pages," where Plato creates his own paradigm of wisdom.[38] "Socrates," "Horace," and "Pope," however, emerge as paradigms with "a language that targets something outside the self," to repeat Polk, "namely the particular object and/or grounds of the emotion."

This focus on the elsewhere-directed language of the self leads Polk to distinguish Jeremiah's confession from the "Petrarchan-Rousseauvian pattern of autobiography, which is marked by self-absorption." He uses Sallie TeSelle's reminder that in another autobiographical pattern, the "interest in the self is vocational." More parabolic in nature than the stricter life story, "the presentation of the self takes place in service of a larger task."[39] Particularly apt here is Maynard Mack's description of the satirist in his heroic voice: the satirist "never lets us forget that we *are* at war; there *is* an enemy [Mack's emphasis]."[40] He has enlisted in a cause. The self-portrait which emerges in such a confession is "more compelling than the self-exalting variety" because—the words are now TeSelle's—

> the mystery of the self, like all mystery, is visible only indirectly, through the encounters of the self with the world. It is the vocationally oriented autobiographies, those that point away from a direct, inward perception of the self to what *drives the self* [my emphasis], drives it concretely in the world, which are most revealing of the self. . . . The peculiarity of the Christian confession [the concern of TeSelle's book] is the denial of the self, its hiddenness in and for the vocation, the calling, to allow the story of the self to be used as an indirect route of

insight for others. It eventuates, however, in a vivid self-portrayal, in an individuality that is not that of an "interesting Personality" but of someone molded by God . . . .[41]

Polk's claim that the book of Jeremiah represents, finally, a paradigmatic self—"an indirect route of insight to others," in TeSelle's phrase—applies very nicely to the satiric apologia and shows equally how prophetic and satiric self-revelation in the pattern of vocational autobiography have a great deal in common. The satirist too defines himself concretely in his relations with the world, with its Bufos and Mathos, its urban ghettos and country retreats. The prophet encounters the golden calves, the phallic deities, worshipers impatient to start cheating after ritual, and the self-assured voices of never-ending weal. If, furthermore, the forms particularly suited for vocational autobiography include "journal, letter, and prayer,"[42] Pope's many verse conversations and Horace in prayerful quiet at the Sabine farm only reinforce the proximity between prophetic and satiric self-presentation.

The paradigms of biblical criticism that reveal the oblique self-presentation of the prophets usefully illuminate a comparable technique in satire. The critical voice in both discourses reveals a craft of insinuation in the best sense of the phrase. The irresistible call to bring others to a better life does not, of course, always occasion an eagerness to hear: "The Virgin [Thel]," Blake writes, "started from her seat, & with a shriek / Fled back unhindered till she came into the vales of Har."[43] The Israelites wandering in the desert whiningly recall, in selective memory, how they "sat round the fleshpots [of Egypt] and had plenty of bread to eat!" (Exod 16:3, NEB). Back in Egypt, several centuries later, in the aftermath of the Fall of Jerusalem, the Israelites utter a cry with a familiar anti-Mosaic echo:

> we are not going to listen to you. . . . we will scrupulously do all that we have vowed to do, and will offer sacrifice to the Queen of Heaven and pour out libations to her, just as we and our fathers, our kings and our princes, used to do in the cities of Judah and in the streets of Jerusalem; for then we had plenty to eat, were prosperous, and experienced no misfortune. [Jer 44:16-17, AB]

Having mastered Adam's cop-out in Genesis—"The woman whom you put by my side—it was she who gave me of that tree, and I ate" (Gen 3:12, AB)—the women add: "Has it been without our husbands' knowledge and consent that we have made cakes depicting her, and poured out libations to her?" (44:19, AB). What Jeremiah says to the fleeing Judahites in response contains, according to John Bright, "the last words uttered by Jeremiah of which we have knowledge."[44] His audience, however, has made it strenuously clear: "we are not going to listen to you."

ii.

> "I hate the man, because he prophesies no good for
> me; never anything but evil."   1 Kgs 22:8 (NEB)

Since much of what the prophet chastises is expressed satirically, the prophet's self-representation reveals striking affinities with techniques of the satiric apologia. Thus the caution Maynard Mack introduces into "The Muse of Satire," his influential study of the satiric persona, can easily be recognized in the assumptions and approaches of biblical critics like Diamond and Polk on the persona of Jeremiah: even in apparently "very personal poems" like Pope's *Epistle to Dr. Arbuthnot*, cautions Mack, "we overlook what is most essential if we overlook the distinction between the historical Alexander Pope and the dramatic Alexander Pope who speaks in them." The usefulness Mack finds in the term Muse to underscore this distinction has relevance to the prophet, possessed by Yahweh, or at least by the word of Yahweh: the term Muse is

> our reminder that it is not the author as man who casts these
> shadows on our printed page, but the author as poet: an
> instrument possessed by and possessing—Plato would have
> said a god, we must at any rate say an art . . . .

If *Muse* further reminds us "that in any given instance the shadow may not delineate even the whole poet, but only [a partial] angle of his sensibility," the reminder forces us to consider the self in the text as a self defined in the terms of the vocation in the text.[45]

The similarities do not end here, however. Drawing on Mary Claire Randolph's study of the structure of formal verse satire, Mack draws attention to the two-layer approach of satire, a layer of attack and a layer of "ideal norm." Prophetic satire, which often and quickly shifts within the same oracle from practice blamed to ideal recommended, shows in this very characteristic movement an important structural affinity with satire.[46] So Isaiah's oracle which pronounces Yahweh's dismissive rejection of "whole offerings of rams / and of the fat of buffaloes," his impatience with the externally ritual celebration of "new moons and . . . festivals" quickly urges:

> Cease to do evil and learn to do right,
> pursue justice and champion the oppressed;
> give the orphan his rights, plead the widow's cause.
> [Isa 1:11,14,17, NEB]

Or Joel's bluntly laconic contrast: "Rend your hearts and not your garments" (2:13, NEB). The pastiche nature of the completed prophetic text—its sewing together in succession of a number of oracles—brings out even more repeatedly than formal verse satire the movement within prophecy from attack to exhortation, from corrupt practice to asserted ideal. The rapid shift of scenes in Juvenalian satire often involves such a movement from the reprehensible to the attractive, from the gross to the desirable.

Although the persuasive elements of any communication demand forceful argument and the engaging of the audience's interests and concerns, the most imperative element, in Mack's judgment, is the ethos of the speaker: "the weight of authority that comes from the hearer's estimate of the speaker's character." The audience must accept the speaker as "fundamentally virtuous and tolerant"; "the audience must be assured that its censor is a man of good will who has been . . . *forced* into action [Mack's emphasis]."[47] It is difficult not to prophesy.

While not limiting myself in what follows to the paradigm proposed by Mack—the satirist as the naive or good or heroic man—[48] I do claim that the techniques of self-presentation he finds in satire also appear in prophecy and that paradigms which emerge in the biblical criticism of prophetic personae

163

restate and expand this paradigmatic common denominator. This becomes particularly apparent if it is kept in mind that the prophets frequently speak as satirists, a focus that is not the concern of biblical criticism like that of Diamond and Polk. Like satirists, prophets project a persona designed to counter the animosity they expect. Their message arouses hostility or contemptuous dismissal. Elijah—the text of whose message is not preserved—is called a "troubler of Israel" (1 Kgs 18:17, NEB) and forced to go into hiding because Jezebel seeks his life. The obscurity of Hosea's attacks on a corrupted and corrupting priesthood may be a deliberate self-protecting vagueness. Amaziah, priest in Israel, tells his king, Jeroboam, that the prophet Amos conspires against him. In face-to-face meeting Amaziah tells Amos to return to his home in the southern kingdom (Amos 7:10-17), Amos perhaps, thus, the first in a long line of "outside agitators." The prophecy of Jeremiah is filled with instances of hostile reception: his patriotism is questioned; he is arrested; the king destroys his prophecy as it is being read to him (Jeremiah 36). Ezekiel complains that his audience disregards his message because they deem him merely a wordsmith, a crafter of parables, a teller of stories (Ezek 20:49). Jonah, archetype of the reluctant prophet, receives God's command to go to Nineveh and responds by traveling in the opposite direction. Indeed, the prophetic call to Jeremiah, Isaiah, and Amos also appears as an interruption in a life that had been proceeding otherwise, and the interruption occasions protests of unworthiness and fear of possibly dangerous consequences. The analogies to the self-defensive anxiety, reluctance, and protests of satirists like Horace, Juvenal, Pope, and Swift are striking.

In the face of such real or anticipated opposition, what image, what character, do the prophets construct of themselves? The image often resembles the satirist's frequently assumed roles as the good or heroic man. As defenders of traditional religion, the prophets claim that the simple, decent, demanding worship of God has been corrupted by the laying on of so much superfluous, irrelevant obligation that the real demands of religion have been obscured. Here is the prophet as the good man, ironically radical in calling for a return to simpler, more decent religious values. Each of the prophets, secondly, can lay claim as well to speaking as the heroic man. The prevailing tone of Hebrew prophecy is Juvenalian: disaster is imminent; moral disintegration is widespread and prevails in the highest places; radical reform is in order; the prophet's is a solitary, unheeded, but dangerous calling. Whether any of the prophets appears as Mack's naive man—disarmingly puzzled by his involvement in controversy—poses a separate examination in what follows. At any rate like the satirists, the Hebrew prophets present themselves not as self-appointed aggressors, but as messengers of something higher, some principle within and without themselves, urging them to accept an admittedly difficult task.

Like Horace in the satire that opens each book of his *Satires*, or like Pope in his *Arbuthnot*, prophets occasionally fashion a self-revelation comparable to the satirist's. Indeed, even more elements, also familiar from satiric self-presentation, appear in the Hebrew prophets: the reluctance to assume the burden of judgment; the fear of reprisal; the insistence on the ultimately healthful nature of the message, however much pain it causes along the way; the prophetic career itself portrayed as a turning from a more desired, albeit unspecified, alternative— the prophetic career, in other words, like the satirist's, as something unexpected, unanticipated. How striking it is that the Hebrew tradition that has so painstakingly preserved the message of these prophets has also taken great care—especially in the cases of Amos, Jeremiah, and Ezekiel—to preserve a good deal of the way in which these prophets presented themselves to their times. The artfulness of this and related techniques in Hebrew prophecy bears unmistakable resemblance to the techniques of self-revelation and image-fashioning in the satirists.

Before, however, pursuing the more direct applicability to the Hebrew prophet of Mack's paradigm of the satirist as a good or heroic or even naive man, I want first to consider what might be termed a group alignment in the rhetoric of the prophets, the fear and reluctance of the prophets to follow their call, and their insistence on the ultimately beneficial aims of what they preach. These three features of prophetic self-presentation are as common in and important to the prophet as they are to the satirist.

iii.

"Can it be that any man has skill to fabricate himself?"
St. Augustine, *Confessions*

To emphasize, as Maynard Mack does, how the satirist shapes himself into a naive, or good, or heroic figure—a "public defender," in the last case—, or to picture his function, as Northrop Frye does, in terms of a giant-killer or David taking on Goliath[49] is to leave perhaps an impression even rhetorically misleading that the satirist is always a solitary, isolated figure, climbing the beanstalk alone or standing in an otherwise empty field with nothing but a slingshot in hand. In commenting on letters that were exchanged between Alexander Pope and Jonathan Swift, Samuel Johnson was certainly left with this impression:

> In the letters both of Swift and Pope [he writes], there appears such narrowness of mind as makes them insensible of any excellence that has not some affinity with their own, and confines their esteem and approbation to so small a number, that whoever should form his opinion of the age from their representation would suppose them to have lived amidst ignorance and barbarity, unable to find among their contemporaries either virtue or intelligence, and persecuted by those that could not understand them.[50]

What is rhetorically significant in these comments is Johnson's awareness that the satirist does not stand alone: sometimes he speaks for a group small in number.

a.

"The prophets who were of old . . . prophesied against many countries and great kingdoms of war, of disaster and plague."   Jer 28:8 (AB)

In an important pattern of self-presentation which Maynard Mack does not consider in "The Muse of Satire," the satirist speaks of a double alignment: first, virtuous persons past and present—a support group, which, of course, may indeed be actual; and, second, with earlier practitioners of his art. Part of a remnant and part of a tradition and speaking as either, he is not alone. Mack has recognized in his biography of Pope the presence of this small-group sense whose rhetorical power to win sympathy as part of a challenged minority seems clear: "that 'saving-remnant' syndrome," he calls it, "which has so often throughout history stiffened the spines of men and women who either were or perceived themselves to be repositories of some variety of 'true faith.'"[51] The satirist is one of few who embodies threatened values, and only the most recent to speak in their defense. The number may not be many, but it is not one.

The prophet's persona shows traces of this same paradigm. Although the popular view of his calling, according to Robert R. Wilson, regards it as a personal process "taking place in relative isolation," he insists rather that "there can be no socially isolated intermediaries."[52] Wilson's concern is sociological, here with small support groups that mainstay the prophet. In prophetic utterance, however, the remnant becomes the very shape of the consolation ultimately promised by the prophets, a remnant with whom the prophets identify and whose values they share.[53]

What even more directly concerns the self-presentation of the prophets is their aligning themselves with and invoking the prophetic tradition itself. Like the Horace who exonerates himself by pleading the example of the earlier Lucilius, or Persius and Juvenal later invoking Horace, the Hebrew prophets often find their own voice by incorporating echoes of their prophetic forebears to justify themselves. This adapting and assimilating of the past to the present strengthens both the character of the prophet and his indictment. Such a use of the authority of the past, however, pertains very particularly to prophecy and to satire because it constitutes a form of precedent in prophecy, which often uses legal forms, and to the frequent legal and quasi-legal fictive context in which much satiric self-defense occurs. The quasi-legal quality of satire and prophecy, discussed in Chapter One, also affects the presentation in the text of the character of the prophet and the satirist.

The prophet and satirist engage in a legal action of sorts which moves a criminal through the rhetorical process of indictment, evidence, verdict, and sentence.

First of all, the legal contexts in satiric self-defense occur easily to mind. Horace talks with his lawyer-friend Trebatius, who is keenly disturbed at the possible legal ramifications of Horace's satire. Pope's imitation of this poem has him conversing with the lawyer Fortescue, who like his Roman counterpart, can cite chapter and verse of the relevant statute. Swift's most devoted servant includes in his Pseudo-Discourse on Satire assurances about the impunity of writing satire as long as no names are mentioned. Whoever unfortunately gets specific "must expect to be imprisoned for *scandalum magnatum*; to have challenges sent him; to be sued for defamation; and to be brought before the bar of the house." Juvenal asks: "Who says now: 'I dare name names, and if they don't like it, / What does it matter to me?'" Swift's *Verses* describes his interventions in politics as a "crime of state," and he takes understandable satisfaction that although "two kingdoms . . . / Had set a price upon his head," and a handsome price at that, " . . . not a traitor could be found / To sell him for six hundred pound." Quasi-legal touches appear in the "Prologue" to John Oldham's *Satyrs Upon the Jesuits*. Oldham uses, for instance, an Amos-like series of hyperbolically stated impossibilities—e.g., "Sooner shall false Court favourites prove just"—to emphasize the greater unlikelihood that he, "with utmost spite, and vengeance" will "cease / To prosecute." He styles his writing a "severe and exemplary doom," a judicial sentence or judgment, as Johnson defines it, a reminder that in satire as in prophecy doom is both form and content. The satirist's persona appears often in a courtroom context, with threats of action at law prominently in the foreground.[54]

Even more integral to prophecy, as noted in Chapter One, legal forms are actually a genre through which the prophets direct judgment at individuals and at nations. Narrative sections introduced into the text, furthermore, sustain the impression of the legal dialog which often emerges from the satiric apologia. Often the hint remains that however conveniently danger is rhetorically surmounted, triumph may not be so easy outside the confines of the text.

Take, for instance, the reinforced sense of danger that nevertheless shadows Jeremiah's apparent vindication. The prophet has blisteringly condemned the Judahites' unflappable assurance about the eternal endurance of the Jerusalem Temple. Jeremiah, however, counters that Yahweh "will make this house like Shiloh," the Northern Temple destroyed by the Assyrians over a century earlier, and that "this city [will be] a curse word to all the nations of the earth" (Jer 26:6, AB). Seized immediately by priests and prophets alike, Jeremiah is hauled before the princes of Judah, who refuse to execute him. Just as Horace not only claims that Lucilius spoke severely against many prominent Romans, but also that these victims took no umbrage at what he said of them, so here "certain of the elders" plead the example of the earlier Micah and remind those in attendance that he too had spoken of the coming destruction of Jerusalem. Despite that deeply disturbing message, neither King Hezekiah nor anyone else in Judah dared lay a hand against the prophet (26:17-19). Precedent notwithstanding, the narrative concedes that "it was only the fact that Ahikam ben Shaphan lent his support to Jeremiah that prevented his being handed over to the people to be put to death" (26:24, AB). This grim concession is made even more shaky with the addition of the story about the flight, extradition, execution, and dishonorable burial of Jeremiah's contemporary, the prophet Uriah ben Shemaiah (26:20-23). Language reinforces a distinction between verbal vindication and real triumph.

Summoning, so to speak, the shades of the prophetic dead buttresses the living prophet. Their authority becomes a mantle that falls on his shoulders: he is Yahweh's current speaker, sharing the power of past utterance and knowledgeable about its transmission. The satiric technique parallels the prophetic and is worth mentioning here: Horace, for example, not only discusses the pros, cons, and exemplary protection of Lucilius' earlier satire (*Satires*, I, iv, x, and II, i) but implies in a single text (*Satires*, II, iii) his familiarity with and study of old masters of his craft like Plato and Menander, Eupolis and Archilochus, the last instance stretching far back into the darkest recesses of the origin of satire. Rhetorically, it is quite a leap. The Jeremiah who advisedly reminds his more comforting brother-in-prophecy Hananiah that earlier prophets spoke messages of woe, not of weal (Jer 28:8), lays open his own familiarity with that tradition and the conformity of his utterance with that past as his own epistemological norm of prophecy. Jeremiah, in fact, affords the most extensively developed instance in the Hebrew Scriptures of a prophet seeking his authority in and shaping himself by the prophetic past. Like the young Alexander Pope of the *Essay on Criticism*, who discovers a voice in the tradition of the Ancients and especially in that of Horace—whose poetry supplies the epigram of the poem—, so the young Jeremiah begins with a voice incorporating other prophetic voices on the way to maturing into a uniquely recognizable voice that assimilates other prophets without blurring its own identity.

For a study like this concerned with the parallels of satiric and prophetic self-presentation, Joseph Blenkinsopp's *History of Prophecy in Israel* indirectly provides a rich mine of rhetorical technique. The early Jeremiah, for him, is a prophet seeking to find his own voice by using the voice of others. The emerging pattern of Moses in the prophet's lifetime as the exemplar of all prophets most influences the shaping of the Jeremiah of the text. Moses plays Horace to Jeremiah's Pope, although the patterning in the prophet is likely much closer than in the poet. Indeed, Blenkinsopp contends that the close affinities between the account of Jeremiah's call (Jer 1:14-19) and that of Moses (Exod 3:1-4:17) "confirms the impression that Jeremiah is being presented from the beginning of his career as a 'Mosaic' prophet." The two calls display much structural similarity:

> divine address, expostulation of the one addressed, confirmation and encouragement designed to overcome his hesitation, an act of installation accompanied by a form of words, specification of the mission entrusted to the prophet designate, and a visionary experience.[55]

Jeremiah speaks with striking similarities to Hosea: the account of the two bad sisters, Israel and Judah (Jer 3:6-18), is for John Bright "a further development of Hosea's theme of the adulterous wife," a theme Ezekiel twice pursues (Ezekiel 16 and 23).[56] Blenkinsopp further argues that Jeremiah deliberately links himself to the entire prophetic tradition: "in his denunciations and recapitulations of a long history of national infidelity [Jeremiah] is in the process of assimilating the prophetic tradition and bringing it to bear on the contemporary situation." This rhetorical pattern is evidently as old as the "written" prophets themselves: "It is clearly an essential part of [Hosea's] own self-image to be within a tradition of chosen intermediaries that has unbroken links with the past." Hosea's opposition to monarchy, in particular, has links with Ahijah of Shiloh, Micaiah, and Elijah, whose activities appear as narratives in 1 Samuel and 1 and 2 Kings.[57]

Hosea is echoed and alluded to in Isaiah, who may have prompted in his southern counterpart "the theme of the unfaithful sons (Isa 1:2-3) and the harlot city (1:21-26)" and whose denunciation of fertility cults (10:1) may have echoes in Isaiah's love song of the vineyard (5:1-7). Isaiah's condemnation of the upper classes sounds very much like Amos' indictment of "the same kind of social irresponsibility"; his poem on the divine anger (5:24-25; 9:8-10:4) opens with a passage Blenkinsopp believes "very probably an indirect allusion to Amos." Indeed, the stylistic similarities "suggest that Isaiah has taken up where Amos left off and that his intent is to apply the message of his older contemporary to the Kingdom of Judah." In a history that asserts the legitimacy of speaking of a prophetic tradition, Blenkinsopp succinctly summarizes this prophetic inter-awareness and assimilation:

> A careful reading of Hosea suggests that he was familiar with the public activity of Amos; Isaiah appears at one stage of his career to be applying the message of Amos to Judah; Jeremiah's debt to Hosea, especially in the early stage of his career, is easily verifiable; Ezekiel borrows from his older contemporary Jeremiah, and so on.[58]

Although the prophets do not explicitly quote one another, they allude, they repeat, they use and invert established patterns, they invoke the authority of earlier prophets—in short, they constantly employ the language of the past to strengthen their present position. These assimilations, adaptations, and echoes of a prophetic yesteryear become, in the overall context of the prophecy, mini-imitations along the lines of those very popular among eighteenth-century British satirists. These texts translate and transfer the indictments of the past into a contemporary situation. In a context as highly and as morally charged as the prophetic, this assimilation and echo unmistakably warn against imitating the heedlessness of earlier times and suffering a comparable doom. To reject Jeremiah is to reject Moses, and with similar consequences.

Robert R. Wilson does not find the traditional quality of this utterance and self-presentation at all unusual. The continuing evocation of one prophet by another constitutes the stereotypical quality of prophetic speech which Wilson finds characteristic of the intermediary. Micah, he notes, quotes Isaiah, while Zephaniah quotes or uses the language of Hosea, Amos, Isaiah, Micah, and Jeremiah.[59] The intermediary thus defines himself considerably according to a pattern of language already available and expects that familiarity to expand the definition of the prophetic office at least enough to include him. The prophet defines himself not only by his vocation, but also by the language which has traditionally defined his calling. A verbal genetics emerges that shows any one prophet bearing family resemblances, to have, as it were, the rights and the authority of kinfolk—an ironic situation, in a way, because none of the "written" prophets appears to have been a hereditary prophet. Amos, in fact, explicitly denies being a family practitioner of prophecy (Amos 7:14). In the sense I am speaking of it, however, language achieves what biology has not effected. Jewish legend confirms the impression.

Louis Ginzberg's *The Legends of the Jews* reveals a motif of prophetic interrelatedness and status that goes back even to patriarchal times in Israel, a full millennium before the advent of the "written" prophets. The prophets claim a descent from important figures in Israel's history; they are related to one another and to important religious and political figures, not always the most exemplary; and they interact with one another in that telescoping of time and distance that legend easily admits. Hosea, one of the earliest of the "written" prophets, is the son of the priest and prophet Beeri, the only two surviving verses of whose prophecy are preserved by Isaiah (IV, 260).[60] Hosea's ancestry extends as far back as Reuben, a brother of Joseph, who was the first to attempt rescuing his brother from the pit into which he had been thrown. Hosea is promised him in posterity as a reward for his good offices (II, 12-13). The son whom Elijah restores to the widow is Jonah, her late husband the prophet Obadiah, and the widow herself a survivor of one of the sons of the prophets (IV, 196-197, 240). Obadiah descends from Eliphaz, one of the disputing friends of Job, whom legend makes into a prophet as well as the firstborn son of Esau (I, 422). Jonah becomes one of the most prominent of many thousands of disciples of Elisha (IV, 246). Micah had earlier numbered himself among the followers of Elijah (IV, 343).

Amóz, the father of Isaiah in the prophecy (Isa 1:1), becomes the prophet Amos (VI, 357). Isaiah's daughter marries King Hezekiah, who has forebodings about the future behavior of his sons, Rabshakeh and Manasseh. Although the first dies, Manasseh as king fulfills all the dread expectations of his father. To avoid having to witness his abominations, Isaiah, Micah, Joel, and Habakkuk flee Jerusalem. Manasseh succeeds in capturing Isaiah, whom he condemns to death. The prophet flees again and, for protection, is swallowed up by a cedar tree. Isaiah dies when the tree is sawn in pieces at the order of Manasseh, who is, after all, Isaiah's grandchild (IV, 277-279). Isaiah himself descends from the Tamar who confronted Judah and whose modesty was rewarded with a posterity that includes King David as well as the prophet (II, 33-34). Active in Jeremiah's lifetime, Zephaniah is one of the four prophets whom God commissions to proclaim punishment to the posterity of Lot— the others, Isaiah, Jeremiah, and Ezekiel (I, 257). Zephaniah is a great grandson of Hezekiah—hence related to Isaiah—and the teacher of Jeremiah (VI, 386, 388). Uriah, the prophet executed by King Jehoiakim, is a relative of Jeremiah (IV, 296). Both Jeremiah and Ezekiel claim descent from Rahab, and legend identifies Ezekiel's priest-father—(so Ezek 1:3)—as a prophet as well (VI, 371, 386). Daniel seeks advice from Ezekiel, who cites the authority of his teacher Isaiah (IV, 331). Habakkuk brings food to Daniel in Babylon, whose friends there include Haggai, Zechariah, and Malachi (IV, 348-349). Ezra is a disciple of Jeremiah's secretary, Baruch, who leads the exiles back only after Baruch's death (IV, 323). Joel is a son of Samuel (IV, 64-65).

One of the most important features of satiric self-presentation in the text of Hebrew prophecy and in legends about the prophets is the continuing aligning of the prophet with his ancestry in prophecy. Whenever the prophet speaks, he stands with the company of his prophetic forebears. Rhetorically, it is a powerful platform from which to speak. In concluding "The Muse of Satire," Maynard Mack draws on a phrase of Louis Bredvold's about "'the invisible church of good men' everywhere, 'few though they may be—for whom things matter.'"[61] Precisely. But that church is a community bound by shared value regardless of time and transcending the limits of time. In evoking echoes of their prophetic past, the Hebrew prophets repeatedly fashion and refashion small support groups from the past that carry their weight, authority, and assistance into contemporary danger. The technique is a very important part of prophetic, and I would add, satiric, self-presentation.

b.

> " . . . let each, sure enough, take the price of his
> blood; let his paleness / Be like a man's who steps on
> a snake, barefoot . . . . "   Juvenal, *Satire I*

On 18 December 1679, John Dryden was the victim of what Edward and Lillian Bloom call "one of the most notorious beatings in literary history."[62] A satiric target of Dryden's evidently retaliated. The danger everywhere feared in the rhetoric of satire had become a reality. To the best of my knowledge, however, the incident is unique. Not so among the Hebrew prophets. Yahweh sends Elijah into hiding (1 Kgs 17:3) shortly before the prophet's archenemy Jezebel is recorded as having "massacred the prophets of the LORD" (18:4, NEB). This "troubler of Israel," as Jezebel's husband King Ahab calls him (18:17, NEB), understandably fears for his life. Micaiah is struck in the face by the priest Zedekiah (22:24), and the physical

174

threats to Jeremiah need no rehearsing. Second Isaiah's "satire directed at the Babylonian imperial cult," speculates Blenkinsopp, "could not have been free of risk."[63] The most poignant feature of Jeremiah's story, for me, is that the text leaves Jeremiah in Egypt, that false assurance alliance with whom the prophet had steadfastly preached against. Jeremiah leaves the text with all the painful ambiguity and haunting irresolution of a missing person, a holocaust victim of sorts last seen heading in a direction that promises no hope.

If the prophets travel so often in the company of their prophetic forebears, as I have just insisted, they are merely seeking allies on a mission of confrontation. However intense and private their anxiety, the assumption of and need for public action and public utterance plays no small part in their fear of danger. Those convulsions so graphically limned by Jeremiah—

> O my bowels, my bowels! I writhe!
> O walls of my heart!
> My heart is in storm within me
> I cannot be still.

—move quickly to an awareness of the imminent public disaster apparent in "the trumpet blast / The battle shout . . . . / the standard, . . . [and] the blast of the horn" (Jer 4:19-20, AB).[64] The prophet's dangerous mission calls forth violent language; truculently persisted in misaction and misadventure, the prophet warns, will bring violent consequences. "Therefore have I lashed you through the prophets," Yahweh says through Hosea, "and torn you to shreds with my words" (Hos 6:5, NEB). In their translation of this passage, Andersen and Freedman transform the prophets themselves into weapons:

> That is why I hacked them with my prophets;
> I killed them with the words of my mouth. [Hos 6:5, AB]

Yahweh readily admits that he is sending his prophets on a dangerous mission: Ezekiel, for instance, who will "sit on scorpions" (Ezek 2:6, AB), or Jeremiah, who comes to warn of "poisonous snakes / That cannot be charmed away" (Jer 8:17, AB).

Yahweh, however, is himself a source of terror and danger. Ezekiel sees "a stormy wind" coming from the north, and "out of it—out of the fire—appeared something that looked like *hashmal*" (Ezek 1:4, AB), a word which Moshe Greenberg explains as "the heart of the vision of the Majesty . . . [which] later came to be regarded as endowed with holy and dangerous properties."[65] The call's source is more fearful than the audience to be warned, a point Yahweh makes specifically to Isaiah:

> You shall not say "too hard" of everything that this people calls hard; you shall neither dread nor fear that which they fear. It is the LORD of Hosts whom you must count "hard"; he it is whom you must fear and dread. [Isa 8:12-13, NEB]

The point is even more threateningly made to Jeremiah:

> Don't lose your nerve because of them,
> > Lest I shatter your nerve right before them. [Jer 1:17, AB]

Like Jonah, the prophet courts danger in either direction. There is no exit.

When the prophet projects himself, consequently, as a "censor . . . of good will . . . *forced* into action [Mack's emphasis]," to use Maynard Mack's phrase,[66] his compulsion rests as much in the fearful origins of his call as in anxiety about its necessary consequences. In describing this impulse, the image of fire, a consuming fire, comes to the foreground. Michael Fishbane points out that Jeremiah uses the image of fire

> to distinguish authentic prophetic speech from the slick-styled lingo of prophetic pretenders . . . . The true prophet . . . is consumed by the scorching power of his uncontainable task and bellows forth words which sear the security of the nation.[67]

Fire and heat dominate Ezekiel's account of his prophetic call (Ezek 1:4-15). A glowing coal touches Isaiah's lips (Isa 6:6-7). The LORD's voice in Amos scorches the shepherds' pastures and dries up the top of Mount Carmel (Amos 1:2). When Micah's God "walks on the heights of the earth / Beneath him mountains dissolve like wax before the fire. . ." (Mic 1:3, NEB). The anger of Nahum's God "pours out like a stream of fire, and the rocks melt before him" (Nah 1:6, NEB). These images of fiery consummation hint at the threat to the prophet himself, who must handle this flame. The curse of this situation, as Geoffrey

Hartman points out, the curse as always uttered by the word, "is the word itself, the violence done by it to the prophet. He feels it in his heart and bones as a burning fire."[68] While the prophetic "I," like the satiric, stands out prominently in a canvas that distinguishes him from the follies and abominations that threaten to overwhelm the picture, the prophet characteristically registers fear and hesitation about accepting a call to labor in a field of snakes.

The prophet's hesitation rings changes on Moses' "Send whom thou wilt" (Exod 4:13, NEB), i.e., send anyone but me. Isaiah pleads that he is "a man of unclean lips," no inconsiderable limitation in one called to utter (Isa 6:5, NEB). Amos is following the flock when the LORD takes him (Amos 7:15), snatched, as it were, into alternative service: the prophet as conscript. Jonah sets out, not for Nineveh, but for Tarshish "to escape from the LORD" (Jonah 1:3, NEB). The context of the call, furthermore, often implies other, less convulsive possibilities. If Juvenal, Horace, and Pope can turn to the safer, more profitable alternative of praising Caesar or reciting the familiar, Jeremiah and his kind make clear that professional and paid prophecy, merged with the institutions of temple and monarchy, afford a prophetic way out. Indeed, the Northern Kingdom's priest Amaziah suggests exactly such a career to Amos (Amos 7:12). That, however, is precisely the option that cannot be pursued. Neither prophet nor satirist can stay on good terms with the great. As Swift says in his *Verses*:

> With princes kept a due decorum,
> But never stood in awe before 'em.
> He followed David's lesson just,
> In princes never put thy trust.[69]

Jeremiah's reluctance to be a prophet is a significant feature of his self-presentation. Jonah flees from a single mission; Jeremiah seeks escape for a lifetime. He is staggered by the force of God's word (Jer 23:9), weary of the prophet's task (Jer 6:10-11), and, like Qoheleth and Job, disturbed by the success of the wicked (Jer 12:1-2). With its many voices and moods, the prophecy of Jeremiah assumes the form of a dialog in which the prophet argues with himself, with Yahweh, or with the Israelites.

177

He shares his people's sense of abandonment:

> "Is Yahweh not in Zion?
>> Is her King no longer there?" [Jer 8:19, AB]

Like Pope's invocation at the beginning of Book IV in *The Dunciad*, Jeremiah envisions only darkness that will encompass him as well:

> I saw the earth—lo, chaos primeval!
>> The heavens—their light was gone.
> I saw the mountains—and lo, they were quaking,
>> And all the hills rocked to and fro,
> I looked—and behold, no human was there,
>> And the birds of the skies had all flown.
> I looked—and behold, the tilled land was desert,
>> Its cities all lying in ruins—
> Before Yahweh,
>> Before his fierce anger [Jer 4:23-26, AB]

He chastises Yahweh for this call and for the sense of abandonment that has come with it: "For thy sake I suffer abuse" he pointedly reminds Yahweh, as he now asks for revenge: "Avenge me of those that harass me!" (Jer 15:15, AB).

Jeremiah's is a not untypical complaint of isolation as the result of the prophet's office. The prophetic text often brings out the personal sacrifice demanded by the response to God's call. As mentioned earlier, Hosea's marriage and resultant children enter the prophet's life only as puns or parables. Isaiah begets three children each of whose names reinforces a prophetic lesson (Isa 7:3, 7:14, and 8:2). The mourning and despair Ezekiel is ordered to withhold at his wife's death instructs the Judahites how to respond to the coming destruction of the Temple (Ezek 24:16-24). The unrelenting confining of the prophet and all the facets of his life to the word he preaches reinforces the sense of isolation which the rhetoric of prophetic self-presentation often employs. "Bitter, my spirit raging, overpowered by the hand of YHWH, I came to the exiles at Tel Abib," Ezekiel recalls, and "there I sat seven days, desolate among them" (Ezek 3:14-15, AB). Moshe Greenberg glosses the passage:

the tension between the task of the prophet and the retreat
into himself induced by exposure to the divine wrath led
immediately to a week-long lonely muteness; in modified form
the prophet's withdrawal continued for many years afterward.[70]

This passage, as Greenberg notes, has affinities with Jeremiah's own complaint about the isolating effect of his call:

> Not for me to sit with the crowd,
>   Laughing and merry.
> Gripped by thy hand I did sit all alone,
>   For with rage thou didst fill me. [Jer 15:17, AB]

Jeremiah too has been instructed to make major personal
sacrifices: "You are not to marry and have sons and daughters
in this place" (Jer 16:2). Prophet is wedded to his word, as poet
to his wit, but, for either, it is a sexless union: "What is this
Wit," Pope can ask, in the *Essay on Criticism*, "which must our
Cares employ? / The *Owner's Wife*, that *other Men* enjoy"
(Pope, p. 51, ll. 500-501, Pope's emphasis). The joy of uttering
God's word—

> There were thy words, and I ate them;
>   And it was my joy, my heart's delight,
> That I bore thy name, was thine.
>   O Yahweh, thou God of Hosts. [Jer 15:16, AB]

—has turned to ashes in his mouth:

> Why, O why, is my pain without end,
>   My wound ever worse, defying all cure?
> Ah, truly you are a dry wadi to me,
>   Whose waters have failed. [Jer 15:18, AB]

The Yahweh who enters this dialog promises renewed strength,
but only if the prophet repents these doubts of his call. Then he
will become "an impregnable wall of bronze" (Jer 15:19-21,
AB). Jeremiah sees himself as the continuing object of plot and
conspiracy—

> like an innocent lamb
> Led to the slaughter,
> Not knowing that it was against me
> They had hatched their plots. [Jer 11:19, AB]

—and projects himself into the mindset of those seeking his harm:

> They said [the prophet recounts], "Come! Let us lay plans against Jeremiah. For priestly instruction, and the counsel of wise men, and the prophetic word will never cease. Come, let us bring charges against him, and let us pay no heed to anything that he says." [Jer 18:18, AB]

Jeremiah knows, like Isaiah, that he is ridiculed:

> Who is it that the prophet hopes to teach
> [ask the drunken apers of Isaiah],
> to whom will what they hear make sense?
> Are they babes newly weaned, just taken from the breast?
> It is all harsh cries and raucous shouts,
> "A little more here, a little there!" [Isa 28:9-10, NEB]

He knows, like Ezekiel, that he is dismissed. More strenuously and more terrifyingly than any other of the prophets, Jeremiah registers the isolating consequences of a dedication to judgment, the bitterness at roads taken and not taken, the keenness of being ridiculed, and the savagery of demanding vindication:

> Let them that hound me be shamed—not *me*!
> Let it be their courage that snaps—not *mine* [AB emphasis]!
> Bring thou upon them the day of disaster!
> Break them, and break them again! [Jer 17:18, AB]

A Juvenalian outrage dominates this picture: horror at the abominations and bitter fearfulness about the call. Small wonder the prophet complains about being duped.

c.

" . . . with his stripes we are healed." Isa 53:5 (KJV)

The prophet's image as a reluctant scourge, terrified even by the impulse to censure, not only undercuts imputations of bitterness and malice but works as well with a more explicitly affirmative quality which he projects. The prophet pleads unwillingness also because he does not seek to inflict pain or effect violence. If these come, they come as necessary and deserved means of healing. Prophecy, thus, claims to be one of the healing arts, like satire, a moral potion, however disagreeable to drink. The promised healing assuages fear of the technique. The fire that consumes prophet and victim is also a cleansing fire. If the healing or refining fail of purpose, neither Yahweh nor his prophet is at fault. With vivid, strenuous language, reminiscent of Blake, Yahweh says to Jeremiah:

> "I have made you my people's assayer,
>   To observe and assay their conduct."
> They are all the most stubborn of rebels [Jeremiah counters],
>   Peddlers of slander,
>   Corrupt to the very last man.
> The bellows blow fiercely,
>   But the lead comes whole from the fire.
> It's useless to go on refining,
>   The wicked are not removed.
> Refuse silver men will call them,
>   Because Yahweh's refused them. [Jer 6:27-30, AB]

Isaiah too calls Yahweh's work a process of refinement—

> Once again I will act against you
> to refine away your base metal as with potash
>   and purge all your impurities . . . . [Isa 1:25, NEB]

—while Obadiah reverses the image of consuming fire into an enhancement of God's people and a means of destruction for their enemy:

> Then shall the house of Jacob be fire,
>   the house of Joseph flame,
>   and the house of Esau shall be chaff;
> they shall blaze through it and consume it,
> and the house of Esau shall have no survivor. [Obad 17-18, NEB]

Uttering the LORD's consolation and promise of a restored Jerusalem, Jeremiah transforms Yahweh's fury into "his heart's desire," scorching the wicked to effect healing and recovery (Jer 30:23-24, NEB).

Not only does a significant portion of the text of Jeremiah promise hope, consolation, and renewal, but does so with touching use of the language of healing:

> Yes, this is what Yahweh has said [the prophet affirms]:
> "Your hurt is mortal,

> Your wound past cure,
> No salve for your sore,
>   No healing for you . . . .
> Why cry o'er your hurt,
>   Your incurable pain? . . .
> Yes, cure I'll bring you,
>   Of your wounds I'll heal you—Yahweh's word—
> Because they called you, 'Outcast—
>   That Zion, for whom nobody cares!' " [Jer 30:12-17, AB]

Isaiah even reverses the use of legal form: the LORD encourages dispute with Israel now not to affirm destruction but the possibility of redemption. The victim can escape his doom:

> Come now, let us argue it out,
>   says the LORD.
> Though your sins are scarlet,
>   they may become white as snow;
>   though they are dyed crimson,
>   they may yet be like wool.
> Obey with a will,
> and you shall eat the best that earth yields. [Isa 1:18-19, NEB]

Virtually all the prophetic texts, indeed, affirm a promise of something better to come; a number of the texts, like Hosea, Second Isaiah, and Amos, conclude with such affirmation. Hosea promises: "the Israelites will return and seek Yahweh their God and David their king. And they will come trembling to Yahweh and his goodness at the end of the age" (Hos 3:5, AB). He concludes with Yahweh's promise to "heal their apostasy" and "love them generously" (Hos 14:5, AB). In Joel, consuming love triumphs over consuming anger—

> Then the LORD's love burned with zeal for his land,
>   and he was moved with compassion for his people. [Joel 2:18, NEB]

—and the prophet's particular perception becomes a widespread gift:

> your old men shall dream dreams
>   and your young men see visions. [Joel 2:28, NEB]

Even the stern Amos promises a never-to-be-shaken implanting in the land:

> Once more I will plant them on their own soil,
> and they shall never again be uprooted
>> from the soil I have given them. [Amos 9:15, NEB]

The saving potentialities of Yahweh's word occasion in the prophets an occasional buoyancy and vivacity of language not unlike the later affirmations of William Blake. The consoling Jeremiah anticipates a time when

> maidens shall dance and be gay,
> Youths and graybeards as well;
> For I'll turn their mourning to mirth,
>> Give them comfort and joy for their grief. [Jer 31:13, AB]

Zechariah's God pledges:

> Old men and old women will again sit
>> in the open places of Jerusalem,
>> each with a staff in hand because of great age.
> The open places of the city will be filled with boys and girls
>> playing in its open places. [Zech 8:5, AB][71]

This "Echoing Green" of the prophets admits no ominous, lurking shadows from a World of Experience. That dreadful time is past. Such powerful and graphic affirmations do much to project the prophet, not as a chastening scourge, but as an affirming healer. He insists that a more desirable future is possible. Jeremiah is called not only

> To uproot and tear down,
> To destroy and to raze,

but also "to build and to plant" (Jer 1:10, AB). Yahweh makes that clear in the very summoning of the prophet and in the statement of his mission.

The compellingly attractive image projected of the prophet by the positive nature of his objectives receives corollary support from an inescapable inference that emerges from the prophetic text: those who heed the word will gain. The prophet seeks to advantage others, not himself. However institutionally or traditionally warranted, the paid prophet, the prophet as retainer, is precisely the kind of prophet the likes of Amos or Hosea dissociate themselves from. The "written" prophets, and their immediate ninth-century forebears like Elijah and Elisha, always stand apart from the community of cultic prophets. However thorny a question it is to determine the cultic status of the classical or "written" prophets, a major reason for the difficulty in determining the question is the virtual absence of a cultic context for any of them. Explicitly or implicitly, these great prophets of Israel keep the retainer-prophets at arm's length.

In prophetic narrative, the dissociation goes back at least to the time of Elijah, and the prophet's disinterest in monetary gain appears in an incident recounted of Elijah's successor, Elisha. When Gehazi, the prophet's servant, seeks to advantage himself by taking from the cured leper Naaman some of what Elisha had refused as a gift, the prophet inflicts Naaman's leprosy upon Gehazi as a punishment (2 Kgs 5:15-27). Amos, as Bruce Vawter points out, appears to the high priest "like the other prophets with whom he was familiar and many of whom were in his stable for comfortable prophecies," a prophet Amaziah thought of "in conventional terms, of prophets who were in the hire of courts, sanctuaries, and the like, prophets for favorable oracles, who could be dismissed at will for their defects" (Amos 7:10-17).[72] Micah extensively attacks self-interested prophets "who promise prosperity in return for a morsel of food" (Mic 3:5, NEB). Malachi upbraids the priest who brings "a damaged victim to the LORD, though he has a sound ram in his flock" (Mal 1:14, NEB). The prophets not only question and chastise prophecy for profit; they repeatedly denounce the abuse of institutional status and privilege they find in priests and prophets alike. Hosea is critical of greedy and promiscuous priests (Hos 4:10) and aware of the infectious example of their behavior upon their own children (Hos 4:9). The prophets, on the contrary, seek no gain and flaunt no institutional privilege.

d.

"Your primary obligation
Lies in goodness of soul."   Juvenal, *Satire VIII*

The analyses so far of the prophet's evocation of his past, the fear of and reluctance about his calling, and the insistence on the finally healthful aims of his utterance demonstrate in the

Hebrew prophets that concern with favorably establishing one's character which Maynard Mack claims is an essential feature of satiric self-presentation. The current analysis, however, will show that the Hebrew prophets also project themselves as good or heroic men, very closely along the lines Mack discovers in the satirists. The prophet as naif will conclude this chapter.

In Mack's analysis, the good-man image projected by the satirist pictures him as a plain-living individual of high thinking, scornful of lies and slander and loving above all "the language of the heart." His taste is simple, his loyalty persistent, his formation along "the good old-fashioned ways," and his pieties natural.[73]

The Hebrew prophet projects a comparable image. His simplicity often distances him designedly from the insidiously corrupting influences of Temple and Court.[74] He shares the satirist's disdain for the courtiers of religion and politics, the retainers who frame their words to win the smiles and avoid the frowns of the great. On occasion, the prophet satirically contrasts the corruption of the metropolitan centers with the assumed simplicity of the country. Jeremiah, for instance, anticipates Juvenal's Umbricius in his desire to escape the corrupted and corruptions of the town:

> O that I had in the desert
>   A wayfarer's lodge,
> And so could leave my people,
>   Get away from them!
> For they're all adulterers,
>   A gang of crooks,
> They bend their tongue like a bow;
>   Lies and not truth prevail in the land.
> They proceed from evil to evil,
>   And know not Yahweh.
> Be on guard against one another!
>   Distrust every brother!
> For every brother's as crafty as Jacob,
>   Every friend a peddler of slander.
> Everyone cheats his neighbor,
>   Never speaking the truth.
> They've trained their tongues to falsehood,
>   Perverted, too weak to change.

> Wrong on wrong, deceit on deceit,
> They refuse to know Yahweh. [Jer 9:1-5, AB][75]

Zephaniah announces a doom which includes "all who ape outlandish fashions" and "all who dance on the temple terrace" (Zeph 1:8-9, NEB). The apparent provenance of the prophets as it emerges from the text reinforces the image of the prophet as a man of simple, unaffected character: Amos is the provincial, "a herdsman and a dresser of sycamore-figs" (Amos 7:14, NEB), put off by the style and antics of the wealthy and powerful in the Northern Kingdom and speaking for the dispossessed and the excluded; Micah, perhaps of the land himself, fiercely defends the rights of small farmers;[76] Jeremiah finds no religious integrity in high places (Jer 5:30-31). Like satire, prophecy also employs the contrast between urban (bad) and rural (good). Except for Isaiah, whose access to and familiarity with the centers of power pervades the text, a repeated feature of prophetic self-presentation is their sometimes even physically distancing themselves from Court and Temple, the "Town" of satirists like Pope, Swift (in self-styled exile in Dublin), and Waugh (no lover of London), which, in the tradition of satire, is repeatedly the center of corruption and folly. Horace and Juvenal are likewise pervaded with this anti-urban bias. Rural simplicity, directness, and wholesomeness contrast with the moral squalor of the city.

The tradition so often appealed to by the prophets also underscores the "good old-fashioned" formation which the good man projects. The prophet defends these old ways, he finds values in these old ways—a nostalgia of sorts, radical rather than sentimental in its effect. The complex present the prophet sees as an encrustation which has layered over basic yet demanding challenges of faith with religious minutiae and formalities and the cocksureness that comes from appealing to a lifeless and disembowelled tradition. The prophets see that Yahweh has become a fossilized God, appealed to formally rather than vitally. The prophet strips away these obfuscating layers of a dead tradition and demands dynamic, imaginative perception in its stead. In the words of biblical scholar R. B. Y. Scott, "The prophets bear witness to [God] as the great Intruder in human affairs."[77] John Bright observes that the prophets brought a new word "in its essence not new, but a very old word radically re-interpreted and adapted to the new situation," a word "rooted in the traditions of Israel's distant past."[78] When, consequently, they echo, assimilate, and allude to the prophetic past, the Hebrew prophets not only establish their authority but assert as well the demanding, dynamic qualities of the prophetic word, past and present. The "good old-fashioned way" is an exacting, but promising path:

> I will again make your judges what once they were
> [Yahweh promises through Isaiah]
> and your counsellors like those of old. [Isa 1:25, NEB]

The promise, however, makes clear that the real shadows and empty ghosts are the judges and counsellors of today.[79] Jeremiah passes on Yahweh's exhortation to

> Stand at the crossroads, and look;
> Ask for the ancient paths,
> Where the good way lies. That take,
> And find for yourselves repose. [Jer 6:16, AB]

Yahweh later remarks that his people have "stumbled from their way, / The Ancient trails" (Jer 18:15, AB). The prophetic text, consequently, is haunted by an exacting simplicity, the dictates of whose piety shatter the brittle and complicated fabric of ethical rationalization and ritual assurance. Basic decency is the need:

> Cease to do evil and learn to do right,
> pursue justice and champion the oppressed;
> give the orphan his rights, plead the widow's cause. [Isa 1:17, NEB]

Set aside, says Amos, the unwarranted confidence in "pilgrim feasts" or "sacred ceremonies." Forget the "songs" and "the music of . . . lutes." Instead, "Let justice roll on like a river / and righteousness like an ever-flowing stream" (Amos 5:21-24, NEB).

Nowhere does the prophet's challenge to the false confidence of a life-less tradition appear more prominently than in Jeremiah's Temple Sermon (Jer 7:1-34). Standing in the place that is the very embodiment of Judah's faith, the prophet excoriates a ritual assurance that disregards conduct while appealing to traditional status as a security:

> Reform the whole pattern of your conduct [Yahweh says], so
> that I may dwell with you in this place. Do not put your trust
> in that lie: "This is Yahweh's temple, Yahweh's temple!" No!
> Only if you really reform the whole pattern of your conduct—
> if you really behave justly one toward another, no longer op-
> press the alien, the orphan, and the widow [nor shed innocent
> blood in this place], nor follow other gods to your own hurt—
> only then can I dwell with you in this place, in the land that I
> gave to your fathers of old for all time to come. [Jer 7:3-7, AB]

Yahweh pointedly accuses his people:

> You think you can steal, murder, commit adultery, perjure
> yourselves, burn sacrifices to Baal, and follow other gods of
> whom you know nothing, and then come and stand before me
> in this house, which bears my name, and say, "We are
> safe!"—just so you can go right on doing all these abomina-
> tions? [Jer 7:9-10, AB][80]

The Temple has become the mere tomb of a dead faith. Ethical
responsibility is its living embodiment. Over and over again, the
Hebrew prophet emerges as the good man, urging decency,
despising false confidence, persistent in his loyalty to and
understanding of a past carried vitally into the contemporary,
and never blind to the elementary demands of piety and devotion. The Hebrew prophet is, indeed, the *vir bonus*.

e.

> "Whom shall I send? Who will go for me?"
> And I answered, "Here am I; send me." Isa 6:8 (NEB)

The most common role assumed by the prophet, however, is
that of defender of the city of God. The prophet is, above all,
the heroic man, be he alone or the challenging and representative voice of the faithful remnant. In this role he easily displays
qualities of the satirist as hero. Maynard Mack notices, first of
all, how the heroic voice in satire speaks with a sense of high
moral purpose.[81] If it seems exaggerated to infer the equivalence of satiric and divine voices in this mode, there is, after all,
Pope's boast in *Dialogue II* of the *Epilogue to the Satires*:

> Yes, I am proud; I must be proud to see
> Men not afraid of God, afraid of me.[82]

Jeremiah's enemies are God's enemies, an identification that pervades that prophetic text.[83] The satirist as hero, furthermore, couples "the discernment of evil" with "the courage to strike at it." In this role, "he never lets us forget we *are* at war; there *is* an enemy [Mack's emphasis]." However attractively disguised, the satirist is not taken in. Sporus, finally, is only one of the many shapes of Satan. The satirist as "public defender" confronts this serpent in the garden.[84]

That the prophet frequently assumes the heroic role derives to a great extent from the prevailingly Juvenalian quality of prophecy. In Israel or in Judah, catastrophe of incalculable dimensions is at hand, yet social injustice, ritual prostitution, and human sacrifice go on unchecked. "When was there ever a time more rich in abundance of vices?" the prophet can as cogently ask as Juvenal in *Satire I* (p. 20). The unspeakable abominations, however, go hand in hand with a false sense of security in privileged position which outrages the prophet as much as the satirist. The true Roman is as conspicuously absent as the true Israelite. The prophet's ridicule will thus prove doubly insulting and dangerous. In his satire of the high norm, to use Northrop Frye's classification, the prophet, as we have seen, defies "customary associations with things" that have provided an apparently stable base for interpreting the present and predicting the future.[85] As Ezekiel 16 so graphically illustrates, the prophet will insult the traditional securities of faith even with near-obscene reductiveness.[86]

The heroism demanded in such attacks appears as well in the imagery of weaponry and violence that pervades much prophecy and assumes particular importance in accounts of the prophet's call. "Gird up your loins," Yahweh orders Jeremiah, as he prepares him for battle:

> And I—see! I have made you today
> A fortified city,
>   An iron pillar,
> A wall of bronze
>   Against all the land;

> Against Judah's kings and princes,
>   Its priests and landed gentry.
> Attack you they will; overcome you they can't,
>   For I'm with you to come to your rescue—
>   Yahweh's word. [Jer 1:18-19, AB][87]

Hosea's words are weapons (Hos. 6:5). Isaiah's God has battered his people:

> Where can you still be struck
>   if you will be disloyal still?
> Your head is covered with sores,
>   your body diseased;
> from head to foot there is not a sound spot in you—
> nothing but bruises and weals and raw wounds
> which have not felt compress or bandage or soothing oil.
>   [Isa 1:5-6, NEB]

The prophet claims to have entered the war between good and evil, but with the historical consciousness—like Pope in his attack on Sporus—that evil is here and now, not an abstraction, and if the prophet finds evil in high places, then he will strike high. The involvement of the prophets in the events of their time, that historical awareness inescapably theirs, is the prophets' seeking, in Eliot's phrase, to redeem the time. That time is now. So Ezekiel is urged to courage—

> You, man, do not be afraid of them,
>   and of their words do not be afraid . . . . [Ezek 2:6, AB]

—and appointed watchman over Israel (3:16-21). The second of the accounts of this particular commissioning (Ezek 33:1-9) details extensively in military imagery the significance and responsibility of the task. As heroic defender of the city of God, the prophet and his word are the major weapons of the LORD. Prophecy is a call to battle.

f.

> What, said Amos, I a prophet? Nay, not that, nor a prophet's
> son neither; I am one that minds cattle, one that nips the
> sycamore-trees . . . .   Amos 7:14 (Knox)

If the prophet, however, is a good man called to the heroism of ethical warfare, can he also be a naif, one of the three roles Mack finds possible in the satirist's persona? A prevailing playfulness in this pose seems to render it almost totally unsuited for the direct and Juvenalian approach that dominates prophetic satire. Understatement doesn't seem to be the prophet's forte. According to Maynard Mack, the satirist as naif feigns an inability to fathom matters; he is puzzled by his involvement in the arts and especially in controversy; he offers joking explanations for persisting in his career; but, finally, "he makes us see the ulcer where we were accustomed to see the rouge. He is the child in the fairy story forever crying, 'But mamma, the king *is* naked [Mack's emphasis].'"[88]

Horace, Pope, and Geoffrey Chaucer stand out prominently as artists who have transformed themselves into shrewd eirons pretending a bafflement that exposes much vice and folly. Indeed, Chaucer-the-pilgrim provides an excuse a prophet can borrow: forgive my bluntness of speech, he says in *The General Prologue* to *The Canterbury Tales*, because I am only passing on to you the words of another. "My wit," after all "is short." His primary obligation is to render truthfully and faithfully the word as he has heard it. Jeremiah, on at least one occasion, claims unawareness of the hostility he has aroused:

> For I'd been like an innocent lamb
> Led to the slaughter,
> Not knowing that it was against me
> They had hatched their plots. [Jer 11:19, AB]

Coming from a prophet as relentless as Jeremiah in his attack on sacred, but admittedly, not well understood traditions, the remark seems inescapably disingenuous.

Although Moses is not one of the "written" prophets, the Deuteronomic reform that transformed him into Israel's prophet par excellence retains about him a most ironically intriguing feature—for a prophet: "O LORD, I have never been a man of ready speech," Moses begs off, "never in my life, not even now that thou hast spoken to me; I am slow and hesitant of speech." To this disclaimer of at least verbal skills, Yahweh responds by promising that Moses' brother Aaron "will do all the speaking to the people for you, he will be the mouthpiece. . . ." (Exod 3:10-

11, 16, NEB). The exchanges with Pharaoh that follow, however, ironically emphasize Moses' initiative and primacy in challenging the ruler of Egypt and his power to command Aaron. Most ironically, the verbal ineptitude disappears entirely in Moses' direct conversations with the LORD, dialogs in which Aaron does not participate at all. The man of plain and halting speech displays remarkable rhetorical power, even in the most august of presences. However momentarily playfulness enters into this picture, irony is certainly one of the prevailing features in the story of Moses as a prophet.

The "written" prophet most closely approximating this pattern is not Jeremiah but Amos. In a very real sense, Amos registers puzzlement at his involvement in controversy. He shifts abruptly from the present—"I am no prophet . . . nor am I a prophet's son"—to the past—"but the LORD took me as I followed the flock and said to me, 'Go and prophesy to my people Israel' [Amos 7:14-15, NEB]"—with a quick juxtaposition that reinforces the sense of the unexpected turn of events. God's unanticipated taking is the only explanation Amos finds for his suddenly finding himself immersed in the controversy that comes with prophetic function. Secondly, the mention of his background as "a herdsman and a dresser of sycamore-figs" suggests the at least verbal incompatibility with being a prophet. So Amos projects the image of a simple man in a text which, ironically, is a continuing demonstration of the rhetorical skills of its supposed farmer-author.[89]

Amos' disclaimer, finally, about being a prophet has ironic nuances. He is not, admittedly, denying that he is a prophet at all: he disclaims only being a hereditary prophet but makes clear he has been sent to prophesy. In denying that he is a *nabi*—the Hebrew word for prophet in this passage—or the son of a *nabi*, Amos nevertheless uses the verbal form of this word—*hitnabbe*—when he says he has been sent to prophesy. Is Amos subtly redefining prophecy here? Does he hint at a kind of prophecy new certainly to Amaziah, the Northern high priest who wants Amos to go back home to Judah. Like the Horace urged to write something safer, so Amos insists he will prophesy as Horace will write—*scribam*—but the mode will be radically redefined though the word remains the same. In this disclaimer that is and is not a disclaimer, Amos plays an eiron's role. Perhaps Jewish legend recognizes an element of play in Amos' denial of at least one kind of prophecy: he too has "an impediment in his speech,"[90] Moses-like in being devoid of any obvious verbal consequences.

These same Jewish legends recorded in Ginzberg, incidentally, considerably expand a humorous quality about the prophets, Elijah particularly. Elijah, for instance, uses his wit to bring a husband and wife back together again on good terms. He devises a ruse which enables the wife to spit in the eye of the rabbi whose lengthy sermon delayed her return home where she was denied entrance by her husband until she spat in the rabbi's face.[91] Elijah also uses his wit scatologically. Initially repulsed by the wealthier of two brothers, Elijah approaches the rich man a second time—again in disguise. The prophet takes advantage of the man's astonishment at the wealth his poor sibling has secured since his brother's kind treatment of the prophet-in-disguise. On this second occasion, the wealthy brother showers the prophet with all the food he can provide. More than delighted at the prospect of even more wealth, he hears the departing prophet's apparent blessing: "May the first thing you do have no end, until it is enough." Alas, his wife suggests that to be undisturbed in their unending counting of gold, "let us first attend to our most urgent physical needs." And that's what they do until they die.[92] Jewish legend says further that Elijah promised a great future in Paradise to two clowns who

> made it their purpose in life to dispel discontent and sorrow by their jokes and their cheery humor, and they used the opportunities granted by their profession to adjust the difficulties and quarrels that disturb the harmony of people living in close contact with each other.[93]

Frequent instances of quick wit, eiron-like triumph over the wealthy and powerful, and placing evildoers in ridiculous or demeaning situations run through these legends about Elijah. Often he achieves these victories in disguise, pretending to be something less than he is. The Elijah of legend comes close to being a Horace among the prophets.[94]

Although physical disguise is not a technique used by or associated with the "written" prophets, a masked appearance does sometimes figure in narratives about earlier prophets. Ahab, for instance, is tricked into condemning himself by a disguised prophet (1 Kgs 20:35-43). A more common disguise used by the prophets, however, is the use of the apparently innocuous tale or artifact. The prophet shrewdly fashions a verbal trap, a story that figuratively parallels criminal or vicious behavior in the very person whose attention the prophet is simultaneously engaging and distracting with the story. In the legal fashion not uncommon in the prophets, the story is presented as a case about which the unwitting but intended victim is asked to utter a judgment. The judgment, of course, becomes a self-condemnation. Nathan the prophet traps David with the case of the rich man who steals the poor man's one prized ewe (2 Sam 12:1-14). The David angered at this injustice condemns his own vicious murder of Uriah, husband of the Bathsheba he has taken to bed. Isaiah's love song of the vineyard whose owner will destroy it for its unfruitfulness (Isa 5:1-6) quickly makes its point:

> The vineyard of the LORD of Hosts is Israel,
> and the men of Judah are the plant he cherished. [Isa 5:7, NEB]

The prophets also use apparently innocent artifacts: a plumbline in Amos (Amos 7:7-9); a linen waistcloth or a wine jar or a visit to a potter's house in Jeremiah (Jer 13:1-11, 13:12-14, 18:1-12). These apparently harmless things quickly take on condemnatory meaning; they are epiphanic moments in the prophetic text in which apparently insignificant minutiae of daily life carry a dreadful freight of coming judgment.

If the pose of the ingenu or naif, finally, achieves satirical effect by showing the naif unable to accept certain values because he stands outside the frame of reference that gives those significance, the prophets' attacks on the false gods of Israel and Judah sometimes convey the shattering effect of "But mamma, the king is naked." Where others see phallic divinities, Hosea sees only wood and a staff (Hos 4:12); Second Isaiah ridicules the goldsmith called in "to make a god," who neither budges from where he is set, nor answers when he is spoken to (Isa 46:6, AB); for others, what ghosts and familiar spirits provide is guidance: for First Isaiah they only "squeak and gibber" (Isa 8:19, NEB); the worshipped false gods of the Judahites are for Jeremiah nothing but an artisan's handiwork, as mute as "scarecrows in a cucumber patch—can't talk!" and invalids as well: "Have to be carried—can't walk!" (Jer 10:4-5, AB). In deliberately distancing themselves from this falsity, the prophets highlight the ulcers under the rouge. Unlike the boy in the story, however, they know exactly why this false perception has arisen. In legend and in the text of prophecy, the Hebrew prophet does on occasion display the delightful and surprising role of the naif. A very limited role admittedly, but it is not altogether lacking. Its presence among the Hebrew prophets, however, reinforces the awareness that the text of Hebrew prophecy, whose criticism is often satiric, shows careful attention to the construction of a prophetic persona very much like the persona of the satirist. The Hebrew prophet often wears the satirist's mask.

EPILOGUE

"Sing a song of derision
to this people of rebels . . . ."
Ezek 24:3 (NEB)

Privy to a world unseen by mere physical vision, the Hebrew prophet penetrates the apparent but deceptive stability of the space-time dimension with keen imaginative power. The prophet is thus necessarily the artist, for his utterance and his text incarnate his vision: "the poetic work before us," says Walter Brueggemann of the text of Jeremiah, "is knowingly crafted."[1] The prophet's imagination, however, does not often take him to Keats' "realms of gold." He travels, rather, in regions of rust, fields of decay, itineraries useful for their reminder of the darker, ambiguous, and discomfiting qualities of imaginative insight. No wonder Northrop Frye reasserts a centuries-old awareness that "the prophets, explorers of the spiritual world, are notoriously unwelcome in their own countries."[2] However disturbing this imaginative insight for seer and hearer alike, the insight simultaneously establishes the prophet as artist for—Frye again—"the fully imaginative man is ... a visionary whose imaginative activity is prophecy and whose perception produces art."[3] Like the satirist, however, the prophet frequently takes the infernal route to the divine, to the ideal: Dante visits the Inferno before he arrives in Paradise.

But unlike the tragic or comic poet, frequently securing distance through a dramatic medium, or the lyric or elegiac poet, moving to the soothing, the reassuring, or the exulting, the prophet as poet enters with striking immediacy of comment and context: this enemy, this ploy, this abomination, this corrupted priesthood, and the like. Like the satirist, the prophet speaks to yet beyond his time. His damning perception is for a never-ending now. No wonder then that he seeks support among his contemporaries and fashions himself according to prophets of old. No wonder that his message tells us not only what he utters but who he is and what he is like, for his character is the only credentials he bears. So he relentlessly strips away the comfortable bric-à-brac of human and physical temples, the ever-satisfying gewgaws that adorn edifices of complacency and self-assurance. And, as I hope this study has shown, the prophet often shatters the stillness of these now hollow shells with the mocking laughter of God.

NOTES

BIBLIOGRAPHY

INDEXES

NOTES

References, unless otherwise specified: to Horace, *Horace's Satires and Epistles*, tr. Jacob Fuchs, intro. William S. Anderson (1977); to Juvenal, *The Satires of Juvenal*, tr. Rolfe Humphries (1958); to Alexander Pope, *Poetry and Prose of Alexander Pope*, ed. Aubrey Williams (1969); to Jonathan Swift, *Gulliver's Travels and Other Writings*, ed. Louis A. Landa (1960). For publication details, see the Bibliography.

NOTES TO PREFACE

[1]Northrop Frye, *Fearful Symmetry: A Study of William Blake* (1962), p. 201. (Hereafter referred to as *Symmetry*.)

[2]See *Symmetry*, pp. 194-201.

[3]See Northrop Frye, *The Great Code: The Bible and Literature* (1982), pp. 125-129, and *Words with Power: Being a Second Study of the Bible and Literature* (1990).

[4]See Robert Alter, *The Art of Biblical Poetry* (1985), pp. 141-151.

[5]See *Tragedy and Comedy in the Bible*, ed. J. Cheryl Exum (= *Semeia* 32), 1984. Esp. 73-75 (from Martin Buss, "Tragedy and Comedy in Hosea"), p. 83 (where Gottwald, in "Tragedy and Comedy in the Latter Prophets," speaks of prophetic books as "mixtures of genres"), p. 87 (where Gottwald, in effect, describes the "critical laughter"—satire?—of the prophets), and p. 107 (where respondent Yair Zakowitch speaks of "the terms comedy and tragedy" as "alien to the Bible and its sphere of origin."

[6]See *On Humour and the Comic in the Hebrew Bible*, eds. Yehuda T. Radday and Athalya Brenner (1990). (Hereafter referred to as *Humour*.) Some of the essays which appeared earlier and elsewhere I had already been familiar with.

[7]Athalya Brenner and Yehuda T. Radday, "Between Intentionality and Reception: Acknowledgement and Application (A Preview)," in *Humour*, pp. 15, 18.

[8]Athalya Brenner, "On the Semantic Field of Humour, Laughter and the Comic in the Old Testament," in *Humour*, p. 42.

[9]R. P. Carroll, "Is Humour Also Among the Prophets?" in *Humour*, pp. 169, 177, 184, 188, 183. (Hereafter referred to as Carroll.)

[10]Carroll, p. 169.

[11]Carroll, p. 188.

[12]See Martin Grotjahn, "Beyond Laughter: A Summing Up," in Robert W. Corrigan, *Comedy: Meaning and Form*, 2nd ed. (1981), p. 181.

[13]Carroll, p. 169.

[14]See p. 35. Heschel's comment is in *The Prophets* (1971), II, 59.

[15]Carroll, p. 186. A year later Chaucer scholar R. K. Root was raising questions about the moral propriety of things like *The Miller's Tale* and wondering whether *The Canterbury Tales* wouldn't have been a greater work without such an artistic and moral lapse on Chaucer's part. Since seven of the twenty-two completed *Tales* are in this vein, Chaucer obviously lapsed often. See R. K. Root, *The Poetry of Chaucer* (1906), p. 176.

Carroll is likewise unaware of issues raised by the large proportion of satire implicitly acknowledged in his essay. He notes, for example, the "xenophobia and vilification of foreign nations" which inform the oracles against the nations and "provide some black humour in the prophetic books." I agree. He fails to note, however, that his three examples constitute sizeable chunks of the prophetic texts cited: eleven chapters in Isaiah, six chapters in Jeremiah, and eight chapters in Ezekiel. That's a lot of "black humour." See Carroll, p. 183.

[16]Carroll, p. 182. He claims that the "strong sense of the ridiculous in many of the sayings of Isaiah . . . reflects more the negative aspect of humour than its positive side."

[17]One consequence of this hope affects the documentation. Where possible, I cite reliable, accessible editions of the satires I discuss rather than definitive editions, certainly more authoritative, but less handy and more expensive.

[18]I rely very heavily, but not exclusively, on the Anchor Bible commentaries. Except for Amos, I have used Anchor Bible translations of the prophets where available. Otherwise, the New English Bible, for the most part. All of this reflects a literary scholar's biases about the sound of English. An explanation of how I identify the translation used appears in "A Note on Biblical Citations" on p. 17.

NOTES TO CHAPTER 1:
PROPHECY AND SATIRE

[1]*The Satires of Juvenal*, tr. Rolfe Humphries (1958), pp. 176, 175. (Hereafter referred to as Juvenal.)

[2]Michael Patrick O'Connor, "The Weight of God's Name: Ezekiel in Context and Canon," *The Bible Today*, 18/1 (1980), p. 33. (This

article is hereafter referred to as O'Connor.)

[3]John L. McKenzie, S.J., "The Literary Characteristics of Genesis 2-3," *Theological Studies*, 15 (1954), p. 572.

[4]G. L. Hendrickson, for example, asserts that when Quintilian says

> *satura tota nostra est* he means that special type of literature created by Lucilius, dominated by a certain spirit, clothed in a certain metrical form, fixed by the usage of a series of canonical writers, and finally designated by a name specifically Latin, is Roman and not Greek. And in this sense [Hendrickson concludes] the correctness of [Quintillian's] statement requires no qualification.

See "*Satura Tota Nostra Est*," in *Satire: Modern Essays in Criticism*, ed. Ronald Paulson (1971), p. 48. Norman Knox claims that "behind the recent notoriety [about all kinds of irony] is a long, involved, and sometimes important career which began in the age of Socrates." See *The Word Irony and Its Context, 1500-1755* (1961), p. vii.

[5]With the exception of Deutero-Zechariah (i.e., 9-14), which may be as late as the third century BC, 400 BC seems a frequently assumed terminus for the text of the fifteen canonical Hebrew prophets.

[6]James S. Ackerman, "Jonah," in *The Literary Guide to the Bible*, eds. Robert Alter and Frank Kermode (1987), pp. 234, 242. This collection hereafter referred to as *The Literary Guide to the Bible*.

[7]In placing strong emphasis on the conscious decision to write satire (understood as a literary term), Jack M. Sasson far too simply and confidently dismisses the possibility of satire in the Hebrew Bible. Do the Hebrew writers intend to write satire? Probably not. Do they intend to ridicule? Repeatedly. Sasson, I believe, confuses the two questions, the second much more complex than the first. The Hebrew Scriptures repeatedly engage in ridiculing criticism which I call satire. See AB: Jonah, pp. 331-334.

[8]AB: Genesis, pp. xxviii-xxix; 205-213.

[9]AB: Esther, p. liii.

[10]Robert C. Elliott, *The Power of Satire: Magic, Ritual, Art* (1966), pp. 66-78, esp. pp.67-68. (Hereafter cited as Elliott.)

[11]Elliott, pp. 67-68.

[12]See "Psalms," in NEB, p. 569.

[13]See AB: Psalms II, p. 269.

[14]Mitchell Dahood observes: "The moral inability of the Israelites to sing hymns of praise in Babylonia put them in a class with the denizens of the nether world whose keenest sorrow was their inability to sing Yahweh's praises." See AB: Psalms III, p. 270, n. to v. 2, *we hung up*.

[15]The prophecy of Jeremiah—except for the historical note that forms Chapter 52—concludes with a comparable celebration of the anticipated violent, destructive fall of Babylon: the disgrace and dismay of its gods Bel and Marduk (Jer 51:2, AB); the invective of Yahweh against Babylon as "Sir Pride," who "shall stumble and fall" (50:31-32, AB); praise of the Yahweh who directs "a sword on her boasters" (50:35, AB); sneering at her images, "lifeless things, . . . a ridiculous joke" (51:17-18); in fine:

> Heaven and earth shall exult over Babylon,
>> They and all that is in them,
> When there comes from the north upon her
>> The destroyers—Yahweh's word. [51:48, AB]

As in Psalm 137, the efficacious principle of this deeply sought revenge is clear:

> Remember Yahweh from afar,
>> Let Jerusalem come to your mind. [51:50, AB]

And like Psalm 137, Jeremiah's concluding curse against Babylon is studded with sharp recollections of the shame, disgrace, and gloating suffered in the Fall of Jerusalem and the subsequent captivity and exile. See AB: Jeremiah, p. 360.

[16]Archilochus' curse is the following:

> [Let him go to sea, find storm and wreck, and be]
> . . . driven ashore by the waves
> at Salmydessus,
> and may the wiry-haired barbarian Thracians
> seize him bereft of kin and friends,
> where he will suffer great calamities;
> chewing upon the bread of slaves,
> he will shudder stiff-frozen with cold,
>> and let him be befouled
> in a gangle of seaweed from the roaring sea,
> his teeth chattering, as he lies shattered like a dog,
> his mouth stuffed in the sand
> by the water-side, spitting out the brackish sea.
> This exquisite sight would I be enraptured to behold,
> for he abused me and trampled underfoot our bond—
> he, who formerly was my friend.

This translation, by A. L. Motto and J. R. Clark, appears in Satire: That Blasted Art, eds. John R. Clark and Anna Motto (1973), p. 137. The brackets are in the original. A priest and servant of the War God, Ares,

Archilochus obviously fashioned his own appropriate psalms.

[17]See AB: Psalms III, p. 269. In another incident, Gabriel Josipovici mentions that the concluding references to Sisera's mother and her attendant ladies (Judg 5:28-31) are commonly interpreted as a gloating over them because Sisera has brutally fallen victim to the woman Jael, who drove a nail through his head. The gloating, Josipovici insists, "has of course to be understood in the light of primitive cultures, since civilized people cannot condone such sentiments." See Gabriel Josipovici, *The Book of God: A Response to the Bible* (1988), p. 129. (Hereafter cited as Josipovici.)

[18]NEB, p. 628, n. to Ps 83:12-19.

[19]See in particular Pss 12:8; 13:2-4; 22:17; 25:2-3; 37:12-13; 38:15-16; 39:8; 40:14-16; 42:10; 44:10-17; 52:6-7; 55:12; 58:10-11; 59:8-15; 63:11; 64; 69:11-12; 70; 71:13, 24; 74:10-11, 18-19, 22; 79:3-4; 80:6; 92:11; 119:42, 51; 123:4; 139:22.

Formally, virtually all these psalms, according to the NEB, are laments, the largest single group in the Psalter. In the individual laments, which most of these are, "the underlying motive for the prayer," according to Lawrence E. Toombs, "is not the disaster itself but the alienation from God which it produces." In the lament, furthermore, "the victim often denounced his enemies in vigorous terms and heaped terrible curses upon them . . . in the traditional language of Near Eastern denunciations." Toombs explains too that "the violence of the words is due to the fact that in the pagan cultures in which this literary form originated the enemies were often sorcerers attempting to destroy the sufferer by magical means." See Toombs, "The Psalms," in *The Interpreter's One-Volume Commentary on the Bible*, ed. Charles M. Laymon (1971), p. 257. (Hereafter cited as Toombs.)

[20]See Mark Van Doren and Maurice Samuel, *The Book of Praise: Dialogues on the Psalms*, ed. Edith Samuel (1975), pp. 101, 109-128. They draw attention here to a verse from Proverbs—"Death and life are in the power of the tongue" (18:21, KJV)—which nicely epitomizes the central thesis of Robert Elliott's book. They note also that "one of the worst things that the wicked man does . . . is that he takes away the self-confidence and the assurance of the decent man," Toombs' point (above, n. 19) about the emotional prompting of the lament. See pp. 101, 108.

[21]I thank my wife, Barbara, for pointing out this disturbingly triumphant note in perhaps the most familiar and best loved of the 150 psalms.

[22]See Robert Alter, *The Art of Biblical Narrative* (1981), p. 49. Two other variants involve Rachel, the wife Jacob first wanted, and

Hannah, mother of the prophet Samuel. Rachel, remember, had to wait an additional seven years for her marriage to Jacob, and into a situation fraught with the possible perils of sibling rivalry, "when Rachel saw that she had failed to bear Jacob children, she became envious of her sister [Leah]" (Gen 30:1, AB). Elkanah's wife Hannah resents both the other wife, Penninah, and her children because "her rival," as Penninah is called, "provoked and tormented [Hannah] for her childlessness" (1 Sam 1:1-8, AB). Childlessness is a curse and reproach in the Hebrew Scriptures: all of Job's sons and daughters die in a violent storm (Job 1:18-19), and when Job is restored to fortune

> he had twice . . . seven sons and three daughters . . . . In all the land no women were to be found as beautiful as Job's daughters and their father gave them inheritance among their brothers. After this Job lived 140 years and saw his sons and grandsons to four generations. So Job died, old and satisfied with life. [42:13, 15-17, AB]

[23]Of the reference to "outrage," E. A. Speiser notes: "The Code of Hammurabi states explicitly that a slave girl who was elevated to the status of concubine must not claim equality with her mistress . . . . Sarah is thus invoking her legal rights, and she holds her husband responsible . . . for the offense." See AB: Genesis, pp. 117-118, n. to v. 5, *This outrage.*

[24]See Elliott, p. 68.

[25]In John Milton's *Samson Agonistes*, Manoa, Samson's father, says in his last remarks:

> Nothing is here for tears, nothing to wail
> Or knock the breast, no weakness, no contempt,
> Dispraise, or blame, nothing but well and fair,
> And what may quiet us in a death so noble.

See John Milton, *Samson Agonistes*, in *The Student's Milton*, ed. Frank Allen Patterson, rev. ed. (1933), p. 438, ll. 1721-1724. Milton's hero is keenly aware of the humiliation of his captivity by the Philistines. The most eloquent tribute to Saul's heroism appears in David's lament, 2 Samuel 1:17-27 (A comparison between Samson's fate and Psalm 137 also appears in Josipovici, p. 124.).

[26]P. Kyle McCarter, Jr., speculates that "Matthew may have had the death of Ahitophel in mind when he fashioned his report of the suicide of Judas (Matt 27:5)" since major motifs in the earlier account "are all there in Matthew." Furthermore, "Gethsemane, where Jesus was betrayed, cannot have been far from the place on the Slope of Olives where David stood when he learned that Ahitophel had be-

trayed him." See AB: II Samuel, p. 389, n. to v. 23.

[27]See "General Introduction," in AB: Proverbs and Ecclesiastes, p. xvi. Major wisdom writings in the Hebrew Scriptures are Proverbs, Ecclesiastes, and Job, as well as Psalms and the Song of Songs. The Wisdom of Ben Sira (i.e., Ecclesiasticus) and The Wisdom of Solomon are extra-canonical. In concluding his analysis of the canonicity of the Wisdom of Ben Sira among the Jews, Alexander Di Lella says: ". . . the rabbis, the successors of the Pharisees, excluded [it] from the Jewish canon late in the first century A.D., but they nonetheless continued to quote the book, on occasion, paradoxically, even as Sacred Scripture." See "Canonicity of the Book and Place in the Canon," in AB: Wisdom of Ben Sira, p. 20.

[28]See Peter Green, "Introduction," in Juvenal, *The Sixteen Satires*, tr. Peter Green, rev. ed. (1974), pp. 13, 29. (Hereafter cited as Green.) Samuel Johnson's imitation of Juvenal's *Satire III*, "London," provides the forceful line "SLOW RISES WORTH BY POVERTY DE-PRESS'D," which Johnson himself capitalized. See "London," in Samuel Johnson, *Poems*, (The Yale Edition, Volume VI), eds. E. L. McAdam, Jr., and George Milne (1964), p. 56, l. 177. (Hereafter referred to as Johnson, *Poems*.) Johnson's famous letter to the Earl of Chesterfield, 7 February 1755, draws much of its strength from Johnson's dignified response to neglect from one of the wealthy and powerful.

[29]A comparable reversal occurs in the Wisdom of Solomon, where the "oppressors" who "made light of [the just man's] sufferings" will say:

> This was the man whom we once held in derision
> and for a byword of reproach, fools that we were;
> his life we accounted madness,
> and his end without honor. [5:4, AB]

[30]In Alexander Pope's *Dunciad* one of the most treasured awards granted by the Goddess Dulness to the fools who serve her cause is precisely "Want of Shame." See the "Argument" to Book IV, p. 354.

[31]Again from the male point of view, the Book of Proverbs affords a similar warning in 5:15-19. In his own "Proverbs of Hell," William Blake, it seems to me, was specifically answering these verses with his own "The Cistern contains; the fountain overflows." See *The Poetry and Prose of William Blake*, ed. Geoffrey Keynes (1956), p. 184.

[32]The assumed emphasis on social propriety certainly spurs much of Blake's satire on the Book of Proverbs. But R. B. Y. Scott

succinctly and, I think, convincingly challenges readings of that sort. See "Religious and Ethical Teachings of the Book of Proverbs," in AB: Proverbs and Ecclesiastes, pp. 22-27. And Qoheleth's whole point in Ecclesiastes, after all, is that wisdom does not confer happiness.

[33] Marvin Pope explains: "The figure here [i.e., Satan] is not the fully developed character of the later Jewish and Christian Satan or the Devil," but rather "a kind of spy roaming the earth and reporting to God on the evil he found therein." The Satan, from *satan*, to accuse, thus becomes an "enemy and accuser" of human beings. See AB: Job, p. 10, n. to *the Satan*.

[34] Eliphaz later reveals a scarcely more edifying view of God:

> Even his angels he distrusts,
> The heavens are not pure in his sight.
> How then one loathsome and foul,
> Man who gulps evil like water? [15:15, AB]

[35] See Moshe Greenberg, "Job," in *The Literary Guide to the Bible*, p. 296.

[36] Marvin Pope does not discount the possibility that Job's prosperity attracted not only his relatives but "fair-weather friends" as well. See AB: Job, p. 291, n. to v. 11.

[37] See *Nelson's Complete Concordance of the* Revised Standard Version Bible, comp. John W. Ellison (1957), *passim*.

[38] R. B. Y. Scott advances at least eight explanations of suffering in the Hebrew Bible and offers examples of each: retributive, disciplinary, probationary, temporary or only apparent, inevitable, necessarily mysterious, haphazard and morally meaningless, and vicarious. See *The Way of Wisdom in the Old Testament* (1971), pp. 145-147.

[39] See Jonathan Lamb's discussion of Edward Young's paraphrasing of the Book of Job in "Research Reports, VII—Job, Epitaphs, and Blake's Illustrations," *The Clark Newsletter: Bulletin of the UCLA Center for 17th- and 18th-Century Studies*, 16 (Spring 1989), p. 4.

[40] St. Thomas Aquinas, for example, asserts that justice "denotes a kind of equality." See *The Summa of St. Thomas Aquinas*, trs. Father of the English Dominican Province (1947), II-II (i.e., the Second Part of the Second Part), Q. 57, Art. 1, II, 1431. Samuel Johnson's *A Dictionary of the English Language* defines revenge as the "return of an injury," as "the passion of vengeance; desire of hurting one from whom hurt has been received." He adds this distinction: "*Revenge* is an act of passion; *vengeance* of justice. Injuries are *revenged*, crimes are *avenged*." However, Johnson concludes, "This distinction is perhaps not always preserved."

[41]See David B. Morris, "The Muse of Pain: *An Epistle to Dr. Arbuthnot* and Satiric Reprisal," in *Alexander Pope: the Genius of Sense* (1984), pp. 214-240. (Hereafter referred to as Morris.)

[42]Morris, p. 231.

[43]Sporus, as Suetonius notes, was the boy Nero had castrated and turned into a wife. Even Nero was not able to deprive the Romans of a sense of humor, for Suetonius concludes this episode by noting: "A rather amusing joke is still going the rounds: the world would have been a happier place had Nero's father Domitius married that sort of wife." See *The Twelve Caesars*, tr. Robert Graves (1957), p. 223.

[44]Morris, pp. 215, 217-219, 223-224. For Mack's essay see *Yale Review* 41 (1951-1952), 80-92. (Hereafter referred to as Mack.) Northrop Frye, of course, points to the satirist's predilection for the obscene and the scatalogical in what Frye calls "the third phase of satire, the satire of the high norm." See "The Mythos of Winter: Irony and Satire," in *Anatomy of Criticism: Four Essays* (1968), pp. 234-236.

[45]I discuss the presence in the Hebrew prophets of what Frye calls "satire of the high norm" in Chapter 3, below.

[46]Morris, pp. 224-227.

[47]For an analysis of the satire and irony in this lament see Chapter 3, below. Robert Alter offers this same lament to instance "the splendid excess of the historical occasion" where the victim of prophetic satire "occasions a mythological scale of mimicry." This expansion of the immediate subject into mythic status is exactly what Maynard Mack sees in Pope's creation of Sporus in the *Epistle to Dr. Arbuthnot*, pp. 207-208, ll. 305-333. See *The Art of Biblical Poetry* (1985), pp. 146-151; and Mack, 92. I find it revealing that Alter's only discussion of satire in the Hebrew Scriptures occurs in his discussion of prophecy.

[48]Morris, pp. 238-240; Alexander Pope, *The Iliad of Homer: Books X-XXIV*, ed. Maynard Mack (Volume VIII of The Twickenham Edition), pp. 141-142, n. to l. 779. In this instance, by the way, Pope is quoting the KJV.

I do have some reservations with Morris' otherwise compelling analysis. First of all, rhetorical and structural analyses do not deny the disturbing force Morris finds in something like the Sporus sketch. Maynard Mack, for example, not only admits that Pope "passionately disliked" Hervey but insists that "we may justly infer that personal animus entered *powerfully* [my emphasis]" into the motivation of the Sporus sketch. See Mack, 92. But Mack proceeds to make a connection which, I think, Morris obscures: precisely because the satirist convincingly channels his animus into and through moral purpose the lines maintain their power. What we read is not undisciplined rage, but righteous and sometimes fearful indignation. As David Worcester convincingly puts it: "Satire is the engine of anger, rather than the direct expression of anger." See *The Art of Satire* (1960), p. 18.

The point, curiously enough, finds substance in the twentieth-century critical reputation of Juvenal, who, Morris points out, taught the eighteenth century "the validity and power of satirical anger." See Morris, p. 233. Juvenal's failure to convince our time of his moral seriousness, however, has led some critics to regard him as an excellent technician at best or a flimsy, limited, and superficial moralist. For the first view, see H. A. Mason, "Is Juvenal a Classic?" in *Satire: Critical Essays on Roman Literature*, ed. J. P. Sullivan (1968), pp. 93-176. For the second view see Green, pp. 23-24, or Niall Rudd, "Dryden on Horace and Juvenal," in *The Satires of Horace* (1982), pp. 272-273.

[49]See Toombs, p. 257.

[50]Marvin H. Pope's notes on Job's final oath repeatedly bring out the legal character of this climactic chapter. See AB: Job, pp. 199-209.

[51]See Gene M. Tucker, *Form Criticism of the Old Testament* (1971), pp. 66-67. Tucker quotes Micah in the RSV. The brackets in the passage are Tucker's.

[52]See AB: Jeremiah, p. 15, n. to v. 9, *state my case*. John Bright notes here: "The picture of Yahweh making a *rib* against his people occurs repeatedly in the prophetic books."

[53]See Elliott, p. 285. Theodor Gaster explores some of the beliefs underlying the episode of Balaam in *Myth, Legend, and Custom in the Old Testament* (1975), I, 303, where he notes: "Curses are considered to work more effectively if they are uttered by someone who is habitually en rapport with superior beings and who is versed in the appropriate techniques," eventually, the satirist and the prophet. Johannes Lindblom speaks similarly:

> The prophetic word was thought of as charged with energy and power. The prophetic word was an *effective* and a creative word . . . . In the thought of ancient Israel the spoken word was also a deed. The Hebrew word *dabar* often does duty for action as well as for word . . . . This is the reason why prophets who announced prosperity or success were highly appreciated and favoured, while prophets who foretold ill fortune were feared and hated.

He illustrates this last point by referring to Ahab's remarks about Micaiah in 1 Kings 22. See *Prophecy in Ancient Israel* (1965), pp. 51-52.

The evolution in society of the curse into law and in religion into vow and the prayer has intriguing consequences on the structure of prophecy and satire. Although predominantly censorious or negative, both can and do include affirmation of ideals and consoling assurances. Even if the assurance in a given prophetic text is a later addition, the overall effect of the structure remains the same: as evolved forms of the power of the word, curse and blessing appear in both. Consider Samuel Johnson's *Vanity of Human Wishes*, very biblical in its texture, as a quasi-prophetic statement. After more than three hundred lines indicting the folly of recklessly pursued human desire, the poem concludes (ll. 343-368) with an exceptionally powerful affirmation of the happiness available to any human being who disciplines and rectifies the energies of emotion and desire. Like a prophetic consolation, "celestial Wisdom calms the mind, / And makes the happiness she does not find." See Johnson, *Poems*, pp. 107-109.

[54] Morris, p. 238. No one will accuse me, I trust, of implying that prophecy is only "literary discourse," but it is with the language of prophecy that I am concerned.

[55] Abraham J. Heschel, *The Prophets* (1971), II, 59. (Hereafter referred to as Heschel.)

[56] See AB: Ezekiel, p. 135. This divine gloating occurs despite the threat that "the house of Israel . . . shall fall by the sword by famine and by plague." Greenberg is citing Deut 28:63.

[57] See above, p. 204, n. 15.

[58] See Herbert Marks, "The Twelve Prophets," in *The Literary Guide to the Bible*, pp. 216, 223, and Geoffrey Hartman, "The Poetics of Prophecy," in *High Romantic Argument: Essays for M. H. Abrams*, ed. Lawrence Lipking (1981), p. 18.

[59] Heschel, pp. 62, 66, 70.

[60] Morris, p. 235. For the satirist to be effective, Mack notes: "he must be accepted by his audience as a fundamentally virtuous and tolerant man, who challenges the doings of other men not whenever he happens to feel vindictive, but whenever they deserve it." See Mack, 86.

[61] See O'Connor, 33. In addition to Ezek 16:20-21, which I discuss earlier (*ante*, p. 4), explicit accusation of child murder for sacrifice appears in Jer 7:31, also discussed earlier (above, p. 39).

NOTES TO CHAPTER 2:
OF JACOB'S POTTAGE AND HORACE'S FARE

[1] Quoted in Robert C. Elliott, *The Power of Satire: Magic, Ritual, Art* (1960), p. 37.

[2]Walter Brueggemann, "The Book of Jeremiah: Portrait of the Prophet," *Interpretation* 37 (1983), 132-133, 135. (Hereafter referred to as Brueggemann.) Brueggemann's description of such use of language as "subversive activity" (135) is a theme I pursue further in Chapter 4, below. In Chapter 5 I am likewise concerned with Jeremiah's so-called Temple Sermon, offered by Brueggemann as an example of ideological coverup challenged by a prophet's subversive use of language.

[3]In Chapter 5 I discuss this poem as an instance of the prophet's awareness of the danger of his mission.

[4]Brueggemann, 137.

[5]So John Dryden translates Juvenal's *First Satire*, ll. 129-132. See *The Poetical Works of Dryden*, ed. George R. Noyes, new rev. ed. (1950), p. 324. (Hereafter referred to as Dryden, ed. Noyes.) "Olio," that is, a miscellaneous mixture or a miscellaneous collection, is Rolfe Humphries' translation of Juvenal's term in these same lines. See Juvenal (tr. Humphries), p. 20.

[6]Evelyn Waugh, *Vile Bodies* (1977), pp. 283-284.

[7]William Shakespeare, *King Richard II*, 4th ed., rev. and ed. Peter Ure (1956), pp. 49-54 (II, i, 31-68).

[8]Smith Palmer Bovie, "Introduction to Book Two," in *The Satires and Epistles of Horace*, tr. Smith Palmer Bovie (1959), pp. 97-98. (Hereafter referred to as Bovie.) Meals figure prominently in *Satires II*, iv, vi, and viii.

[9]See Dryden, ed. Noyes, p. 311, and Bovie, p. 98.

[10]Johannes Lindblom, *Prophecy in Ancient Israel* (1965), p. 122. (Hereafter referred to as Lindblom.)

[11]Joseph Blenkinsopp, *A History of Prophecy in Israel: From the Settlement in the Land to the Hellenistic Period* (1983), p. 201. (Hereafter cited as *History of Prophecy*.)

[12]Gene M. Tucker, *Form Criticism in the Old Testament* (1971), pp. 54, 66. Tucker elsewhere provides a handy résumé of the growth of scholarly interest in prophetic speech forms, some of the divergent opinions on the matter, and a specification of a number of the diverse forms themselves. See Gene M. Tucker, "Prophetic Speech," in *Interpreting the Prophets*, eds. James Luther Mays and Paul J. Achtemeier (1987), esp. pp. 29-35. (Hereafter referred to as "Prophetic Speech.")

[13]Lindblom, p. 155.

[14]Leon Guilhamet, *Satire and the Transformation of Genre* (1987), p. 13. (Hereafter referred to as Guilhamet.)

[15]"Prophetic Speech," pp. 27-28.

[16]See above, pp. 148-152.

[17]Guilhamet, p. 16. Later, Guilhamet says (p. 165): " . . . it is the characteristic dynamic of satire to de-form those [host] structures [it borrows] as part of their transformation to components of generic satire."

[18]Brueggemann, p. 135.

[19]See Gerald L. Bruns, "Allegory and Satire: A Rhetorical Meditation," New Literary History, 11 (1979-1980), p. 129.

[20]Guilhamet, p. 164.

[21]AB: Hosea, p. 132. The references in the Andersen and Freedman text are to Robert Gordis, Poets, Prophets, and Sages (1971) and to Frederic William Farrar, The Minor Prophets, Their Lives and Times. Men of the Bible 14 (New York: A. D. F. Randolph, 1890).

[22]Under the name of anatomy, Menippean satire has also been a keen interest of Northrop Frye. See Anatomy of Criticism: Four Essays (1965), esp. pp. 308-314. (Hereafter referred to as Anatomy.)

[23]Mikhail Bakhtin, Problems of Dostoevsky's Poetics, ed. and tr. Caryl Emerson, intro. Wayne C. Booth (1984), pp. 121-122. (Hereafter referred to as Dostoevsky's Poetics.)

[24]Quoted in Dostoevsky's Poetics, pp. 106-107, n. b.

[25]Dostoevsky's Poetics, p. 280.

[26]Dostoevsky's Poetics, p. xxxvii.

[27]Mikhail Bakhtin, as quoted in Tzvetan Todorov, Mikhail Bakhtin: The Dialogical Principle, tr. Wlad Godzich (1984), pp. 102, 107.

[28]Northrop Frye points out what happens in literary criticism of the anatomy which tacitly assumes the exhaustiveness of its analytical principles (Anatomy, p. 313):

> It is the anatomy in particular that has baffled critics, and there is hardly any fiction writer deeply influenced by it who has not been accused of disorderly conduct. The reader may be reminded here of Joyce, for describing Joyce's books as monstrous has become a nervous tic . . . . The care that Joyce took to organize Ulysses and Finnegan's Wake amounted nearly to obsession, but as they are not organized on familiar principles of prose fiction, the impression of shapelessness remains.

[29]See Mikhail Bakhtin, Rabelais and His World, tr. Helene Iswolsky (1984), p. 439.

[30]Dostoevsky's Poetics, p. 114.

[31]Abraham J. Heschel, The Prophets (1969), [I], p. 3.

[32]Bakhtin's analysis of Menippean characteristics appears in

Dostoevsky's Poetics, pp. 114-119. In another discussion of Menippean satire, Eugene P. Kirk describes it as

> a medley—usually a medley of alternating prose and verse, sometimes a jumble of flagrantly digressive narrative, or again a potpourri of tales, songs, dialogues, orations, letters, lists, and other brief forms mixed together. In theme, Menippean satire was essentially concerned with right learning or right belief. That theme often called for ridicule or caricature of some sham-intellectual or theological fraud.

See Eugene P. Kirk, "Introduction," to *Menippean Satire: An Annotated Catalogue of Texts and Criticism* (1980), p. xi. The prophets, as I mention, are concerned with right practice rather than "right learning or right belief," in an intellectual sense.

[33]See Jonathan Swift, *A Tale of a Tub*, in Swift, *Gulliver's Travels and Other Writings*, ed. Louis A. Landa (1960), p. 267. This edition hereafter referred to as Swift. Gulliver's lament appears on p. 4, immediately after he describes the yahoos (that's you and me) as "a species of animals utterly incapable of amendment . . . ."

[34]*Dialogue II*, of *Epilogue to the Satires*, in Pope, p. 294, n.to l. 255. Maynard Mack discusses the circumstances of this note in *Alexander Pope: A Life* (1985), pp. 735-736.

[35]See *Anatomy*, pp. 163-167.

[36]David Robertson, *The Old Testament and the Literary Critic* (1977), p. 16. Robertson makes this observation in discussing Exodus 1-15 as a comedy. Incorporation into one's own society, however, is hardly the prophet's fate.

[37]*Anatomy*, pp. 165, 167. In *The Great Code*, Frye applies the paradigm of comedy to the Hebrew and Christian Scripture taken as a whole, a

> U-shaped pattern, approximate as it is, [which] recurs in literature as the standard shape of comedy, where a series of misfortunes and misunderstandings brings the action to a threateningly low point, after which some fortunate twist in the plot sends the conclusion up to a happy ending. The entire Bible, viewed as a "divine comedy," is contained with a U-shaped story of this sort, one in which man . . . loses the tree and water of life at the beginning of Genesis and gets them back at the end of Revelation.

See p. 169. The Biblical comedy ends, appropriately, with a wedding: the Lamb marries the New Jerusalem. I am arguing, in effect, that prophecy, like satire, leads to "a threateningly low point" unrelieved by "a happy ending" achieved within the text.

[38] One of Alexander Pope's most delightful poems is a verse epistle from Mrs. Mary Gulliver to her husband, Lemuel, occasioned by her *"apprehending from his late Behaviour some Estrangement of his Affections* [original emphasis]." The symptoms therein described would certainly test the wisdom of Ann Landers. See "MARY GULLIVER *to Captain* LEMUEL GULLIVER," in Alexander Pope, *Minor Poems* (Volume VI of The Twickenham Edition), eds. Norman Ault and John Butt (1964), pp. 276-279. Who, for example, can remain insensitive to Mrs. Gulliver's anxiety when she asks, "What mean those Visits to the *Sorrel Mare?*" (l. 30). Ll. 39-48 of Pope's poem, Michael O'Connor reminds me, parodies the Song of Songs.

[39] An argument frequently used to support the supposedly later addition of consolation to the prophetic text is precisely the contrast between that and the severe, uncompromising, and threatening quality of the prophetic message. In particular, this contrast has been used to postulate later dates for the consolations that close Amos (9:8-15) or Hosea (14:1-8). In the case of Amos the NEB says: "Many scholars believe that this glowing passage was added to give a positive ending." See NEB, p. 990, n. to 9:8b-15. Andersen and Freedman challenge this view, however. They see the consolation "as part of the prophet's message, . . . an integral part of the book to which he was the principal contributor, and in the compilation of which he may have had a role." See AB: Amos, pp. 80, 82.

[40] Joel Rosenberg, "Jeremiah and Ezekiel," in *The Literary Guide to the Bible*, p. 194. Second Isaiah (i.e., chs. 40-55) seem to pose a striking and significant exception to the claim that prophecy, like satire, leaves us with the unresolved. The pervasiveness of consolation in Second Isaiah is without exception. But what Second Isaiah announces is a future brought into being by Israel's having paid the punishment necessary for her sins. Second Isaiah is commanded:

> Speak kindly to Jerusalem, and proclaim to her,
> That her sentence is served, her penalty is paid,
> That she has received from Yahweh's hand
> double for all her sins. [40:2, AB]

As I point out in n. 46, however, James Crenshaw describes Second Isaiah as "the most noticeable instance of prophetic promise" because the text "is permeated with unfulfilled predictions." See p. 216. However proved wrong, Second Isaiah nonetheless proclaims a morally conditioned future.

[41] *The Great Code*, p. xiii. Later, Frye says: "The New Testament

. . . claims to be, among other things, the key to the Old Testament, the explanation of what the Old Testament really means." See p. 79.

[42] John Barton, *Oracles of God: Perceptions of Ancient Prophecy in Israel After the Exile* (1986), pp. 13, 14. (Hereafter referred to as Barton.)

[43] NEB, p. 734, n. to Isa 8:1-4.

[44] Sheldon H. Blank, "A Job to Do—a Mission," in *Perspectives on Old Testament Literature*, ed. Woodrow Ohlsen (1978), p. 257.

[45] AB: Jeremiah, pp. 359-360.

[46] James L. Crenshaw, for instance, lists several predictions by the Hebrew prophets that proved wrong, including Isaiah's assurance about the despoiling of Israel and Syria. Crenshaw adds: "the most noticeable failure of prophetic promise is II Isaiah, for this poetic masterpiece is permeated with unfulfilled predictions." See *Prophetic Conflict: Its Effect Upon Israelite Religion* (1971), p. 51, n. 39. (Hereafter referred to as Crenshaw.)

[47] Lindblom, pp. 199, 200.

[48] Crenshaw, p. 44.

[49] Barton, p. 13.

[50] At first glance, a statement like Gene Tucker's—"the element of prediction was essential to prophecy"—seems to contradict the argument presented here. But Tucker goes on to insist that the future announced in the prophets is linked to accusation about present behavior. The future thus remains morally conditioned. See "Prophetic Speech," pp. 34, 38-40. Hans Walter Wolff likewise seems to contradict the claim that prediction is not important in the Hebrew prophets. He states categorically that "the decisive content of all call narratives and visions is not contemporary sin, but those coming events brought forth by Yahweh." Later, however, he asserts the prophets' attestation that "the threatened judgment is warranted." See Hans Walter Wolff, "Prophecy from the Eighth Through the Fifth Centuries," in *Interpreting the Prophets*, eds. James L. Mays and Paul J. Achtemeier (1987), pp. 19, 22. (Hereafter referred to as Wolff.) Dropping *prediction* to describe the contents of a prophetic message would be an incalculable gain in clarity, if only because—Tucker and Wolff serve as examples—biblical scholars agree that the future announced in the prophets is a morally conditioned future. With the hesitation of an amateur, I suggest that the phrase *announcement of a morally conditioned future* is clearer than *prediction*.

[51] R. B. Y. Scott says:

The prophets foretell doom in the one case and deliverance in the other—a doom or deliverance which is to befall the people whom the prophet is addressing. More important, they will experience it as an immediate consequence of their moral and spiritual condition at the moment when the prophet speaks . . . . The margins of present time . . . are extended to include a near future which is vitally and morally related to that present.

Such predictions are not glimpses of a predetermined future which is shortly to pass through the present moment into the past, like a motion-picture film passing the lens of the projector. The future is no so mechanically determined. What is about to happen is *the necessary consequence of a moral situation* [original emphasis] at the same time it will be the concrete realization of the prophetic "Word" which expresses in relation to that situation the righteous will of Yahweh.

See *The Relevance of the Prophets* (1968), p. 10.

[52]Let me note but one instance of a predictive reading of satire. In a major nineteenth-century edition of Alexander Pope's *Works*, Whitwell Elwin draws attention to Pope's note·near the end of the Book III of *The Dunciad* (l. 355), where the poet explains how a cultural catastrophe of the magnitude of that described in the poem can be effected "by such *weak Instruments* [original emphasis] as have been (hitherto) described in our poem." Two generations after Eichmann, we can be forgiven a disturbing amusement with Elwin's editorial assurance that "Time has proved that the fears of the poet had no grounds but in his own imagination." See "Introduction," to *The Works of Alexander Pope*, new ed., by Whitwell Elwin (1967 [1871-1889]), IV, 19. Pope's note appears in Pope, p. 352, n. to l. 355.

[53]A. J. P. Taylor provides a grim footnote to Swift's despair in the 1720's about the situation in Ireland:

When British forces entered the so-called "convalescent camp" at Belsen in 1945, they found a scene of indescribable horror: the wasted bodies of 50,000 human beings who had died from starvation and disease . . . . Only a century before, all Ireland was a Belsen. Nearly two million Irish people died of starvation and fever within five years; another million fled, carrying disease to Liverpool and the New World.

See A. J. P. Taylor, "Genocide," in *Essays in English History* (1976), p. 73. Is human sacrifice, in prophecy and in satire, perhaps *the* crime that calls to heaven for vengeance?

[54]Lindblom, p. 199.

[55]Jonathan Swift, *Answer to a Memorial*, in *The Prose Works of Jonathan Swift*, ed. Herbert Davis (1939-1968), XII, 22-23. Although Oliver W. Ferguson claims that Swift's *Modest Proposal* expresses "the full weight" of Swift's "frustration and despair" with the Irish situation after "ten years of warning and exhortation," he finds "even more terrible" the statement in *Answer to a Memorial* from which I draw the epigraph on p. 71. The whole context is worth quoting in full:

> If so wretched a State of Things would allow it, methinks I could have a malicious Pleasure, after all the Warning I have in vain given the Publick . . . to see the Consequences and Events answering in every Particular. I pretend to no Sagacity: What I writ was little more than what I had discoursed to several Persons, who were generally of my Opinion: And it was obvious to every common Understanding, that such Effects must needs follow from such Causes . . . . [ellipsis in Ferguson] *Wisdom crieth in the Streets; because I have called and ye refused; I have stretched out my Hand, and no Man regarded. But ye have set at nought all my Counsel, and would none of my Reproof. I also will laugh at your Calamity, and mock when your Fear cometh* [original emphasis].

Ferguson concludes: "Here is the promise which Swift fulfilled in the day of Ireland's fear; and here, stripped of all irony and grounded in the authority of Scripture, is the moralist's judgment on the Irish people." See Oliver W. Ferguson, *Jonathan Swift and Ireland* (1962), pp. 176-177. This brief citation from a major satirist illustrates a number of points made in my study: the ambiguous relationship the prophet has towards the doom he announces; God's and the prophet's satisfaction with effected punishment; the absence of any real hope that disaster can be avoided; and the announcing of a future seen as the consequence of current behavior (Swift is quoting Prov 1: 20, 24-25 [KJV], a wisdom writing that often threatens humiliation and ridicule as a consequence of shameful behavior.).

[56]Horace, *Horace's Satires and Epistles*, tr. Jacob Fuchs, intro. William S. Anderson (1977), p. 25, l. 50. (Hereafter referred to as Horace.)

[57]Virtually any handbook definition of satire claims that amendment of manners and morals is the aim of satire.

[58]See Barton, p. 13, and Wolff, p. 22.

[59]Robert R. Wilson, *Prophecy and Society in Ancient Israel* (1984), pp. 30, 43. In Chapter 5, I discuss the role of these support groups in the construction of the prophet's and satirist's character.

[60]Persuasive and punitive satire are discussed in Edward W. Rosenheim, Jr., *Swift and the Satirist's Art* (1963), pp. 12-17. Rosenheim, for example, (p. 13) describes the effect of punitive satire in terms very applicable to prophecy as it is heard by the like-minded:

> No new judgment is invited; no course of action is urged; no novel information is produced. The audience, rather, is asked chiefly to rejoice in the heaping of opprobrium, ridicule, or fancied punishment upon an object of whose culpability they are *already* [original emphasis] thoroughly convinced.

NOTES TO CHAPTER 3:
DIVINE DERISION AND SCORN

[1]As a definition of *prophecy* Johnson offers "To preach. A scriptural sense," an important and hermeneutically defensible equivalent. Except for this one denotation, however, all his definitions of *prophecy, prophesy, prophet* and *prophetess, prophetick* (including *prophetical*), *prophetically*, and *prophetize* all stress the ability to see the future. The *Oxford English Dictionary*, however, places greater stress on prophecy as utterance, preaching, proclamation, or interpretation. Coincidentally, the *OED* uses Shakespeare's remark in *Lear* to illustrate a definition of *jester*.

[2]Theodor Gaster, *Myth, Legend, and Custom in the Old Testament* (1975), II, 508. (Hereafter cited as Gaster.) NEB, p. 377, n. to 1 Kgs 18:27, which describes this passage as a "fierce satire."

[3]KJV says: "He that sitteth in the heavens shall laugh: the Lord shall have them in derision." The version here is from the *Book of Common Prayer*.

[4]AB: Hosea, p. 40. Consolation can also be the content of prophetic utterance, e.g., Second Isaiah, and is sometimes so out of keeping with the censorious quality of the rest of the prophecy as to suggest later interpolation, e.g., sections of Amos.

[5]Has Samuel a grisly sense of humor? Lied to by Saul, who assures the prophet that he has extirpated everything belonging to the Amalekites, Samuel asks: "What then is this bleating of sheep in my ears? Why do I hear the lowing of cattle?" (1 Sam 15:14, NEB).

[6]"A red grape of excellent quality." AB: Jeremiah, p. 15, n. to 2:21.

[7]Northrop Frye, "The Mythos of Winter: Irony and Satire," in *Anatomy*, pp. 224, 225. My analysis of the prophets as satirists is heavily indebted to his treatment of satire, esp. pp. 223-239. *Jeremiad* has, of course, entered the language from prophecy as a synonym for

a particular kind of complaint or denunciation and reveals the essentially critical nature of prophecy.

[8]Northrop Frye, "The Nature of Satire," *University of Toronto Quarterly*, 14 (1944-1945), 80. The theological expertise revealed in good swearing leads Frye to remark that "the greatest masters of invective, Rabelais and Swift, have been recruited from the clergy" (80). Ezekiel and, perhaps, Jeremiah, two of the greatest satirists among the prophets, were from priestly families.

In *Satire and the Transformation of Genre* (1987), Leon Guilhamet comments (pp. 22-23):

> Despite the widespread acceptance of the views of Fred N. Robinson and Robert C. Elliott that magic and curse are the roots from which later satire has sprung, many theorists, because of their demands for fiction or irony in satire, have failed to treat curse and invective as satire. It is true that this kind of satire is something of an embarrassment to anyone dealing with the complexities of later masters, but the family resemblance cannot be denied. Further, once it is seen that satire in its primary forms is analogous to rhetorical form, much of the difficulty vanishes. Curse or invective, of course, does not conform to the pattern of demonstrative orations. But the denunciatory format is there, and, indeed, there is use of imagery and other rhetorical techniques.

[9]NEB, p. 385, n. to 2 Kgs 1:2.

[10]AB: Hosea, p. 366, n. to 4:12a, where Andersen and Freedman pass on the suggestion of H. L. Ginsberg on this point. Horace has an extended conversation with his penis in *Satires*, I, ii.

[11]AB: Hosea, pp. 465-466, where Andersen and Freedman consider possible interpretations of this image.

[12]NEB, p. 1006, n. to 2:1-3:19.

[13]*Anatomy*, p. 225.

[14]David Worcester, *The Art of Satire* (1960), p. 8. (Hereafter cited as Worcester.)

[15]Worcester, p. 8.

[16]Samuel Sandmel, *The Enjoyment of Scripture: The Law, the Prophets, and the Writings* (1974), p. 240. (Hereafter cited as Sandmel.)

[17]In *The Way of Wisdom in the Old Testament* (1971), R. B. Y. Scott observes (p. 125) how strange it has always seemed that "the first prophet whose words have been preserved in written form should have spoken with such eloquence and literary mastery, as if he were heir to a highly developed literary tradition," which Scott claims he

was. For William R. Harper, "its artistic character" is one of the features of Amos' style. See his "Amos," in *Perspectives on Old Testament Literature*, ed. Woodrow Ohlsen (1978), p. 192.

[18]Isaiah 3:9 also uses the insulting comparison of Israel to Sodom: "like Sodom they proclaim their sins and do not conceal them" (NEB). *The Enjoyment of Scripture* speaks of the contemptuous or ironic contrasts in Amos' figures of speech. See Sandmel, p. 247.

[19]Jeremiah marvels at the reception given in Judah to false prophets:

> An appalling, a shocking thing
>> Has occurred in the land:
> The prophets—they prophesy falsely,
>> And the priests—they lord it beside them;
> And my people—they love it that way. . . . [Jer 5:31, AB]

[20]Gaster, II, 620.

[21]Gaster, II, 632, 632-636.

[22]Gaster, II, 648-649.

[23]Gaster, II, 679.

[24]AB: Ezekiel, p. 152, n. to 7:19.

[25]Gaster, II, 611, 614-615. AB: Ezekiel, p. 152, n. to 7:17.

[26]See Peter Ackroyd, "The Book of Isaiah," in *The Interpreter's One-Volume Commentary on the Bible* (1971), p. 341, comm. on 14:4b-21. NEB calls this "a satire on the fall of [the exiles'] oppressor" (p. 741, n. to 14:1-23).

[27]See Part IV, chapters five and six, of *Gulliver's Travels*, in Jonathan Swift, *Gulliver's Travels and Other Writings*, ed. Louis A. Landa (1960), esp. pp. 198-200, 203-205. This edition hereafter referred to as Swift.

[28]Gaster, II, 566.

[29]*Anatomy*, p. 236. This is Frye's "satire of the high norm," the "third phase of satire." *Ibid*, p. 234.

[30]*Anatomy*, p. 235.

[31]AB: Jeremiah, p. 16, n. to 2:23.

[32]AB: Jeremiah, p. 23, n. to 3:2.

[33]AB: Second Isaiah, pp. 188, 191, n. to 64:5.

[34]The idiom also appears in 1 Kgs 21:21. Translations differ.

[35]AB: Ezekiel, pp. 297-298.

[36]Because idolatry frequently involved ritual prostitution, the literal and the figurative merge in this usage. Johnson, incidentally, offers idolatry as one of the two definitions of *fornication*: "In Scripture, sometimes. . . ."

[37]AB: Hosea, pp. 46-48.

[38] *Anatomy*, p. 225.

[39] AB: Ezekiel, p. 286. The intense, graphic quality of Ezekiel 16 can prompt the suspicion, of course, that Judah's behavior is nowhere near as hypererotic as the imagination of her censuring prophet. Similar possibilities often arise in Juvenal and in Swift.

[40] Moshe Greenberg includes an excellent commentary and analysis on this chapter, with sophisticated literary awareness. It has influenced my own reading of this passage. See AB: Ezekiel, pp. 270-306.

[41] Juvenal (tr. Humphries), p. 19 (for 11. 36-62 of *Satire I*).

[42] "Because your juice was poured out" (Ezek 16:35 AB) is "a reference to female genital 'distillation' produced by sexual arousal." See AB: Ezekiel, p. 285, n. to 16:36.

[43] *Anatomy*, p. 235.

[44] *Anatomy*, pp. 226-229.

[45] *Anatomy*, pp. 229-234.

[46] *Anatomy*, pp. 223, 237.

[47] *Anatomy*, p. 237.

[48] I have never assumed that Frye's phases of satire and irony are mutually exclusive; rather, that in a good deal of satire, different phases of both can and do appear. The usually low-key Horace, for instance, uses obscene sexual reductiveness in *Satires*, I,ii, and iii.

[49] *Anatomy*, pp. 237-238.

[50] *Anatomy*, pp. 238-239. "The humiliation of being constantly watched by a hostile or derisive eye" appears in Job's angry question to God: "What have I done to you, man watcher?" (7:20, AB).

[51] See James S. Ackerman, "Satire and Symbolism in the Song of Jonah," in *Traditions in Transformation: Turning Points in Biblical Faith*, eds. Baruch Halpern and Jon D. Levenson (1981), p. 220.

[52] See *Anatomy*, pp. 233-234.

[53] AB: Hosea, pp. 66, 59. Prophetic texts, like satiric, are frequently rearranged by editors, translators, and the like to satisfy their convictions about how the original should have been or was written.

[54] AB: Hosea, p. 131.

[55] AB: Hosea, pp. 198-199.

[56] This analysis of irony in the Book of Hosea is much indebted to Harold Fisch's "Hosea: A Poetics of Violence," in *Poetry with a Purpose: Biblical Poetics and Interpretation* (1988), pp. 136-157. (Hereafter referred to as Fisch.) Fisch focusses, however, on the power and violence of the text; my concern focusses on how Hosea's irony easily exemplifies the paradigm of that irony Frye describes in the *Anatomy* as third-phase irony, the irony of the madhouse, of the void, of the quest that ends in nothing. Like other commentators, Fisch does

discuss irony in Hosea, for instance, the ironic appeal to Yahweh (in 6:1-4) as if he were a vegetation deity (149-151), the context in which Fisch also cites James Ackerman about the "highly sophisticated irony" the Bible is capable of. Andersen and Freedman speak of "very bitter irony" in Hosea (271), "bitter parody" (325), sarcasm (406), "the irony of turning away from Yahweh" (516), or Hosea's use of parody terms (527). In *Hosea: A Commentary on the Book of the Prophet Hosea*, tr. Gary Stansell, ed. Paul D. Hanson (1974), Hans Walter Wolff likewise notes features like "a punlike polemic against the cult" (49), ironic undertones in 4:4-19 (82), "bitter irony" in 10:5 (175), or "scornful expressions" in 13 (223). (Hereafter referred to as Wolff.) My objective is to expand these observations and situate them and other such instances of irony into a paradigmatic analysis of irony in the Book of Hosea.

[57]AB: Hosea, pp. 131, 266, 281, 298, 386-387 (where Andersen and Freedman note that Ezek 20:31 makes clear the reference to "the sacrificial burning of children"), 581. Harold Fisch notes that in Hosea, Yahweh becomes a frightening, devouring animal. See Fisch, pp. 151-153.

[58]NEB, p. 964, n. to Hos. 1:4.

[59]Wolff, pp. xxvi-xxvii.

[60]AB: Hosea, pp. 136, 169, 224, 246, 323.

[61]AB: Hosea, p. 232.

[62]AB: Hosea, pp. 235, 355, 410 (where Andersen and Freedman draw attention to "Isaiah's disgusting description of the tables covered with filthy vomit" as "a sickening picture of a helpless drunk," who, by the way, is either prophet or priest!).

[63]Wolff, p. xxv.

[64]AB: Hosea, p. 527. However false the god, Hosea reveals the startling reality of what occurs: "the most horrifying god-food is child sacrifice, and Hosea makes it clear that this practice had entered Israel in his time."

[65]Jonathan Swift, *A Tale of a Tub*, in Swift, pp. 321-322, 324. Although Swift intended his satire in the *Tale* to defend the Church of England, he was roundly criticized for his flippant, irreverent treatment of religion even by some within the Established Church. The "Apology" which Swift added to the fifth edition of the *Tale* (1710) shows unmistakable signs of his defensiveness and uneasiness. The *Tale*, remember, is the work that is supposed to have so offended Queen Anne as to have cost Swift his chance of ever securing a bishopric. She certainly disliked him.

[66]AB: Hosea, pp. 369, 325.

[67]AB: Hosea, p. 442.

NOTES TO CHAPTER 4:
PROPHETS OR PROJECTORS?

[1]A projector in eighteenth-century English parlance is, according to Samuel Johnson, "one who forms schemes or designs, . . . one who forms wild impracticable schemes," the equivalent of a quack or medicine man. I thought this clarification advisable since one early reader of this piece wondered about its connection with the likes of Kodak Carousels.

[2]See, for example, Robert C. Elliott, *The Power of Satire: Magic, Ritual, Art* (1966), which deals, as Elliott himself says, with "the origins of satire in primitive magic and incantation" and which seeks "to elucidate an early connection of satire with magical power and to show how that original connection survives . . . in satire written today" (vii).

[3]The pithy summary of Pope's satiric objective by William John Courthope in his "Introduction to *The Dunciad*" in *The Works of Alexander Pope*, ed. Whitwell Elwin and William John Courthope (1871-1889), IV, 28.

[4]Crispinus is identified in Horace (tr. Fuchs), p. 99. Horace calls him the "sore-eyed Crispinus" in the last line of the opening satire (p. 3). See Persius, *Satire I*, in *Horace, Satires and Epistles [and] Persius, Satires*, rev. ed., Niall Rudd (1979), esp. ll. 13-20, pp. 208-209. See *Satire I* in Juvenal (tr. Humphries), pp. 17-23. Juvenal's attack on bad writers, the theme which opens this satire, recurs often in the poem.

[5]John Bright observes: ". . . of all the classes of people in contemporary Judah, there were few with whom Jeremiah was more irreconcilably at odds than with those who, like himself, bore the title 'prophet.' " See AB: Jeremiah, p. 154. In his *History of Prophecy*, my colleague Joseph Blenkinsopp notes that only in the concluding narrative of First Isaiah (chs. 36-39) is Isaiah called a *nabi*, that is, a prophet, "and presented as a miracle worker"; that Micah, like Amos, disavows his connection with prophecy: ". . . it is highly unlikely that [Micah] would even have wished to be known as a *nabi*"; and that "Habakkuk is the only preexilic prophet identified as a *nabi* in the title." See pp. 109, 123, 151. Amos' disavowal of the title appears at 7:14 (NEB): "I am no prophet . . . nor am I a prophet's son." Blenkinsopp has pointed out to me that the denominative verb "prophesy"— *hitnabbe*, i.e., "to act like a prophet"—also means "to act crazy."

[6]The thaumaturgy that authenticates prophets like Elijah in their conflict with the prophets of other gods does appear in accounts of intrafraternal challenges to authority in earlier times in Israel, e.g., Korah's rebellion against Moses (Numbers 16). Again, such thaumatur-

gical "verification" is conspicuous by its virtual absence in the narratives of the canonical "written" prophets.

[7]So Andersen and Freedman assume. See AB: Hosea, p. 344.

[8]The NEB points out that the sarcastic term for prophecy which it renders *rant* for Mic 2:6 is translated *go drivelling on* in Amos 7:16. See p. 998, n. to 2:6-11.

[9]Such is the interpretation of Bruce T. Dahlberg, "The Book of Micah," in *The Interpreter's One-Volume Commentary* (1971), p. 485.

[10]The phrase is John Bright's. See AB: Jeremiah, p. 154. Stanley Brice Frost, incidentally, speaking of Jer 23:9-40, points out how Jeremiah's conflict with his fellow prophets inadvertently revealed "the undependability of the institution," which, after the failure of realization in Second Isaiah's glowing vision of the future, finished "prophecy as an institution." See "The Book of Jeremiah," in *The Interpreter's One-Volume Commentary* (1971), p. 388. (Hereafter cited as Frost.) This theme is of major concern in Joseph Blenkinsopp's *Prophecy and Canon: A Contribution to the Study of Jewish Origins* (1986). (Hereafter cited as *Prophecy and Canon.*)

[11]This picture of enjoyable, communal delusion reminds me of Samuel Johnson's comments on those who view themselves as exquisitely sensitive lovers of the arts:

> The ambition of superior sensibility and superior eloquence [he writes] disposes the lovers of arts to receive rapture at one time, and communicate it at another; and each labours first to impose upon himself, and then to propagate the imposture.

See *Idler* 50, in Samuel Johnson, *The Idler* and *The Adventurer* (The Yale Edition, Volume II), eds. W. J. Bate, John M. Bullitt, and L. F. Powell (1963), p. 157.

[12]A denotation of *burden* as a recurring idea or theme, and used so in music, makes it possible to approximate this pun in English: that Yahweh's burden is that His people have become a burden whom He will cast off because they find they cannot accept the moral burden of his challenging and threatening burden. Bright discusses the Hebrew pun in AB: Jeremiah, p. 153.

[13]John Bright describes these thirty-some verses as the "classic expression of [Jeremiah's] hostility to the prophets," a passage which as a whole graphically demonstrates "the tension with the prophets . . . [which] reached its peak in the days of [King] Zedekiah," that is, around 600 BC See AB: Jeremiah, pp. 154-155.

[14]I am indebted to Joseph Blenkinsopp for this awareness about the disappearance of *ruah* from the lexicon of Hebrew prophecy. (The

pejoratively used word for wind, air, or breath in Ecclesiastes is not *ruah* but *hebel*, denoting, according to R. B. Y. Scott, "a breath, empty of substance and also transient." See AB: Eccl., p. 209.) A stimulating, brief discussion of the pejorative use of wind imagery in Swift appears in Robert M. Adams, "Candide on Work and Candide as Outsider," in Voltaire, *Candide: or, Optimism: A New Translation, Backgrounds, Criticism* [A Norton Critical Edition], tr. and ed. Robert M. Adams (1966), p. 167.

[15]The *ruah* which he translates here as *whims* is described by Moshe Greenberg as "auto-inspiration and willfulness in pursuit of delusion"—Swift's Jack among the Hebrews. Greenberg notes how "particularly close in themes and language" to Jeremiah 23:9-40 is this somewhat later censure of specious prophecy. See AB: Ezekiel, pp. 235, 243. In the verses that conclude Ezekiel 12 (21-28), immediately preceding this attack, where Ezekiel recounts arguments used to discredit true prophecy, Joseph Blenkinsopp notes an emphasis even stronger in Ezekiel than in Jeremiah on "the grave responsibility of the prophet to the community he must serve" and of "the likelihood of collusion between the prophet and the public which disingenuously solicits his guidance." See *History of Prophecy*, p. 199.

[16]Third Isaiah, "in invectives . . . addressed to the post-exilic community of Palestine," attacks the faithless leaders of the returned community by using pejoratively the watchman image of the prophet unique to Ezekiel (Ezek 33:1-9). A watchman, says Ezekiel, who "does not blow his trumpet or warn the people when he sees the enemy approaching" will be held responsible for those who die because of his dereliction of duty (6, NEB). Third Isaiah says:

> Its watchmen are blind, none of them know;
> All of them are dumb dogs, they cannot bark;
> They dream, they lie down, they love to slumber.
> They are greedy dogs, that cannot be filled;
> And these are shepherds who understand nothing;
> All of them go their own way, each after his own gain.
> [Isa 56:9-12, AB]

Much of the language and accusation of Jeremiah and Ezekiel against false prophets of Yahweh appears in this brief oracle. See AB: Second Isaiah, p. 158; NEB, p. 924, nn. to Ezek 33:1-20.

[17]According to Moshe Greenberg, the strange phrase in Ezekiel 14:3—"these men have raised idols in their thoughts"—expresses "the deliberateness of their guilty thinking." See AB: Ezekiel, p. 248.

[18]The comments are Greenberg's. See AB: Ezekiel, pp. 250, 254.

[19]AB: Ezekiel, pp. 254-255. My analysis of this passage in Ezekiel is heavily indebted to Greenberg's.

[20]See John Bright in AB: Jeremiah, pp. 201-202, 210-211.

[21]Bright speculates that Jeremiah's promise of execution for Ahab ben Kolaiah and Zedekiah ben Maaseiah, "who are prophesying a lie to you in my name" in Babylon—i.e., that the exile will be short—anticipates the punishment Nebuchadnezzar will order for the treason of such a message (Jer 29:21-23, AB). See p. 209.

[22]See Frost, in Interpreter's One-Volume Commentary, p. 391, n. to 29:20-23.

[23]Zephaniah does not discipline Jeremiah. His predecessor Pashhur, however, had Jeremiah flogged and confined (Jer 19:14–20:2) for preaching the same message. Frost observes: "The quarrel between Jeremiah and those who differed from him was bitter and intense. Both sides felt that the future of the nation depended on the prevalence of their point of view." See Frost in Interpreter's One-Volume Commentary, p. 391, n. to 29:24-32. In comments to the preceding section of the text (29:20-23), Frost insists that Jeremiah "is quite clearly well informed on affairs in Babylon."

[24]Hananiah delivers his prophecy in the fifth month of the fourth year of King Zedekiah's reign (28:1) and dies in the seventh month (28:17).

[25]AB: Jeremiah, pp. 201, 203. Bright notes Hananiah's use of the forms of Hebrew prophecy. See AB: Jeremiah, pp. 202-203.

[26]A brief survey of such comments appears in Maynard Mack, "The Muse of Satire," Yale Review, 41 (1951-52), 82-83. And in an essay on sometimes questionably biographical readings of Samuel Johnson's Vanity of Human Wishes, I have pointed out in some Johnsonian criticism assumptions denigrating the literary status of satire. See Thomas Jemielity, "Samuel Johnson, The Vanity of Human Wishes, and Biographical Criticism," Studies in Eighteenth-Century Culture, ed. O. M. Brack, Jr., 15 (1986), 234-235.

[27]John William Wevers says: "The prophet [Ahijah] is called a mad fellow since prophets were held in some contempt because of their ecstatic behavior." See "The Second Book of Kings," in Interpreter's One-Volume Commentary, p. 200, n. to 9:11-13.

[28]Johannes Lindblom, Prophecy in Ancient Israel (1962), pp. 43, 216. William Wordsworth, intriguingly, seems to admit automatisms in the composing of poetry, for he speaks, in the Preface to the Second Edition of Lyrical Ballads, of obeying "blindly and mechanically the impulses" of certain habits of mind developed in those "originally possessed of much sensibility." See The Norton Anthology of English

Literature, gen. ed. M. H. Abrams, 5th ed. (1986), II, 160.

[29]Moshe Greenberg provides the comments about this herme-
neutical embarrassment. See AB: Ezekiel, p. 122. As a contemporary
scholar, Blenkinsopp refers to Ezekiel's "often bizarre symbolic mimes
and gestures." See *History of Prophecy*, p. 194. A surprising statement
of general disappointment with Ezekiel appears in Samuel Sandmel,
general editor of The New English Bible, who finds it "impossible to
turn from Jeremiah to Ezekiel without a vivid sense of disappointment," and whose brief mention of scholarly attempts to make sense
of Ezekiel's text concludes with his admission that "it is as hard to
make sense of their theories as it is to understand the book itself." See
The Enjoyment of Scripture: The Law, the Prophets, and the Writings
(1974), pp. 266, 268.

[30]Although Greenberg admits to some confusion about whether
Ezekiel's bitterness and rage reflect "God's feelings toward Israel . . .
or his own distress over the dismal, thankless, and perhaps dangerous
task imposed on him," he speculates on the symbolic actions so
quickly narrated in this small section of the prophecy (3:22-5:17)
referred to earlier (AB: Ezekiel, pp. 71, 123):

> May it not be that the unusual accumulation of self-afflictions
> in this passage is at bottom a kind of compensation for with-
> drawal from the public fray, a turning upon oneself of stop-
> pled anger and resentment?

[31]The NEB views the verse as an attack on false prophecy. See
p. 971, n. to 9:7-8. Andersen and Freedman believe, rather, that
Hosea here records "his own experience of hostile rejection." They
allude to 2 Kgs 9:11 to argue that the taunts are "old bywords." See
AB: Hosea, pp. 532-533.

[32]AB: Jeremiah, pp. 132-133.

[33]John Bright regards this incident with Micaiah as "the earliest
illustration that we have of something that later seems to have been
distressingly common: prophetic word flatly contradicting prophetic
word, and prophet pitted against prophet." See AB: Jeremiah, p. xxi.

[34]See John William Wever, "The First Book of Samuel," in *The
Interpreter's One-Volume Commentary* (1971), pp. 155-156.

[35]AB: Jeremiah, p. xxi.

[36]I am disappointed that the John Bright who recognizes that
Jeremiah's prophecy had "contradicted a cardinal dogma of the
official state religion," i.e., Yahweh's external protection for the temple
He had chosen as His abode, later defends Jeremiah so weakly and
irrelevantly from charges of "cowardice or defeatism" or pro-Babylo-

nian sympathies. Jeremiah preaches a religiously and politically offensive message. But why should a Biblical scholar have to defend a prophet's integrity? See AB: Jeremiah, pp. 172, 217-218.

[37]Louis Ginzberg, *The Legends of the Jews*, tr. Henrietta Szold (7 vols., 1909-1938), IV, 294, 297-300. According to Jewish legends, by the way, Hananiah was "prophesying pleasant things." See IV, 298.

[38]This analysis of the conflict between institutional and charismatic authority comes, of course, from Max Weber. See *Ancient Judaism*, trs. and eds. Hans H. Gerth and Don Martindale (1952), esp. pp. 278, 284. It figures very prominently in *Prophecy and Canon*. See esp. pp. 22, 27-28, 38, 143-152.

[39]An illuminating analysis of the place of charismatic prophetic authority within the ecclesiastical community appears in Bernard Murchland, "The Prophetic Principle," *Commonweal*, 29 April 1966, pp. 171-175. And, in his review of Thomas J. J. Altizer's *The New Apocalypse: the Radical Christian Vision of William Blake* (1967), Thomas Merton perceptively analyzes Blake as prophet and visionary in terms very appropriate to the vision of the Hebrew prophets and the institutional complacency and confidence they challenged. See "Blake and the New Theology," *Sewanee Review*, 76 (1968), 673-682. The review was, I believe, the last thing written by Merton before his accidental death, in the Far East, later that year.

[40]For the dating of Lamentations see AB: Lamentations, pp. xviii-xix.

[41]Harvey H. Guthrie, Jr., says of Lam 2:14:

the poet explicitly sides with the minority prophets against those in the majority who maintained themselves [a revealing comment on their self-interested motivation] by prophesying the peace and security Israel wanted to hear . . . . Such prophets have been disqualified by events. Reality has voided their credentials, and they can say nothing to comfort Jerusalem now. The poet makes explicit what has been implicit all along: his acceptance of the interpretation given to Jerusalem's downfall by prophets such as Jeremiah and Ezekiel.

See "Lamentations," in *The Interpreter's One-Volume Commentary* (1971), p. 407.

[42]The comment is Joseph Blenkinsopp's. See *Prophecy and Canon*, p. 99. He dates Deutero-Zechariah in "the early Greek period." See pp. 110-111.

[43]For the homosexuality in the allusion see *Prophecy and Canon*, p. 180, n. 30.

NOTES TO CHAPTER 5:
THE PROPHET IN THE SATIRIST'S MASK

[1]Ezekiel begins in the first person, but a third-person voice appears in verses 2 and 3 only to disappear at once. Second Isaiah (i.e., Isaiah 40-55) begins in direct address, while Third Isaiah (i.e., Isaiah 56-66) begins with a voice announcing the word of the Lord. Jonah, of course, is a third-person narrative from start to finish, less a prophecy than an extended exemplum or illustration such as a prophet might fashion. Jonah is, perhaps, a prophet's *Gulliver's Travels*.

[2]The narrative conclusion to First Isaiah (36-39) as well as the narrative conclusion of Jeremiah (52) both come almost in their entirety from 2 Kings. Hosea concludes with a single verse the NEB describes as a "pious postscript" (p. 976, n. to Hos 14:9). Ezekiel, however, ends in speech, as do Second Isaiah, Third Isaiah, and all the remaining Minor Prophets (except Jonah).

[3]The satiric texts I have particularly in mind are apologias or program satires like the opening poem of each of Horace's two books of *Satires*, as well as the fourth and tenth *Satires* of Book One, Juvenal's *First Satire*, the prologue to John Oldham's *Satyrs Upon the Jesuits*, Alexander Pope's first-person satires like the *Epistle to Dr. Arbuthnot*, and Jonathan Swift's *Verses on the Death of Dr. Swift*.

[4]This phrase comes from Joel Rosenberg, "Jeremiah and Ezekiel," in *The Literary Guide to the Bible*, 184.

[5]*Sermo* proves useful with some of the thorny generic problems posed by some of the first-person satires of Pope, e.g., the *Epistle to Dr. Arbuthnot*. An addressee does not directly inject his or her own comments, verbally or in writing, into the letter he or she is receiving. No such problem occurs in a *sermo*, in a conversation.

[6]Thomas Aquinas unites word and knowledge in his analysis of prophecy. He argues that prophecy "first and chiefly consists in knowledge, because . . . prophets know things that are far removed from man's knowledge." Aquinas immediately equates this knowledge, however, with "*apparition*," that is, with perception, with seeing what others cannot. As knowledge, this perception then makes prophecy consist "secondarily in speech, in so far as the prophets declare for the instruction of others . . . ." Thus, for Aquinas, prophecy is uttered perception not shared by the many. Because that perception often criticizes and judges the many, this perspective provided by Aquinas becomes yet another way of seeing the close affinity between prophecy and satire. See *The Summa of St. Thomas Aquinas*, trs. Fathers of the English Dominican Province (1947), IIa-IIae [i.e., the Second part

of the Second part], Q. 171 ["Of Prophecy"], Article 1 ["Whether Prophecy Pertains to Knowledge?"], II, 1889-1890, which begins four questions on prophecy and one on rapture.

[7]See Persius, "Satire I," in *Horace, Satires and Epistles [and] Persius, Satires*, tr. Niall Rudd, rev. ed. (1979), p. 208, 1. 2. The ready availability of vacuously reassuring prophetic message is a common satiric target in the prophets, e.g., Isaiah refers to the "race of rebels" who tell the seers and visionaries: "give us smooth words and seductive visions" (Isa 30:9-10, NEB).

[8]See Horace (tr. Fuchs), p. 1, 11. 25-26.

[9]John L. McKenzie dates Second Isaiah at roughly the middle of the sixth century BC, that is, about thirty-five or forty years after the start of the Babylonian Exile. See AB: Second Isaiah, p. xxviii.

[10]Paul Fussell, *The Rhetorical World of Augustan Humanism* (1965), p. 161.

[11]Robert Goldenberg, for example, calls "direct violent denunciation" Jeremiah's characteristic reaction. See his "The Problem of False Prophecy: Talmudic Interpretations of Jeremiah 28 and 1 Kings 22," in *The Biblical Mosaic: Changing Perspectives*, eds. Robert M. Polzin and Eugene Rothman (1982), p. 90. This collection hereafter referred to as *The Biblical Mosaic*.

[12]In a difficult, stimulating, and rewarding essay, Geoffrey Hartman discusses prophecy as voice, the intensity of prophetic utterance, and the way prophets are taken over by the word they utter. See "The Poetics of Prophecy," in *High Romantic Argument: Essays for M. H. Abrams*, ed. Lawrence H. Lipking (1981), pp. 15-40, esp. pp. 15-16,, 31-34. (Hereafter referred to as Hartman.) In a certain sense, however, Hartman presents from a different perspective a longstanding awareness of the rhetorical and oratorical quality of prophecy.

[13]Jeremiah puns on the Lord's word as burden. See Jer 23:33-40, and also above, p. 125.

Numbers is the editorial result of post-exilic priests who make theologically significant a second wilderness experience (the Babylonian Exile) in the light of a first (the Exodus from Egypt). The figure of Moses emerges most significantly during this time. See J. Kenneth Kuntz, *The People of Ancient Israel: An Introduction to Old Testament Literature, History, and Thought* (1974), pp. 317-321, 128. (Hereafter referred to as Kuntz.) The Jeremiah-like quality of Moses' complaint more likely reflects the Mosaic patterns which influence the career of Jeremiah. William L. Holladay claims that "it was in the light of the figure of Moses that Jeremiah lived out his own ministry." See "The Background of Jeremiah's Self-Understanding: Moses, Samuel, and

Psalm 22," *Journal of Biblical Literature*, 83 (1964), 153. (Hereafter referred to as Holladay.) The entire essay explores that relationship.

[14]The translation is that of Michael Fishbane, who says:

> As if to provide a physical correlative to his sense of being forced, Jeremiah expresses himself with terms . . . which elsewhere refer to sexual seduction and rape (see Exod 22:15 and Deut 22:25, respectively) . . . . The prophet is felt to be a person at once overwhelmed by God's choice of, and control over, him as a prophet; and as one with an acute sense of having been duped, if not actually "had"—for Jeremiah goes on . . . to describe his life as a prophet as an unbroken series of torments.

See "'A Wretched Thing of Shame, A Mere Belly': An Interpretation of Jeremiah 20:7-12," in *The Biblical Mosaic*, pp. 169, 173. (Hereafter referred to as Fishbane.) KJV, NEB, and RSV emphasize the duplicity in the call, with no hint of sexual aggression. Ronald Knox nicely offers this feature with: "Lord, thou hast sent me on a fool's errand; if I played a fool's part, a strength greater than mine overmastered me . . . ."

[15]James Crenshaw observes:

> . . . complaint comes to be the dominant feeling in Jeremiah's oracles, and in the Confessions [i.e., the first-person speeches of the prophet] "there is not one single instance of hope, no occasion when he gives thanks to Jahweh for granting him redemptive insight or for allowing him some success."

See *Prophetic Conflict: Its Effect Upon Israelite Religion* (1971), p. 66. (Hereafter referred to as Crenshaw.) Crenshaw is quoting Gerhard von Rad, *Old Testament Theology*, tr. D. M. G. Stalker (1962-1965), II, 203.

[16]Crenshaw observes, p. 121:

> the nature and mood of [the disputations in prophetic literature] prove that the prophet was engaged in a struggle for self-vindication, hence that his claim to be speaking for the deity did not go unchallenged . . . . The presence of disputes in messages of weal and woe suggests that the prophets were aware that their words did not automatically carry authority, but had to be legitimated by persuasive argument.

[17]Joseph Blenkinsopp claims that the referent of Hosea 1-3 "is the relationship between Yahweh and Israel." See *History of Prophecy*, p. 104. Blenkinsopp finds in these chapters the basis of the gargantuan sexual fantasy in Ezekiel 16.

[18]NEB, 964, nn. *b, c,* and *e* to Hos 1:4, 6, and 9.

[19]See A. R. Diamond, *The Confessions of Jeremiah in Context: Scenes of Prophetic Drama* (1987). (Hereafter referred to as Diamond.) Diamond identifies these confessions as 11:18-12:6; 15:10-21; 17:14-18; 18:18-23; and 20:7-18. See p. 11.

[20]*History of Prophecy*, p. 155.

[21]M. H. Abrams presents such autobiographical searching as one consequence of what he calls the "expressive theory of art." See *The Mirror and the Lamp: Romantic Theory and the Critical Tradition* (1953), p. 23.

[22]Diamond, pp. 11-13. In a sociological study of the prophets, which defines them essentially as intermediaries, Robert R. Wilson says that "stereotypical speech is a common feature of most intermediaries." See *Prophecy and Society in Ancient Israel* (1980), p. 136. (Hereafter referred to as Wilson.) He explains his use of the term intermediary earlier, on p. 28. An important instance in literature of how the apparently private is mediated through the genre of prayer appears in Paul Fussell's discussion of Samuel Johnson's use of the forms of the *Book of Common Prayer* for his own prayers. See *Samuel Johnson and the Life of Writing* (1971), pp. 132-136.

[23]Diamond, pp. 14, 16. Applied to satiric self-presentation, this question epitomizes the interpretative issue posed in Maynard Mack's influential "The Muse of Satire," *Yale Review*, 41 (1951-1952), 80-92. (Hereafter referred to as Mack.)

[24]Diamond, p. 183.

[25]Diamond, p. 182.

[26]Diamond, pp. 185, 187.

[27]Diamond, pp. 183, 190.

[28]With the license such fantasies allow, I am ignoring the question of whether the artistry of Juvenal's *Satires* is really subordinated to an ethical concern. See especially H. A. Mason, "Is Juvenal A Classic?" in *Satire: Critical Essays on Roman Literature*, ed. J. P. Sullivan (1968), pp. 93-176. This collection hereafter referred to as *Satire*. Pp. 123-135 discuss in particular the limitations and weaknesses Mason sees in the portrait of Umbricius in *Satire III*, that is, if a moral aim is assumed to be primary.

[29]See Timothy Polk, *The Prophetic Persona: Jeremiah and the Language of the Self* (1984). (Hereafter referred to as Polk.) In an approach described as an "intensive rather than extensive" reading of "first-person, so-called autobiographical passages," Polk focusses on Jer 4:19; 8:18-9:25; 10:19-25; 14:1-15:4, and two of the Confessions, 17:12-18 and 20:7-18. See p. 8.

[30]Polk, pp. 163, 165.

[31] Mack, 88; Pope, p. 282, l.63.

[32] Polk, p. 165.

[33] Polk, pp. 165-166.

[34] Polk, p. 166.

[35] Polk, pp. 167-169.

[36] The phrase is from W. S. Anderson, "The Roman Socrates: Horace and His Satires," in *Satire*, p. 37.

[37] From Samuel Holt Monk and Lawrence Lipking, "Alexander Pope [Introduction]," in *The Norton Anthology of English Literature*, 4th ed., gen. ed. M. H. Abrams (1979), I, 2192.

[38] Polk, p. 171; Horace, p. 91, l. 310.

[39] Polk, p. 171.

[40] Mack, 91.

[41] Polk, p. 169, where he quotes from Sallie TeSelle, *Speaking in Parables: A Study in Metaphor and Theology* (1975), pp. 165-166, 169.

[42] Polk, p. 169.

[43] The concluding lines of William Blake's "The Book of Thel," in *Poetry and Prose of William Blake*, ed. Geoffrey Keynes (1956), p. 165.

[44] AB: Jeremiah, p. 264.

[45] Mack, 83. Diamond, the subtitle of whose study is *Scenes of Prophetic Drama*, discusses the manner in which the effect of what he calls "the double-axis pattern" in Jeremiah "could be styled as a prophetic drama." See pp. 181ff. Prophecy also affords a dramatic "I" speaking in the text.

[46] Mack, 84-85. See also Mary Claire Randolph, "The Structural Design of Formal Verse Satire," *Philological Quarterly*, 21 (1942), 368-384. Reversal "from curse to blessing" which Joseph Blenkinsopp finds in Hosea and in Amos he describes as "a regular feature of preexilic prophetic books." See his *History of Prophecy*, p. 101.

[47] Mack, 86.

[48] Mack, 88-92.

[49] See Northrop Frye, "The Nature of Satire," *University of Toronto Quarterly*, 14 (1944-1945), 80.

[50] Samuel Johnson, "Pope," in *Lives of the English Poets*, ed. George Birkbeck Hill (1967 [1905]), III, 212.

[51] Maynard Mack, *Alexander Pope: A Life* (1986), p. 473. (Hereafter referred to as *Alexander Pope*.)

[52] Wilson, pp. 43, 30.

[53] Charles T. Fritsch says that "this important concept" of the remnant is hinted at in Isaiah's inaugural vision (6:13), announced in the name of his son Shearjashub, i.e., a remnant shall return (7:3), and fully expanded in Isa 10:20-23. The remnant in this case, in Fritsch's

speculation, may be "the small group" of Isaiah's disciples. See "The Prophetic Literature," in *The Interpreter's One-Volume Commentary*, (1971), p. 1099. Maynard Mack calls the remnant motif in Pope and Swift a form of "triumphant vindication by posterity." See *Alexander Pope*, p. 473.

[54]See Horace, pp. 24-25; Pope, pp. 213-218; Juvenal, p. 23; Swift, pp. 471, 468-469. The prose citation from Swift appears in "The Preface," to *A Tale of a Tub*, Swift, pp. 269-270. John Oldham's comments appear in the "Prologue," to *Satyrs Upon the Jesuits*, in *A Collection of English Poems*, 1660-1800, ed. Ronald S. Crane (1932), p. 198, ll. 38-50. In drawing attention to a 1734 letter in which Alexander Pope claims an increased effectiveness by specifying names in satire, David Nokes comments: "It is worth noting Pope's explicit identification here of satire with a kind of legal or judicial responsibility." See his *Raillery and Rage: A Study of Eighteenth Century Satire* (1987), p. 52.

[55]*History of Prophecy*, pp. 162-163, 160, 159. In affirming the Mosaic pattern in Jeremiah's sense of self, Blenkinsopp is reiterating William L. Holladay's insistence that "it was in the light of the figure of Moses that Jeremiah lived out his own ministry," that "Moses . . . seems to have loomed largest in the mind of Jeremiah." See Holladay, 153, 154.

[56]AB: Jeremiah, p. 26.

[57]*History of Prophecy*, pp. 159-160, 98-99.

[58]*History of Prophecy*, pp. 112-113, 15.

[59]Wilson, pp. 136, 275, 280-281.

[60]Parenthetical references in this and the following paragraph are to the appropriate volume of Louis Ginzberg, *The Legends of the Jews* (7 vols., 1909-1938), hereafter referred to as Ginzberg. The text of Hosea, it should be noted, identifies Beeri only by name (Hos. 1:1).

[61]Mack, 91. He does not identify his source in Bredvold, nor have I been able to locate it.

[62]See Edward A. Bloom and Lillian D. Bloom, *Satire's Persuasive Voice* (1979), pp. 209-210.

[63]*History of Prophecy*, p. 210.

[64]Walter Brueggemann discusses this quick shift from the private to the public in this passage from Jeremiah. See "The Book of Jeremiah: Portrait of the Prophet," *Interpretation*, 37 (1983), 137. (Hereafter referred to as Brueggemann.)

[65]AB: Ezekiel, p. 43.

[66]Mack, 86.

[67]Fishbane, pp. 175-176.

[68]Hartman, pp. 33-34. J. Kenneth Kuntz points out the tension apparent in the Confessions of Jeremiah between "his natural desires

and his deep commitment to his calling." The conflict makes of Jeremiah a most compelling "personality" (p. 349):

> Jeremiah's moods varied [Kuntz notes]. When he was hurt, he wanted Yahweh to know that. He wanted Yahweh to realize that his enemies deserved the worst conceivable forms of punishment. He also complained that he was not at all pleased about his alienation from his fellowmen. He felt excluded from the common joys and satisfactions of life. He was extremely vulnerable to feelings of failure and persecution.

[69]See Swift, p. 468.

[70]AB: Ezekiel, p. 79.

[71]Carol L. Meyers and Eric M. Meyers offer this instructive gloss on the passage from Zechariah (AB: Haggai, Zechariah 1-8, p. 415):

> The mention of old men *and* old women [original emphasis], along with the suggestion of the physical infirmity of aging, perhaps adds a socio-economic nuance. The labor value of humans is, after all, established according to sex as well as age . . . . This passage shows both men and women *not* at work [original emphasis]. In an agrarian society, such a situation could only represent, whether in a city or on a farm, the existence of a healthy and stable economy whereby the senior citizens are relieved of the necessity of contributing substantially to subsistence tasks. In other words, the phrase "old men and old women" is not only part of the stylized pairing of old and young but also contributes specifically to the prophetic depiction of the future. Older people will be released from the demands of productive labor and will have leisure to gather in a public place.

[72]See Bruce Vawter, *Amos, Hosea, Micah, with an Introduction to Classical Prophecy* (1981), p. 68.

[73]Mack, 88, 86-87. "The language of the heart" and its importance as a major image of the constituting self in Jeremiah are major considerations in Polk's study. See in particular Chapter 2, "The Metaphor of the Heart and the Language of the Self," Chapter 3, "The Heart in Context: Jer 4 and the Enactment of Identity," and "Self-Constitution and the Language of the Heart" in Chapter 6, i.e., Polk, pp. 25-34, 35-57, and 167-169.

[74]A notable exception is Isaiah. Blenkinsopp sees the prophet as "a well-known public figure with access to leading members of the court." See *History of Prophecy*, p. 115.

[75]William Neil says of Jeremiah: "His love of country life, so prominent in the allusions of his oracles, is one of his most attractive charac-

teristics." See "Jeremiah," in *Harper's Bible Commentary* (1975), p. 257.

[76] The information about Amos and Micah appears in *History of Prophecy*, pp. 95-96, 121-122.

[77] See R. B. Y. Scott, *The Relevance of the Prophets*, rev. ed. (1968), p. 130.

[78] See AB: Jeremiah, p. xxiii.

[79] In Evelyn Waugh's *Vile Bodies*, Mrs. Hoop, with heart a-flutter as she enters Anchorage House (!), residence of the appropriately named Duke and Duchess of Stayle, insists to Lady Circumference that she sees the ghosts of "Pitt and Fox and Burke and Lady Hamilton and Beau Brummel and Dr. Johnson." But, the narrator laconically observes, Lady Circumference "saw no ghosts." See Waugh, *Vile Bodies* (1977), pp. 174, 176.

[80] The importance of the Temple Sermon in Jeremiah's attack on falsely grounded security is discussed in Thomas W. Overholt, *The Threat of Falsehood: A Study in the Theology of the Book of Jeremiah* (1970), pp. 1-24, the chapter entitled "The False Conception of Security."

[81] Mack, 89-90.

[82] See Pope, p. 293 (ll. 208-209).

[83] Polk, p. 134, discusses one instance of such an identification.

[84] Mack, 91-92.

[85] See Northrop Frye, *Anatomy*, p. 234.

[86] See above, pp. 112-117.

[87] For the graphic military imagery in Jeremiah, see Brueggemann, 136. Military imagery occurs often in the satiric apologia, especially in Juvenal's *Satire I* and even in the opening satire of Horace's Book II of the *Satires*.

[88] Mack, 89-91.

[89] For discussion of the rhetorical skills of Amos as they are used satirically see Chapter 3, above.

[90] Ginzberg, IV, 261.

[91] Ginzberg, IV, 209.

[92] Ginzberg, IV, 212.

[93] Ginzberg, IV, 226.

[94] For other legends of this kind about Elijah see Ginzberg, IV, 227-233. Close parallels and connections between Jeremiah and Moses also figure in Jewish legend. See Ginzberg, IV, 385-386.

NOTES TO EPILOGUE

[1] Walter Brueggemann, "The Book of Jeremiah: Portrait of the Prophet," *Interpretation*, 37 (1983), 136.

[2] Northrop Frye, *Fearful Symmetry: A Study of William Blake* (1962), p. 57.

[3] Frye, *Fearful Symmetry*, p. 59.

BIBLIOGRAPHY

[For commentaries published in the Anchor Bible series, see the Note on Biblical Citations, at the end of the Preface, above, p. 17.]

Abrams, M. H. *The Mirror and the Lamp: Romantic Theory and the Critical Tradition*. New York: Oxford Univ., 1953.

Ackerman, James S. "Jonah," in *The Literary Guide to the Bible*. Eds. Alter & Kermode (below), 1987. Pp. 234-243.

———. "Satire and Symbolism in the Song of Jonah," in *Traditions in Transformation: Turning Points in Biblical Faith*. Eds. Baruch Halpern & Jon D. Levenson. Winona Lake: Eisenbrauns, 1981. Pp. 213-246.

Ackroyd, Peter. "The Book of Isaiah," in *The Interpreter's One-Volume Commentary on the Bible*. Ed. Laymon (below), 1971. Pp. 329-371.

Adams, Robert M. "Candide on Work and Candide as Outsider," in Voltaire, *Candide: or, Optimism: A New Translation, Backgrounds, Criticism* (A Norton Critical Edition). Tr. and ed. Robert M. Adams. New York: Norton, 1966. Pp. 165-173.

Alter, Robert. *The Art of Biblical Narrative*. New York: Basic Books, 1981.

———. *The Art of Biblical Poetry*. New York: Basic Books, 1985.

Alter, Robert & Frank Kermode, eds. *The Literary Guide to the Bible*. Cambridge: Harvard Univ., 1987.

Anchor Bible. Gen. eds. William Foxwell Albright & David Noel Freedman. Garden City: Doubleday, 1964-. [See note on biblical citations, at the end of the Preface, above, p. 17.]

Archilochus. "Curse," in *Satire: That Blasted Art*. Eds. John R. Clark & Anna Motto. New York: Capricorn Books, 1973. P. 137.

Bakhtin, Mikhail. *Problems of Dostoevsky's Poetics*. Ed. and tr. Caryl Emerson. Intro. Wayne C. Booth. Minneapolis: Univ. of Minnesota, 1984.

———. *Rabelais and His World*. Tr. Helene Iswolsky. Bloomington: Indiana Univ. (Midland Books), 1984.

Barton, John. *Oracles of God: Perceptions of Ancient Prophecy in Israel After the Exile*. London: Darton, Longman & Todd, 1986.

Blake, William. *The Poetry and Prose of William Blake*. Ed. Geoffrey Keynes. London: The Nonesuch Library, 1956.

Blank, Sheldon H. "A Job to Do—a Mission," in *Perspectives on Old Testament Literature*. Ed. Woodrow Ohlsen. New York: Harcourt Brace Jovanovich, 1978. Pp. 251-260.

Blenkinsopp, Joseph. *A History of Prophecy in Israel: From the Settlement in the Land to the Hellenistic Period*. Philadelphia: Westminster, 1983.

———. *Prophecy and Canon: A Contribution to the Study of Jewish Origins*. Notre Dame: Univ. of Notre Dame, 1986.

Bloom, Edward A. & Lillian D. Bloom. *Satire's Persuasive Voice.* Ithaca: Cornell Univ., 1979.

Brenner, Athalya. "On the Semantic Field of Humour, Laughter, and the Comic in the Old Testament," in *On Humour and the Comic in the Hebrew Bible.* Eds. Radday & Brenner (below), 1990. Pp. 39-58.

Brenner, Athalya, & Yehuda T. Radday. "Between Intentionality and Reception: Acknowledgment and Application (A Preview)," in *On Humour and the Comic in the Hebrew Bible.* Eds. Radday & Brenner (below), 1990. Pp. 13-19.

Brueggemann, Walter. "The Book of Jeremiah: Portrait of the Prophet," *Interpretation,* 37 (1983), 130-145.

Bruns, Gerald L. "Allegory and Satire: A Rhetorical Meditation," *New Literary History,* II (1979-1980), 121-132.

————. "Canon and Power in the Hebrew Scriptures." *Critical Inquiry,* 10 (1984), 462-480.

Buss, Martin J. "Tragedy and Comedy in Hosea," in *Tragedy and Comedy in the Bible.* Ed. Exum (below), 1984. Pp. 71-82.

Carroll, R. P. "Is Humour Also Among the Prophets?" in *On Humour and the Comic in the Hebrew Bible.* Eds. Radday & Brenner (below), 1990. Pp. 169-189.

Cassem, Ned H. "Ezekiel's Psychotic Personality," in *The Word of God in the World: Essays in Honor of Frederick L. Moriarty, S.J.* Eds. Richard J. Clifford, S.J., & George W. MacRae, S.J. Cambridge: Weston College, 1973. Pp. 59-69.

Childs, Brevard S. "The Canonical Shape of the Prophetic Literature," in *Interpreting the Prophets.* Eds. Mays & Achtemeier (below), 1987. Pp. 41-49.

Courthope, William John. "Introduction to *The Dunciad,*" in *The Works of Alexander Pope.* Eds. Whitwell Elwin & William John Courthope. London: Murray, 1871-1889. Vol. IV.

Crenshaw, James L. *Prophetic Conflict: Its Effect Upon Israelite Religion.* Berlin: Walter de Gruyter, 1971.

Dahlberg, Bruce T. "The Book of Micah," in *The Interpreter's One-Volume Commentary on the Bible.* Ed. Laymon (below), 1971. Pp. 483-490.

Davies, Philip R. "Joking in Jeremiah 18," in *On Humour and the Comic in the Hebrew Bible.* Eds. Radday & Brenner (below), 1990. Pp. 191-201.

Diamond, A. R. *The Confessions of Jeremiah in Context: Scenes of Prophetic Drama.* Sheffield: JSOT, 1987.

Di Cesare, Mario A. *Poetry and Prophecy: Reflections on the Word.* The Robert Frost Library Lecture. 9 April 1976. Amherst, Massachusetts: Friends of the Amherst College Library, 1977.

Elliott, Robert C. *The Literary Persona.* Chicago: Univ. of Chicago, 1982.

————. *The Power of Satire: Magic, Ritual, Art.* Princeton: Princeton Univ., 1966.

Elwin, Whitwell. "Introduction" to *The Works of Alexander Pope.* New ed., intro., and nn. Whitwell Elwin. New York: Gordian, 1967 (Reprt. London: 1871-1889). IV, 3-38.

Exum, J. Cheryl, ed. *Tragedy and Comedy in the Bible.* (= *Semeia*, 32). Decatur, GA: Scholars, 1984.

Exum, J. Cheryl, & J. William Whedbee. "Isaac, Samson, and Saul: Reflections on the Comic and Tragic Visions," in *Tragedy and Comedy in the Bible.* Ed. Exum (above), 1984. Pp. 5-40.

Feinberg, Leonard. *Introduction to Satire.* Ames: Iowa State Univ., 1967.

Ferguson, Oliver W. *Jonathan Swift and Ireland.* Urbana: Univ. of Illinois, 1962.

Fisch, Harold. *Poetry with a Purpose: Biblical Poetics and Interpretation.* Bloomington: Indiana Univ., 1988.

Fishbane, Michael. "'A Wretched Thing of Shame, A Mere Belly': An Interpretation of Jeremiah 20:7-12," in *The Biblical Mosaic.* Eds. Polzin & Rothman (below), 1982. Pp. 169-183.

Fritsch, Charles T. "The Prophetic Literature," in *The Interpreter's One-Volume Commentary on the Bible.* Ed. Laymon (below), 1971. Pp. 1095-1100.

Frost, Stanley Brice. "The Book of Jeremiah," in *The Interpreter's One-Volume Commentary on the Bible.* Ed. Laymon (below), 1971. Pp. 372-404.

Frye, Northrop. *Anatomy of Criticism: Four Essays.* New York: Atheneum, 1968.

――――. *The Great Code: The Bible and Literature.* New York: Harcourt Brace Jovanovich, 1982.

――――. "The Nature of Satire," *Univ. of Toronto Quarterly*, 14 (1944-1945), 75-89.

――――. *Words with Power: Being a Second Study of the Bible and Literature.* San Diego: Harcourt Brace Jovanovich, 1990.

Fussell, Paul. *The Rhetorical World of Augustan Humanism.* Oxford: Clarendon, 1965.

――――. *Samuel Johnson and the Life of Writing.* New York: Harcourt Brace Jovanovich, 1971.

Gaster, Theodor. *Myth, Legend, and Custom in the Old Testament.* 2 vols. New York: Harper & Row (Harper Torchbooks), 1975.

Ginzberg, Louis. *The Legends of the Jews.* Tr. from the German. 7 vols. (with Index by Boaz Cohen). Philadelphia: Jewish Publication Society of America, 1909-1938.

Goldenberg, Robert. "The Problem of False Prophecy: Talmudic Interpretations of Jeremiah 28 and 1 Kings 22," in *The Biblical Mosaic.* Eds. Polzin & Rothman (below), 1982. Pp. 87-103.

Good, Edwin M. "Apocalyptic as Comedy: The Book of Daniel," in *Tragedy and Comedy in the Bible.* Ed. Exum (above), 1984. Pp. 41-70.

――――. *Irony in the Old Testament.* Philadelpha: Westminster, 1955.

Gottwald, Norman K. "Tragedy and Comedy in the Latter Prophets," in *Tragedy and Comedy in the Bible.* Ed. Exum (above), 1984. Pp. 83-106.

Green, Peter. "Introduction" to Juvenal, *The Sixteen Satires.* Tr., intro., and nn. Peter Green. Rev. ed. New York: Penguin Books, 1974. Pp. 9-63.

Greenberg, Moshe. "Job," in *The Literary Guide to the Bible.* Eds. Alter & Kermode (above), 1987. Pp. 283-304.

Grotjahn, Martin. "Beyond Laughter: A Summing Up," in Robert W. Corrigan, *Comedy: Meaning and Form*. 2nd ed. New York: Harper & Row, 1981. Pp. 180-184.

Guilhamet, Leon. *Satire and the Transformation of Genre*. Philadelphia: Univ. of Pennsylvania, 1987.

Gunn, David M. "The Anatomy of Divine Comedy: On Reading the Bible as Comedy and Tragedy,"in *Tragedy and Comedy in the Bible*. Ed. Exum (above), 1984. Pp. 115-129.

Guthrie, Harvey H., Jr. "Lamentations," in *The Interpreter's One-Volume Commentary on the Bible*. Ed. Laymon (below), 1971. Pp. 405-410.

Harper, William R. "Amos," in *Perspectives on Old Testament Literature*. Ed. Woodrow Ohlsen. New York: Harcourt Brace Jovanovich, 1978. Pp. 190-192.

Hartman, Geoffrey. "Jeremiah 20:7-12: A Literary Response," in *The Biblical Mosaic*. Eds. Polzin & Rothman (below), 1982. Pp. 184-195.

———. "The Poetics of Prophecy," in *High Romantic Argument: Essays for M. H. Abrams*. Ed. Lawrence Lipking. Ithaca: Cornell Univ., 1981. Pp. 15-40.

Heinemann, Joseph. "A Homily on Jeremiah and the Fall of Jerusalem (*Pesiqta Rabbati, Pisqa 26*)," in *The Biblical Mosaic*. Eds. Polzin & Rothman (below), 1982. Pp. 27-41.

Hendrickson, G. L. "*Satura Tota Nostra Est*," in *Satire: Modern Essays in Criticism*. Ed. Ronald Paulson. Englewood Cliffs, N.J.: Prentice-Hall, 1971. Pp. 37-51 [Reprinted from *Classical Philology*, 22 (1927), 46-60.].

Heschel, Abraham J. *The Prophets*. 2 vols. New York: Harper & Row (Harper Torchbooks), 1971.

Holbert, John. "Deliverance Belongs to Yahweh: Satire in the Book of Jonah," *Journal for the Study of the Old Testament*, 21 (1981), 59-81.

Holladay, William L. "The Background of Jeremiah's Self-Understanding: Moses, Samuel, and Psalm 22," *Journal of Biblical Literature*, 83 (1964), 153-164.

Horace. *Horace's Satires and Epistles*. Tr. Jacob Fuchs. Intro. William S. Anderson. New York: Norton, 1977.

———. *Horace, Satires and Epistles [and] Persius, Satires*. Tr. Niall Rudd. Rev. ed. New York: Penguin Books, 1979.

———. *The Satires and Epistles of Horace*. Tr. Smith Palmer Bovie. Chicago: Univ. of Chicago (Phoenix Books), 1959.

Jemielity, Thomas. "Samuel Johnson, *The Vanity of Human Wishes*, and Biographical Criticism," in *Studies in Eighteenth-Century Culture*. Ed. O. M. Brack, Jr. 15 (1986), 227-239.

Johnson, Aubrey R. *The Cultic Prophet in Ancient Israel*. 2nd ed. Cardiff: Univ. of Wales, 1962.

Johnson, Samuel. "Idler 50," in *The Idler* and *The Adventurer* (Volume II in The Yale Edition of the Works of Samuel Johnson). Eds. W. J. Bate, John M. Bullitt, & L. F. Powell. New Haven: Yale Univ., 1963. Pp. 155-158.

————. "London," in *Poems* (Volume VI of The Yale Edition of the Works of Samuel Johnson). Eds. E. L. McAdam, Jr., & George Milne. New Haven: Yale Univ., 1964. Pp. 45-61.

————. "Pope," in *Lives of the English Poets*. Ed. George Birkbeck Hill. New York: Octagon, 1967 (reprt. Oxford: Clarendon, 1905). III, 82-276.

Josipovici, Gabriel. *The Book of God: A Response to the Bible*. New Haven & London: Yale Univ., 1988.

Juvenal. "The First Satire of Juvenal," tr. John Dryden, in *The Poetical Works of Dryden*. Ed. George R. Noyes. New ed., rev. Boston: Houghton Mifflin, 1950. Pp. 322-327.

————. *The Satires of Juvenal*. Tr. Rolfe Humphries. Bloomington: Indiana Univ., 1958.

Kirk, Eugene P. "Introduction" to *Menippean Satire: An Annotated Catalogue of Texts and Criticism*. New York: Garland, 1980. Pp. ix-xxxiii.

Knox, Norman. *The Word Irony and Its Context, 1500-1755*. Durham: Duke Univ., 1961.

Kuntz, J. Kenneth. *The People of Ancient Israel: An Introduction to Old Testament Literature, History, and Thought*. New York: Harper & Row, 1974.

Lamb, Jonathan. "Research Reports, VII—Job, Epitaphs, and Blake's Illustrations," *The Clark Newsletter: Bulletin of the UCLA Center for 17th- and 18th-Century Studies*, no. 16 (Spring 1989), 4-7.

Landy Francis. "Are We in the Place of Averroes? Response to the Articles of Exum and Whedbee, Buss, Gottwald, and Good," in *Tragedy & Comedy in the Bible*. Ed. Exum (above), 1984. Pp. 131-148.

————. "Humour as a Tool for Biblical Exegesis," in *On Humour and the Comic in the Hebrew Bible*. Eds. Radday & Brenner (below), 1990. Pp. 99-115.

Laymon, Charles M., ed. *The Interpreter's One-Volume Commentary on the Bible*. Nashville: Abingdon, 1971.

Levin, Harry. *Playboys and Killjoys: An Essay on the Theory and Practice of Comedy*. New York: Oxford Univ., 1987.

Lindblom, Johannes. *Prophecy in Ancient Israel*. Philadelphia: Fortress, 1965.

Mack, Maynard. *Alexander Pope: A Life*. New York: Norton, 1985.

————. *The Garden and the City: Retirement and Politics in the Later Poetry of Pope*. Toronto: Univ. of Toronto, 1969.

————. "The Muse of Satire," *Yale Review*, 41 (1951-52), 80-92.

Marks, Herbert. "The Twelve Prophets," in *The Literary Guide to the Bible*. Eds. Alter & Kermode (above), 1987. Pp. 207-233.

Mason, H. A. "Is Juvenal a Classic?" in *Satire: Critical Essays on Roman Literature*. Ed. J. P. Sullivan. Bloomington: Indiana Univ. (Midland Books), 1968. Pp. 93-176.

Mays, James Luther & Paul J. Achtemeier, eds. *Interpreting the Prophets*. Philadelphia: Fortress, 1987.

McKenzie, John L., S.J. "The Literary Characteristics of Genesis 2-3," *Theological Studies*, 15 (1954), 541-572.

Merton, Thomas. "Blake and the New Theology, [A Review of Thomas J. J. Altizer, *The New Apocalypse: the Radical Christian Vision of William Blake* (Lansing, Mich.: Michigan State, 1967)]." *Sewanee Review*, 76 (1968), 673-682.

Miles, John A. "Laughing at the Bible: Jonah as Parody," *The Jewish Quarterly Review*, 65 (1974-1975), 168-181.

Milton, John. *Samson Agonistes*, in *The Student's Milton*. Ed. Frank Allen Patterson. Rev. ed. New York: Appleton-Century-Crofts, 1933. Pp. 404-439.

Monk, Samuel Holt, & Lawrence Lipking, "Alexander Pope [Introduction]," in *The Norton Anthology of English Literature*. 4th ed. Gen. ed. M. H. Abrams. New York: Norton, 1979. I, 2188-2194.

Morris, David B. "The Muse of Pain: *An Epistle to Dr. Arbuthnot* and Satiric Reprisal," in *Alexander Pope: the Genius of Sense*. Cambridge: Harvard Univ., 1984. Pp. 214-240.

Mottu, Henri. "Jeremiah vs. Hananiah," in *The Bible and Interpretation: Political and Social Hermeneutics*. Ed. Norman K. Gottwald. Maryknoll, N.Y.: Orbis, 1983. Pp. 235-251.

Murchland, Bernard. "The Prophetic Principle," *Commonweal*, 29 April 1966, pp. 171-175.

Neil, William. "Jeremiah," in *Harper's Bible Commentary*. New York: Harper & Row, 1975. Pp. 256-260.

Nelson, T. G. A. *Comedy: The Theory of Comedy in Literature, Drama, and Cinema*. New York: Oxford Univ., 1990.

Nelson's Complete Concordance of the Revised Standard Version Bible. Comp. John W. Ellison. New York: Thomas Nelson, 1957.

Nokes, David. *Raillery and Rage: A Study of Eighteenth Century Satire*. Brighton: Harvester, 1987.

O'Connor, Michael Patrick. "The Deceptions of Hosea," *The Bible Today*, 20, no. 3 (May 1982), 152-158.

―――. "The Weight of God's Name: Ezekiel in Context and Canon," *The Bible Today*, 18, no. 1 (January 1980), 28-34.

Oldham, John. "Prologue," to *Satyrs Upon the Jesuits*, in *A Collection of English Poems*, 1660-1800. Sel. and ed. Ronald S. Crane. New York: Harper, 1932. Pp. 197-198.

Overholt, Thomas W. *The Threat of Falsehood: A Study in the Theology of the Book of Jeremiah*. Naperville, Illinois: Alec R. Allenson, 1970.

Paulson, Ronald. *The Fictions of Satire*. Baltimore: Johns Hopkins Univ., 1967.

Polk, Timothy. *The Prophetic Persona: Jeremiah and the Language of the Self*. Sheffield: JSOT, 1984.

Polzin, Robert M., & Eugene Rothman, eds. *The Biblical Mosaic: Changing Perspectives*. Philadelphia: Fortress & Chico, CA: Scholars, 1982.

Pope, Alexander. "MARY GULLIVER *to Captain* LEMUEL GULLIVER," in Alexander Pope, *Minor Poems* (Volume VI of The Twickenham Edition of the Poems of Alexander Pope). Eds. Norman Ault & John Butt. London: Methuen, 1964. Pp. 276-279.

―――. *Poetry and Prose of Alexander Pope*. Ed. Aubrey Williams.

Boston: Houghton Mifflin (Riverside Editions), 1969.

Radday, Yehuda T. "Humour in Names," in *On Humour and the Comic in the Hebrew Bible*. Eds. Radday & Brenner (below), 1990. Pp. 59-97.

Radday, Yehuda T., & Athalya Brenner, eds. *On Humour and the Comic in the Hebrew Bible*. Sheffield: The Almond Press, 1990.

Randolph, Mary Claire. "The Structural Design of Formal Verse Satire," *Philological Quarterly*, 21 (1942), 368-384.

Robertson, David. "Micaiah ben Imlah: A Literary View," in *The Biblical Mosaic*. Eds. Polzin & Rothman (above), 1982. Pp. 139-146.

———. *The Old Testament and the Literary Critic*. Philadelphia: Fortress, 1977.

———. "Tragedy, Comedy, and the Bible—A Response," in *Tragedy and Comedy in the Bible*. Ed. Exum (above), 1984. Pp. 99-106.

Rosenberg, Joel. "Jeremiah & Ezekiel," in *The Literary Guide to the Bible*. Eds. Alter & Kermode (above), 1987. Pp. 184-206.

Rosenheim, Edward W., Jr. *Swift and the Satirist's Art*. Chicago: Univ. of Chicago, 1963.

Roth, Wolfgang. "The Story of the Prophet Micaiah (1 Kings 22) in Historical-Critical Interpretation 1876-1976," in *The Biblical Mosaic*. Eds. Polzin & Rothman (above), 1982. Pp. 105-137.

Rudd, Niall. "Dryden on Horace and Juvenal," in *The Satires of Horace*. Berkeley: Univ. of California, 1982. Pp. 258-273.

Scott, R. B. Y. *The Relevance of the Prophets*. New York: Macmillan, 1968.

———. *The Way of Wisdom in the Old Testament*. New York: Macmillan, 1971.

Seutonius. *The Twelve Caesars*. Tr. Robert Graves. Baltimore: Penguin Books, 1957.

Shakespeare, William. *King Richard II*. 4th ed. Rev. and ed. Peter Ure. Cambridge: Harvard Univ., 1956.

Shero, Lucius Rogers. "The Satirist's *Apologia*," *Classical Studies*, 15 (1922), 148-167.

Stinespring, W. T. "Humor," in *The Interpreter's Dictionary of the Bible*. Gen. ed. George A. Buttrick. New York: Abingdon, 1962. II, 660-662.

Stuhlmueller, Carroll, C.P. "Prophet, Who Are You?" in *The Biblical Heritage in Modern Catholic Scholarship*. Eds. John J. Collins & John Dominic Crossan. Wilmington, Delaware: Michael Glazier, 1986. Pp. 58-84.

Swift, Jonathan. *Answer to a Memorial*, in *The Prose Works of Jonathan Swift*. Ed. Herbert Davis. Oxford: Shakespeare Head, 1939-1968. XII, 15-25.

———. *Gulliver's Travels and Other Writings*. Ed. Louis A. Landa. Boston: Houghton Mifflin (Riverside Editions), 1960.

Taylor, A. J. P. "Genocide," in *Essays in English History*. New York: Penguin Books, 1976. Pp. 73-79.

Thomas Aquinas, Saint. "Whether Right Is the Object of Justice?" II-II (i.e., the Second Part of the Second Part), Q. 57, Art. 1, in *The Summa of St. Thomas Aquinas*. Trs. Fathers of the English Domini-

can Province. New York: Benziger Brothers, 1947. II, 1431-1432.
———. "Whether Prophecy Pertains to Knowledge?" II-II (i.e., the Second Part of the Second Part), Q. 171, Art. 1, in *The Summa of St. Thomas Aquinas.* Trs. Fathers of the English Dominican Province. New York: Benziger Brothers, 1947. II, 1889-1890.

Todorov, Tzvetan. *Mikhail Bakhtin: The Dialogical Principle.* Tr. Wlad Godzich. Minneapolis: Univ. of Minnesota Press, 1984.

Toombs, Lawrence E. "Introduction" to "The Psalms," in *The Interpreter's One-Volume Commentary on the Bible.* Ed. Laymon (above), 1971. Pp. 253-261.

Tucker, Gene M. *Form Criticism of the Old Testament.* Philadelphia: Fortress, 1971.
———. "Prophetic Speech," in *Interpreting the Prophets.* Eds. Mays & Achtemeier (above), 1987. Pp. 27-40.

Van Doren, Mark, & Maurice Samuel. *The Book of Praise: Dialogues on the Psalms.* Ed. and nn. Edith Samuel. New York: John Day, 1975.

Vawter, Bruce. *Amos, Hosea, Micah, with an Introduction to Classical Prophecy.* Wilmington: Michael Glazier, 1981.

Waugh, Evelyn. *Vile Bodies.* Boston: Little, Brown & Co., 1977.

Weber, Max. *Ancient Judaism.* Trs. and eds. Hans H. Gerth & Don Martindale. Glencoe, Ill.: Free, 1952.

Wevers, John William. "The First Book of Samuel," in *The Interpreter's One-Volume Commentary on the Bible.* Ed. Laymon (above), 1971. Pp. 155-169.
———. "The Second Book of Kings," in *The Interpreter's One-Volume Commentary on the Bible.* Ed. Laymon (above), 1971. Pp. 197-207.

Williams, James G. "Irony and Lament: Clues to Prophetic Consciousness," *Semeia,* 8 (1977), 51-74.

Wilson, Robert R. *Prophecy and Society in Ancient Israel.* Philadelphia: Fortress, 1984.

Winnett, F. V. "Irony and Satire," in *The Interpreter's Dictionary of the Bible.* Gen. ed. George A. Buttrick. New York: Abingdon, 1962. II, 726-728.

Wolff, Hans Walter. *Hosea: A Commentary on the Book of the Prophet Hosea.* Tr. Gary Stansell. Ed. Paul D. Hanson. Philadelphia: Fortress, 1974.
———. "Prophecy from the Eighth Through the Fifth Centuries," in *Interpreting the Prophets.* Eds. Mays & Achtemeier (above), 1987. Pp. 14-26.

Worcester, David. *The Art of Satire.* New York: Russell & Russell, 1960.

Wordsworth, William. *Preface to the Second Edition of Lyrical Ballads,* in *The Norton Anthology of English Literature.* Gen. ed. M. H. Abrams. 5th ed. New York: Norton, 1986. II, 155-170.

Young, Robert. *Analytical Concordance to the Bible.* 22nd American ed. Rev. William B. Stevenson. Grand Rapids: Eerdmans, 1970.

Zakovitch, Yair. "∪ and ∩ in the Bible," in *Tragedy and Comedy in the Bible.* Ed. Exum (above), 1984. Pp. 107-114.

INDEXES

AUTHORS

SUBJECTS

BIBLICAL REFERENCES

EBREI

Va, pensiero, sull'ali dorate;
Va, ti posa sui clivi, sui colli,
Ove olezzano tepide e molli
L'aure dolci del suolo natal!
Del Giordano le rive saluta,
Di Sionne le torri atterrate.
Oh, mia patria sì bella e perduta!
Oh, membranza sì cara e fatal!
Arpa d'or dei fatidici vati,
Perché muta dal salice pendi?
Le memorie nel petto raccendi,
Ci favella del tempo che fu!
O simile di Solima ai fati
Traggi un suono di crudo lamento,
O t'ispiri il Signore un concento
Che ne infonda al patire virtù!

❦

HEBREWS

Go gently, pensiveness, on golden wings;
Go, seat yourself on slopes and hills
Where the lovely airs, soft and mild,
Of our native land breathe forth their fragrance.
Greet the banks of Jordan
And the fallen towers of Zion.
Oh, my homeland so beautiful and so fallen!
Oh, remembrance so dear and so deadly!
Golden harps of our far-seeing prophets,
Why hang you mute upon the willows?
Rouse again the memories within our hearts!
Tell us tales of times gone by!
Picture again Jerusalem's doom!
Bring us songs of bitter lament!
May the Lord impel you to the harmony
That brings resolve to birth in us.

—"The Chorus of the Hebrew Slaves,"
Giuseppe Verdi, *Nabucco*, III, ii